some just clap their hands

SOME JUST CLAP THEIR HANDS

raising a handicapped child

MARGARET MANTLE

ADAMA BOOKS

Library of Congress Cataloging-in-Publication Data

Mantle, Margaret.
   Some just clap their hands.

   1. Child rearing—United States—Case studies.
2. Mentally handicapped children—United States—Family
relationships—Case studies.   3. Mentally handicapped
children—United States—Home care—Case studies.
I. Title. [DNLM: 1. Child Care—case studies.
2. Child, Exceptional—case studies.   3. Mental
Retardation—case studies.   WS 107.5.C2 M292s]
HQ773.7.M36   1985   649'.1528   85-15026
ISBN 0-915361-24-8

ADAMA BOOKS, 306 WEST, 38 ST., NEW YORK, N.Y. 10018

acknowledgments

There are many people who have contributed to Victoria's story in one way or another, and although I do not list them by name they will know who they are and, I hope, accept my gratitude. Particularly, of course, I want to extend my most sincere gratitude to everyone who had the courage and the sense of adventure to agree to be part of this book; I am proud to know them all.

My father deserves my thanks not only for having given me whatever writing ability I possess, but for waiting so patiently for me to do something substantial with it.

There are two other people to whom I owe a singular and personal debt: they are Beatrice Grabowski and Carol DeChant.

*this book is dedicated to
Victoria and Emma Kate,
whose mother it is my
great good fortune to be*

All God's critters got a place in the choir,
Some sing low, some sing higher,
Some sing out loud on the telephone wires,
And some just clap their hands. . . .

contents

PART ONE

finding out

retrospect: *Victoria at fourteen*

On the windowsill is a photograph of Victoria at the age of five. A charming child with long blonde hair that falls to her shoulders smoothly except for an enviable wave or two. Her head is slightly to one side and in her eyes, which are blue, there is a question that may concern the nearness of lunchtime, or the intentions of the photographer, or life. If I ever did know what was in her mind at that moment I do not remember it now.

It is a small photograph, a snapshot in a cheap frame, and it has spent many months in my desk drawer because the cats kept jumping up on the windowsill and knocking the picture down. I put it back on display last week for some reason of my own, as then undetermined but now clearly interpreted as regression. On my part. I am more familiar with the five-year-old blonde than I am with the crop-haired adolescent who is Victoria today, and on the tip of my tongue are words I was convinced I'd never say—something about wanting my baby back.

Today is Victoria's fourteenth birthday and we are having a party. There are few occasions that unhinge me more thoroughly than my children's birthday parties. They present a threat to the precarious control that I maintain over my domestic situation. In the presence of other people's children I will surely be revealed in my true form as an inadequate mother. The young guests will reject the cake (before they trample it into the rug); the party favors will be inferior to those distributed at the last party they went to (their social life is a lot more crowded than my own); the games will be too juvenile, or too difficult, or guaranteed to cause a riot. The visitors will be bored and the social status of my children therefore jeopardized.

No, I do not enjoy children's birthday parties. And on this occasion I am doubly distressed because, having insisted for years that I can't wait for my young to grow up, I now find that Victoria at fourteen is growing up in ways I had not anticipated and do not know how to handle. Victoria at fourteen is someone I do not know very well and am rather disinclined to know better.

She is wearing a blue woolen dress which clings all too lovingly (for my comfort, anyway) to her brand new breasts and delightful little bottom. Her tights match the dress but the shoes she is wearing are inappropriately heavy because I have not gotten around to buying party shoes and she hasn't asked me to. Her hair has darkened considerably since she was a child, and is now cut short in a feathery style which everyone loves, including Victoria. Everyone, that is, except me. We lopped off the other twelve inches recently in an effort to ease everyone's life by giving this moody teenager one less cause for complaint: she cannot look after long hair alone, and having me brush it for her does not accord with her new adolescent rage for independence. With long or short hair she's a very pretty girl, especially when she smiles. These days she's more inclined to pout.

So, what with one thing and another, I am finding Victoria's fourteenth birthday a bit of a trial. At twelve a child is demonstrably still a child, even in these precocious times. At thirteen the young feet are just testing the cool waters of impending adolescence. But at fourteen the waters are indisputably rising.

Victoria's birthdays have been emotionally loaded ever since we discovered that she is retarded—even before that, in fact, when all we knew was that something about this beautiful child was not quite right. Nobody's ever been able to give us a reason for her being retarded. She was born in a terrific hurry at one of the most reputable maternity hospitals in England. Her father and I had just eaten a dinner of roast veal (I'd never cooked it before and never have since) and had gone to bed when it became apparent that the baby was about to join us. Pausing only to drape the seats of our spanking new car with blankets against a possible obstetrical emergency which would seriously mess up the upholstery, we made it to the hospital. But only just.

And every March twelfth, as I wrap gifts for her birthday on the thirteenth, I embark on an annual exercise in hindsight. Did I do something wrong? Should I have rested more during the pregnancy, or quit my job sooner? Should I have refused anesthesia during the delivery? What if I had done my homework better and been more consciously in control of the process of childbirth? Would any of those variables have made any difference and made her not be retarded?

Probably not. Probably not. But I don't *know*. . . .

Whatever the truth of the matter, I believe that Victoria was normal at conception. I have no grounds for believing otherwise. But at some point, something went wrong. I will never know what it was, and at this stage it doesn't matter. I could, conceivably, go back to the hospital where she was born and demand to see and analyze their records—what drugs was I given, what happened, did something go wrong? Maybe nothing went wrong. Maybe my perfect pregnancy wasn't perfect after all. Maybe something happened after she was born. I don't know. All I know is that Victoria is my daughter, and she is mentally handicapped.

After Victoria was diagnosed as retarded I got to talk to a lot of parents of retarded children, and they alerted me to the problem areas. They said it would be more difficult as the child grew up and that adolescence would almost certainly be a time of crisis. It seems that they were right. Being Victoria's mother was easier when she was little. I suppose that's why I keep picking up the portrait of Victoria at five each time the cats knock it down and putting it back on the windowsill.

but where does the disguise end
and the blessing begin?

Very many parents of retarded children harbor a deep suspicion of people who say things like, "I'm glad my child is retarded." A statement like this is usually qualified, there's a "because"—"because the family has learned so much from him," or "because she is so innocent," or "because he's one of God's special children." A father who appeared on a television show angered many of us by claiming that he wouldn't have his mentally handicapped son any other way because it had been so good for the family to have a retarded child among its members.

We knew what he was trying to say, but we wished he had chosen his words with a little more precision. We feel that, on the whole, we have had a bad press. The home life of retarded children and their families has seldom been addressed by the media, and such representations as do appear frequently offer rosy pictures that have little to do with the reality we experience. We are not saints or martyrs, far from it, but that is the way we are often depicted. And it's bad for our image because it puts us firmly beyond the pale of ordinary parents. It makes us outsiders.

It is certainly true that the birth of a child who is "different" makes for a lot of differences in us as parents—in our priorities, in the way we approach life, in our defense and survival systems. We also do a lot of practical things that most parents don't have to do: we learn to interpret the private language of a child who has limited comprehension or limited communication; we may still be changing diapers when the child is six (or sixteen) years old; we have to get a baby-sitter although our "baby" is of an age when ordinary children are baby-sitting for the neighbors.

With the birth of an exceptional child we become exceptional parents and there's even a magazine of that name—*The Exceptional Parent*—to prove it. As the child is labeled, so is the parent.

Frequently in the eyes of others, and sometimes in our own eyes, the ways in which we are different from other parents negate the ways in which we are just the same. So we fight the label, we resent it, we reject it. We insist that we're not exceptional, that we're just as ordinary as the next person. Indeed, the parents of retarded children have a lot of trouble with the label "exceptional," as with a good number of other labels.

This sense of being set apart, however, adds significantly to the loneliness experienced by most parents of retarded children, and it doesn't help to hear someone declaim, as if speaking for us all, "I'm glad my child is retarded."

I read recently about a woman who died of lung cancer. She was quoted as saying, "I am happy I got lung cancer." She was a strong and determined woman who, before she died, did a great deal to help other cancer patients. She derived great satisfaction from this work, and I can believe that it made her happy. But I don't believe that, given the choice (which of course she wasn't), she would have chosen to have cancer. Or that "happy" precisely described the way she felt about having it. Resigned, accepting, well-satisfied with what she was doing with the rest of her life—all these I can accept. But I find it difficult to accept that she was happy about having cancer. And it's hard to relate to someone who is professing an improbably high-minded attitude toward a personal trauma. It is not particularly helpful to talk to a saint; a regular, plain sinner is easier to get along with.

Similarly, parents who over-romanticize the task of living with a retarded child have little to say to a lot of us who are coping on a more down-to-earth level. When I broached the subject of this book I met with much suspicion (and some hostility) until I assured my potential contributors that I did not plan to paint a halo around my head or theirs. "Tell it like it is," they said. "For God's sake, don't get cute. Don't leave out the shitty parts."

Another thing about the story of the woman with cancer— it did leave out one shitty part. After she got cancer, and while she was plunging into involvement with others in the same predicament, her marriage broke up. Her story was not all hearts and flowers and noble suffering. There was some human failure there, too, but it would have spoiled the story so the writers left it out. When I learned about that I felt thoroughly cheated. They'd tried to put something over on me. What's more, had I known about some of the shitty parts of that woman's life I think I could have gotten something valuable out of her story. Because I would have been able to see her as someone like me, not a saint with a halo but an ordinary person doing her best to cope with an extraordinary situation.

Having a retarded child is not a hearts-and-flowers matter. It is a painful reality. It hurts, and it costs. There's not one of us parents who can, in total honesty, pretend to be glad or happy about being the parent of a handicapped child. We would infinitely prefer, for our child's sake and for our own, that the child be normal. It is possible to be resigned, to recognize that many families do indeed discover unexpected resources of love and strength and compassion in the presence of a handicapped child, while recognizing also that, given one's druthers, it would be altogether nicer if the child were not handicapped.

All the parents I know reject the assumption that the birth of their retarded child was an undisguised blessing. A blessing in disguise, possibly—sometimes in very heavy disguise at that—but a blessing that a lot of the time they'd just as soon have done without. A blessing, moreover, that may have taken a tremendous emotional toll of one or more family members or even torn the whole family structure apart. The pressure of having a mentally handicapped child is a major factor in the break-up of a distressingly high number of marriages.

It doesn't take much deep thought to figure out why some parents romanticize the presence of their retarded child in their lives. Parents who adopt the "I'm glad" strategy may be lying for some good and sufficient reason of their own, perhaps to end an unwanted discussion or to ward off someone's well-meant sympathy. They may still be denying the child's condition to themselves. It is also possible to selfishly overlook the child's losses in appreciation of the fact that one has not been destroyed by one's own. But I am not glad about Victoria's condition, and I'm not going to make any pretense of being glad. I wish my daughter were normal. I wish it for my own sake. And I wish it more and more for hers as I watch her grow up and am forced to recognize the things she will never have because she is retarded.

Even her adolescent strivings for independence will not follow a strictly normal course. She won't be able to storm out of the house in a tantrum and worry me sick by staying out all night. She's too closely supervised for that. Anyway, she cannot travel alone. The only journey she's ever made independently has been the six-block walk to school, with three crossing guards on the route primed to keep an eye on her and the other children who attend the local school for mentally handicapped children.

Similarly, Victoria won't have the sort of freedom a teenager usually has to conduct forays into the delightful but dangerous field of sex. I suppose it is not impossible that she might marry someone like herself, although I find the idea very difficult to accept. But who knows what may happen ten or fifteen years down the road? She's making progress all the time. But she will never have a child if I have any say in the matter. Victoria loves babies; she loves to mother little kids. But there's no way she will ever be capable of giving a child of her own the physical or emotional care necessary for the child's normal development.

Victoria will never be fully and independently mobile. She will never be able to say to herself, "I think I'll get on a plane and go someplace," and experience the delicious thrill of doing so. She will never drive her own car, or anyone else's for that matter. It's not likely, or so it seems at present, that she'll ever even ride a bus or subway alone.

The jobs that will be available to her are likely to be extremely boring, and she is as susceptible to boredom as the rest of us. She'll be lucky to get a job at all outside a sheltered workshop, although I shall do my damnedest—if she seems capable of it—to help find her a job in the community, and her school is training her to that end. She will never be in control of her own life. Most of the major decisions of her life, and even some of the choices, will be made for her. All these limitations are laid on Victoria by the fact of her retardation.

And then, of course, there are the things that *I* miss for her—worlds explored in books; lines from a poem where the words wash over you with a marvelous cold shock like a wave you've got your back to at the beach. Victoria will never read *Jane Eyre. Hamlet* to her will be a closed book. The lyrics of Cole Porter and Stephen Sondheim will never be anything more than nice songs. She won't discover the south of France, or the Greek islands. She probably won't experience the more refined, because more intellectual, torments of being in love.

All this, naturally, meshes inextricably the regrets I have for Victoria with the regrets I have for myself. Because what I'd really like is for her to enjoy books with *me*, travel with *me*, cry on *my* shoulder when she's in love. Perhaps, despite all the warnings I've given her younger sister, Emma (assuming her to be the more likely of the two to reproduce), that I have no intention of taking care of her offspring, I would actually quite like to dandle Victoria's child on my grandmotherly knee.

No, I can hardly be glad that Victoria is retarded. I can be glad she is who she is, because on the whole she's a very nice person. She has some lovely qualities. She's very sensitive to other people, and very kind. Because she doesn't love books or music on my terms doesn't mean she doesn't love them as much. She has as much capacity for enjoyment as I do—maybe more, for her pleasure is not sullied by the anticipation of loss. She is less beset by "ifs" and "buts" and "shoulds."

I put myself through a good deal of inappropriate misery when she was smaller by assuming that the knowledge of her disability was causing her pain on the same intellectual level as my own. But she's not as bright as I am; I have, for what it's worth, a higher IQ. Victoria, who is certainly smart enough to realize that she's different and sensitive enough to be hurt by that knowledge, suffers in her own way. I suffer in mine. Neither one of us can suffer for the other although for years I was sufficiently arrogant to attempt to measure her experience by my own.

Victoria is my daughter, but she isn't me. She's nicer in a lot of ways than I am. She has virtues I lack. She is more honest than I am, and more generous. She is not judgmental, and she is quick to forgive. She is less suspicious than I am. She does not expect too much of people or bear grudges. She has the virtue of simplicity. It's a great shame that *simple* is often considered to be a synonym for *stupid*. The two are worlds apart. To be simple is a gift, and my daughter has it. She may be retarded, but Victoria is no fool.

But believe me when I say that Victoria's retardation has cost me pain and loss on a scale that, had I anticipated it, I would never have believed myself capable of surviving. I would be the fool if I tried to kid myself or anyone else into believing that I'm glad my daughter is retarded.

major crisis number one: the diagnosis

It is generally accepted that there are three major crises in
the lives of the parents of a mentally handicapped child.
There are innumerable other crises of different sizes, of
course, but these are commonly acknowledged to be the top
three. They occur at the time the child is diagnosed as mentally impaired, when the child reaches puberty, and when the
child leaves home. They occur in that order for the families
of kids like Victoria—children whose level of retardation
enables them to live at home until they are approaching
adulthood. These are the children whose handicap is loosely
defined as mild or moderate retardation. Victoria falls within
the moderate range. Lower functioning children fall into the
categories of severe or profound retardation. For the parents
of such children crises one and three may occur simul-
taneously; in fact, the child may never live at home. Having a
child who is severely or profoundly retarded, however, is a
totally different experience from having a child like Victoria
who is far nearer normal than not, and this book does not
primarily address the concerns of parents of those more
severely handicapped children who can never really be part
of a family structure.

Major crisis number one, the diagnosis, is an emotional
minefield. This is due, in part, to the fact that a large proportion of mentally retarded children are not obviously retarded
at birth. Many appear normal for months, or years, until the
creeping realization that something is not quite right begins
to nag at the back of someone's mind—the parent's, the
pediatrician's, the teacher's. More than two hundred and fifty
causes of retardation are known, but, according to the Association for Retarded Citizens of the United States, these account for only one-fourth of identified cases. There is, therefore, a vast speculative area to be acknowledged.

In certain cases, retardation can be identified at birth. Down syndrome, which is the leading cause of retardation in the United States, occurring in one out of six hundred babies born, is accompanied by recognizable physical characteristics. An informed doctor can diagnose Down syndrome in a newborn at a glance, and the diagnosis can be confirmed by a chromosome test; Down syndrome is a chromosomal abnormality.

· So with a baby who has Down syndrome, it should be possible to let the parents know at once what they are dealing with—an identifiable physical condition that causes retardation to some degree or other—and, if they're lucky, lock them into a support system as soon as the mother and baby leave the hospital. The support system can include not only the society of other parents who are dealing with the same thing, but also "early intervention" programs through which the parents work with the child to minimize the effects of the retardation and allow the child to realize his or her full potential.

A great number of retarded children, however, are not so easily diagnosed. An estimated fifty percent of retardation is of unknown cause: the baby appears to be perfectly normal at birth and it may not be for months or even years that evidence of something out of the ordinary begins to appear. In a frighteningly large number of cases the baby *is* normal at or immediately before birth; then something goes wrong. Or someone makes a mistake. Unknown numbers of retarded people, probably Victoria among them, certainly Emily and Katherine whom you will meet in these pages, should be normal today. Victoria, I believe, was normal at conception. Emily was normal for the first five months of her life, then developed hypothyroidism which her pediatrician failed to diagnose and treat; had the condition been diagnosed in time, the brain damage that wrecked Emily's life might have been avoided or minimized. Katherine contracted spinal meningitis in the hospital nursery; her mother believes that Katherine's present handicap—cerebral palsy accompanied by retardation—could have been avoided if the child had been treated in time.

These are among the children whose diagnosis is not as straightforward as recognizing the physical characteristics that accompany Down syndrome, or taking a brain scan that reveals brain damage that will cause the child to be, to some extent or other, mentally handicapped. Who makes the diagnosis in many of these cases? The obstetrician, or the pediatrician, or the psychologist? No, none of these. Frequently, the one who makes the diagnosis, not in medical terms but in terms of the certain knowledge that "something is wrong with this child's brain," is the child's mother. Years of talking to parents of retarded children who were the subject of late diagnoses have convinced me that when there's something wrong with a child's brain, a mother usually knows first. And any pediatrician who refuses to listen to a mother who says, "There's something not right about this child," is, at best, doing the God-playing doctor act and, at worst, possibly laying himself or herself open to a medical malpractice suit.

Victoria was not diagnosed as mentally retarded until she was seven years old. Nobody ever so much as mentioned the word. She sat up, crawled, cut teeth, and walked at more or less the right times. Her developmental milestones were appropriate up to the time when she should have been talking. She made pre-speech sounds at the expected times, but she didn't seem to be able to get much further.

"That's no problem," people told me. "Winston Churchill didn't speak until he was four." Or maybe it was Albert Einstein. Don't listen, ever, to that sort of stuff unless it comes from a professional in whom you have total confidence. The people who tell you such comforting tales are usually trying to be just that—comforting. Some are trying to get off the hook because they don't want to talk about the possibility that there really might be something wrong with your child. Either way, they do you no service by paying lip-service to the conventional clichés of reassurance.

Years later another parent told me that one of the earliest things she noticed was that her son didn't smile. "That's okay," the pediatrician said. "He'll smile when he's got something to smile about." Sure.

Our comprehension of Victoria's condition was probably retarded by a number of circumstances. I was an only child and had no experience with small children. I'd been a solitary, bookish child and I had never done much that brought me in contact with babies or young children. That, I realize now, was a serious disadvantage. But baby-sitting was not something that kids did in my neighborhood when I was young. My mother baby-sat for our next door neighbors, and I went with her. But I wasn't responsible for the young children in a way that might have made me aware of what little kids were like and how they grew.

My husband, John, was the younger of two children whose father had walked out when they were very small. His mother raised the children alone until she remarried when John was twelve. He didn't know much about babies either.

And there we were, two woefully ignorant young professional people who suddenly found ourselves married, with a baby, and living in—of all places—Moscow, USSR. John, then a photographer for United Press International, was posted to Moscow a few weeks after Victoria's birth. I followed shortly thereafter with the baby in a carrier that looked exactly like a shopping basket (it *was* a shopping basket, with a mattress inside) that caused much merriment on the plane journey. I got off the plane at Moscow's Sheremetyva airport, flanked by one fellow passenger carrying the baby in her basket and another carrying my wide-brimmed straw hat, and at times when I'm feeling cynical I look back upon that moment as the end of a rather protracted adolescence.

Moscow was not a nurturing environment. Tension was a way of life. The phones were bugged. Suspicion hung in the air. Moscow, for me, was instant culture shock and for years after I had to grit my teeth at the very suggestion that travel broadens the mind. Many Westerners found that Moscow life did not broaden the mind—it shrank the mind. Some of the people I knew there took to drink, or Valium, or both. It was a very difficult place in which to be a new mother with a new baby. So when I noticed, in Moscow, that Victoria did not seem to be a very outgoing baby I attributed it to the fact that I was not a very outgoing mother under those circumstances. I assumed that when we got out of there we would both blossom like the flowers in spring.

It was not that simple, of course. Things seldom are when you've got a mentally handicapped child. But to this day I wonder whether we'd have gotten Victoria diagnosed and on the right track sooner if we had stayed in London, where she was born, instead of living in the unreal, almost surrealistic, world which most foreigners inhabited in Moscow.

Two years in Moscow were as much as I could handle, so we moved back to London to await reposting. John would come home and say things like, "What about Beirut? There's an opening in Beirut." And I would say, "No way."

It was not conducive to marital bliss. Nor was the fact that Victoria still wasn't talking the way a two-going-on-three year old ought to talk. We took her to a speech therapist, who splashed Victoria's chubby little hands in a basin full of water and tried to get her to imitate the sound.

"Yes, what we've got here is a slow talker," I was assured. And that was all. Nobody said anything about retardation or brain damage. None of those dirty words ever surfaced. But there were hints. The problem was that I didn't hear them. Today, they would strike my ears like sounding brass or clashing cymbals, but I did not know then what I know now.

While we were in London awaiting reposting we sent Victoria to a nursery school, partly because we wanted her to have companions, and partly because I was having a hard time mothering this child who had a vague, undefined "problem" and I needed time to myself. I know now that the woman who ran the playschool suspected that Victoria was retarded, but she never came right out and said so. She said, "She seems to fall a lot, have you noticed that?" And she said, "She doesn't seem to have any sense of danger; she doesn't seem afraid that she might get hurt on some of the playground equipment."

Words like that, today, would set lights flashing along every nerve from my little toe to the innermost regions of my brain. Then, they slid right by me. I wish that pleasant, intelligent woman had said straight out that she suspected something was wrong and that we should take our daughter to see a neurologist.

We were still working with the speech therapist, with Victoria splashing around in the water and having a lot of fun, when the speech therapist suggested that we might want to get another opinion and suggested a well-reputed London clinic, where I made an appointment. But a couple of days later John came home and said, "What about Buenos Aires?" It sounded so totally unlikely a place to live that I said, "Okay." Anyway, my mother had told me frequently about a Spanish-speaking boyfriend of hers who had, for some reason I don't recall, been put up against a wall and shot. And I had studied Spanish for a year at school and found the language utterly beguiling. These were the romantic motivations for accepting such a proposition. The practical motivation was that John could not go on indefinitely rejecting the professional opportunities offered to him. So we packed our bags again and went to Buenos Aires.

Once arrived, of course, we were once more in the position of knowing nobody, so in order to help Victoria find same-age companions and to put myself in touch with other parents we enrolled her in another nursery school.

This time I got lucky. The principal of the nursery school told me, "I think you should take this child to a neurologist because it seems to me something in her brain isn't working right." The clues on which the principal based her observations were simple enough: Victoria had trouble adjusting socially; her gross motor coordination didn't seem good; she suffered periods of confusion, and she seemed to need more structure than the other children.

We heard what the principal of the nursery school was saying, and we took Victoria to a neurologist. Thus we entered a world that we should have entered several years earlier—a world of neurologists and psychologists and social workers and therapists of sundry persuasions. The problem was that none of them actually told us anything. They ran an electroencephalogram which came out normal (although with the more sophisticated equipment available today the readings would have been different). They talked in terms of speech delay, learning disability, and emotional disturbance. Emotional disturbance is the real bummer; that's the one you *know* has got to be your fault. But nobody ever mentioned retardation.

As a result of all the testing we were advised to send Victoria to a school for learning disabled children. She got along okay. How many of those children were learning disabled and how many were mentally retarded I'll never know. Victoria adapted to the school environment and learned her colors and her numbers. She seemed to be having a reasonably good time.

In the meantime, Victoria and I were in therapy. Victoria saw a speech therapist and a counselor who was supposed to help her general emotional adjustment. I went to the same counselor, ostensibly to learn how to be a decent parent. It was suggested that John should join these sessions, thereby turning them into what they were originally supposed to be, family counseling sessions. This, however, was not in his canon of acceptable things to do. If I wanted to go into therapy, he indicated, that was my business. If I had a problem and wanted to deal with it that way, that was fine. He, however, didn't have a problem, and therefore therapy was not necessary to him. Anyway, he had a job to do.

In retrospect, I see that for me this was the beginning of the end of our marriage. We did, however, have another child. I wanted another child. Having been an only child, I didn't want Victoria to be one. Also, to be honest, I had recognized by now that I had a child who was impaired in some way and I wanted to see if we could get it right.

With Emma Kate, we did.

Throughout my pregnancy with Emma I was afraid. Not terrified, but afraid. This time I went to childbirth classes and tried to learn to breathe properly. I felt I had not been in control of the process of childbirth when Victoria was born and I wanted to do right by this baby. This time, I wanted to know what was going on.

It never occurred to me that there might be some way to discover if the new baby was likely to have the sort of problems we now acknowledged Victoria to have—even though we still didn't know exactly what sort of problems she had. I had never heard of amniocentesis and the doctor never suggested that or any other test. Anyway, whatever the test results, I wouldn't have had an abortion. I had never heard of genetic counseling, so the idea of investigating what had happened to Victoria before risking getting pregnant again was not really an issue.

I told the doctor who would deliver my second child that if anything were seriously wrong I would not want him to resort to extraordinary means to make the baby live.

He said, "The chances that this baby will not be perfectly fine are so remote as to be negligible, but nothing I say will make you believe that."

I understand now that he had no right to make the assumption that the second child would be fine, because he didn't know why the first child wasn't. At the time, however, I was duly reassured.

Emma was in just as much of a hurry to enter the world as her sister had been, and the most vivid memory I have of Emma's birth is of the obstetrician belting down the corridor, pulling on his surgical gloves as he ran, as I was wheeled into the delivery room.

Victoria was just over five when Emma was born. She loved

having a little sister, and Emma was a most rewarding baby, cheerful and charming. She appeared—and I was certainly on the watch—bright, alert, and curious. But the signs that Victoria was not normal were becoming more and more apparent. For one thing, the very fact that both Victoria and I were in therapy was a clear enough indication that there was a reason for us to be there. And we were getting to be very good friends with the speech therapist, who came to the house twice a week.

It was also becoming less possible to avoid recognizing that the developmental gaps between Victoria and other children her age were getting wider. Her first nursery school teacher's prediction that she couldn't comprehend danger was being established as accurate. Victoria didn't understand that it was not part of pool-time fun to push other little kids in the deep end. (The other children's parents didn't find that too amusing, either.) Her social behavior was not appropriate to her age. When we went to the market she would wrap her arms around any small child she met, and she could not assimilate information about hugging friends being kind and nice but hugging strange children being something a lot of people didn't like. Once she greeted a totally strange toddler in a stroller with such enthusiasm that she tipped the child onto the cobblestones.

She did not grasp play routines or games as quickly as other children. When she went to birthday parties her hostesses would report that she'd had a good time but was reluctant to join in the activities. She seemed to get confused easily. There were physical signs, too, beyond her limited speech. Her coordination was off. She walked with her knees turned in and her feet splayed. Her movement wasn't right. But she was a charmer, and such a pretty little girl couldn't have much wrong, could she? And still nobody mentioned retardation. They talked about the speech problem and the poor gross motor coordination, and possible emotional repercussions from all the traveling we'd done. And the EEG had been okay.

I can't believe I could have been so ignorant. Looking at the photographs we have of the children from our Buenos Aires period—because their father was a photographer we don't have happy snaps, we have glossy eight-by-elevens—I can see so clearly what I couldn't, or didn't choose to, see then. There are two photographs in particular. One was taken at her fifth-birthday party (I laid on a very comprehensive social life for her). It's right there in her eyes. Today it would take me all of three seconds to recognize that the child was probably mentally retarded. The other photograph was taken when Victoria was six and Emma about eighteen months. The two of them are charging across one of Buenos Aires' beautiful cobblestone plazas. Victoria looks bright and happy and thoroughly well-adjusted, but her legs are all over the place, her body movement is clearly not normal, and that something in her eyes is definitely there.

All these years people have been telling me, "Oh, but to look at her you'd never know. . . ." And I get angry at their lack of observation until I recall how long it took me to look into my own child's eyes and recognize that something was getting in the way of the workings of her mind.

But still nobody mentioned retardation.

Because the school Victoria attended was in downtown Buenos Aires and we lived in one of the affluent suburbs, I had no contact with the parents of other children who attended the school. In any case, the children—including Victoria—were labeled as learning disabled, and my experience of labeling was not sufficiently developed (as it is now) to make many distinctions among different handicapping conditions.

My husband had come to regard any therapeutic programming for Victoria as exclusively my business. That's what mothers were for. I think he regarded my own therapy as a nice little indulgence for a bored wife dumped in a country not her own (there may have been something in that). And my therapy probably cost less than the dedicated spending which occupied the extended leisure hours of some of my expatriate acquaintances.

So there weren't many people, socially speaking, from whom I could get much support in dealing with what was becoming more and more apparent as "Victoria's problem." As a consequence I became increasingly dependent on the professionals involved in the case, and this is a dependency I've had a hard time shaking. It's an easy situation to get into.

The only real understanding I encountered from non-professionals came from a couple who had a son a little older than Victoria, an incredibly good-looking boy whom I had privately written off as a spoiled and obnoxious brat. He had visited us on several occasions and had spent his time wrecking the playroom and pulling the lemons off my cherished lemon tree (having been raised in England, I'd never seen lemons growing on a tree). In my ignorance I took it for granted that the parents were over-permissive and couldn't keep the child under control. As it happened, the child suffered from hyperactivity.

In all my five years in Argentina, those were the only parents I ever met who had any personal experience of what I might be dealing with, a child with special needs. The boy's father was particularly helpful. He would often sit with me at the many parties we attended (our Buenos Aires period was a highly social one) and talk about how to meet the needs of a special child. He talked about trying to get in touch with what the child was feeling and trying to understand that what other people viewed as socially unacceptable behavior was, in fact, a disorder the child needed to be helped with. He told me that my having the child in therapy and doing practical things to deal with Victoria's problem proved that I was a good and loving mother, not the inadequate creature that I then felt myself to be. The very idea was a revelation, the first chink of light through a closed door.

There was no one else, though, who understood. Or so I perceived it at the time. It was, as I said earlier, the professionals in Victoria's life to whom I ran for support and reassurance, thus reinforcing the dangerous dependency that can so easily prove a trap for parents of mentally handicapped children.

So there we were, with Victoria six years old and the victim of some unidentified handicap for which, most of the time, I still felt responsible. I dealt with it, I suppose, as best I could. There were a lot of negatives. On the positive side lay the fact that both the children were healthy, pretty, and apparently happy. Victoria was a sweet and loving child. Emma was developing a crop of strawberry blonde curls and a very determined personality. The latter would stand her in good stead in the years to come.

When Victoria was nearly seven, John decided that he wanted to stop being UPI's photo chief in Latin America and become a North American executive. He announced that we would take the first reasonable American posting that presented itself.

"But what about Victoria?" I wailed. "What about special schools? How do we make sure she will get the chances she needs?"

His reply was that she would take the chances that were offered, like the rest of us. Thus we moved to Chicago.

When we arrived in Chicago I was determined to make the adjustment more easily than I had in Moscow or Buenos Aires (I came to love Buenos Aires, but it took a long time). I was also determined to get Victoria into the right kind of setting—whatever that might be—as soon as possible. I did a great deal of running around to educators and social workers, and Victoria was placed in a special education classroom in a Chicago public school. Her teacher was a very pleasant young lady who assured me that the one thing she was going to achieve with the child, even if she achieved nothing else, was to teach her to recognize the color red.

"What are you talking about?" I asked, much put out. "She's known her colors since she was three."

"No, she does not know her colors; she does not recognize the color red." The teacher was very insistent and it turned out that, indeed, for this teacher Victoria had no intention of recognizing the color red, or any other color for that matter. She was also angry and hostile in school, and she wet her pants regularly (which she sometimes still does, as a five-foot-four young adult, when she's mad).

For someone who had come to accept, as I had, that teacher or neurologist or therapist or social worker knows best, this was a most enlightening experience. I learned something that every parent with a retarded child, or perhaps it would be more accurate to say any parent with any child, needs to know from day one: even professionals make mistakes.

It was clear that Victoria needed to be out of that school, and as John and I were looking for a house to rent in the suburbs I began asking where would be the most appropriate place to live if schooling, possibly special schooling, were a priority. The consensus was Evanston, a pleasant suburb on the northern fringes of Chicago.

Meanwhile, I had been recommended to a clinic at an Evanston hospital where Victoria could be tested, and that was when our luck—Victoria's and mine—began to turn. An amiable, greying, round-faced doctor chatted with Victoria and watched her for a while and then told me, "Well, what we're dealing with here is a retarded child, so we'd better start looking at what we can do for her."

It was the first time anyone had ever told me that my child was retarded. I should have been appalled. But even as the doctor spoke I felt the clouds of ignorance begin to clear from around my head. I had no doubt whatsoever that he was right. It didn't even cross my mind to question his diagnosis. I felt enormous relief. At last I knew what I was dealing with. After all those years someone had finally come out and said to me, "Lady, this kid is retarded." Now we could start working on what to do to help her overcome the limitations that had been placed upon her by whatever caused her to be retarded.

It seems that it should have been possible to diagnose Victoria's mental retardation before she was two years old. Although most of the time I no longer feel personally responsible for her retardation, still I wish I had been more aware of the possibility of brain damage, or retardation, or mental handicap, or whatever. I wish I'd been consciously aware of the possibility of a child's being born not perfect. I wish I'd been exposed to some sort of knowledge that would have prepared me to recognize the warning signs. How I managed to grow up without any vestige of such awareness I still find incredible. However, when I look around and see how society reacts to Victoria and people like her, I realize that most people still don't deal in that kind of language. It is not a reality until it happens to you.

Culpable ignorance is a term I learned during my rigidly Roman Catholic upbringing. If there's anything I feel guilty about when I look at my mentally handicapped daughter it is that I was culpably ignorant. The warning signs were there, quite apart from the obvious speech problems: the play-school teacher's comment about Victoria's lack of awareness of danger; the difficulty Victoria had in integrating herself into a group of same-age children on their own terms; the lack of coordination; the flapping movements she made with her arms when she was excited. And those photographs.

Retardation is a very threatening subject, and it's no wonder that people shy away from it. But it exists, and the parents to whose children it happens might have an easier time dealing with the reality of it if somewhere, at some point, they'd acknowledged the possibility that, yes, it could happen to their child.

A couple of years ago I was talking to the mother of Emily, whose story comes next, about the professionals who are part of the lives of parents with retarded children. I told her that I felt I had been fortunate in encountering—with the exception of that teacher who was obsessed with teaching Victoria the color red—only helpful and compassionate professionals. (The statement was true at the time of that conversation, although it is no longer true.) I told her about some of the people I'd worked with on my long and painful search for a diagnosis of Victoria's condition, and she asked a question that made me look at my situation, as it was then, rather differently:

"But do you really feel you were fortunate just because people were nice to you? Don't you feel that they withheld a lot of information you were entitled to have, because they were afraid to tell you the truth?"

And yes, that was probably the case. Avoidance takes a lot of different forms, and it's not easy to come out and tell a parent that a child is permanently damaged, mentally retarded, and will never lead a normal life. It's rough on the parent who is hearing the news, and it's rough on the person who has to impart it. But for the parent, not knowing is worse. Moreover, it can have serious repercussions for the child. There are a lot of retarded people in our society for whom the effects of retardation might have been minimized had someone leveled with the parents and told them the truth.

As soon as you know that a child is mentally handicapped, you can start looking for appropriate educational and treatment programs. In the case of mildly or moderately retarded children, the sooner you know, the less devastating the effects of the retardation are going to be later on. Since the introduction of "early intervention" programs for children with Down syndrome, for instance, the children who have been exposed to those programs have made significant gains over other children who lacked that exposure.

I know youngsters whose handicap was not obvious or identifiable and who were not placed in the special schools they required until they were in their teens. Along the way they missed out on programming that would have concentrated on developing their particular strengths and helping them hone the survival skills that they would need in later life. Some of these youngsters suffered severely by having to make the effort to compete in areas where success was impossible. They suffered educationally and socially, because a mentally handicapped child in a classroom full of ordinary kids sticks out like a sunflower in a field of daisies. And although it would be pleasant to believe that ordinary children will nurture a less able peer, that's not necessarily the way it happens. Mainstreaming, the policy of integrating handicapped children into ordinary schools, sounds like a wonderful idea. In practice it can be a whole lot less than wonderful.

When a child's mental handicap is a fact from day one, lack of information can seriously hamper the parent's chances of seeking services that will help the child. Ignorance is not bliss.

Ignorance is even less blissful in those cases where a normal child develops some potentially harmful condition which is either not recognized or not taken seriously by the professionals responsible for the child's well-being. Donna, Emily's mother, found this out the hard way—the very hard way.

"hey, what a cute little girl!"

Emily was the first child of Donna and her husband Gary, a commercial film producer. This is what Donna has to say about what happened after Emily's birth.

Emily was meant to be a perfectly normal child. She was normal when she was born, and she ought to be normal today. What happened to her was a terrible mistake. There is no excuse for it.

By the time Emily was four months old she was reaching for things and smiling at me. Then she stopped doing those things. That was the first sign. And one day when I picked her up I saw strange movement in her eyes, like an electrical interference. My heart just went down to my stomach. I knew it wasn't right.

I told the pediatrician about her eyes, and that she seemed to be regressing. He answered that I was an over-anxious first-time mother and expected far too much from a four-and-a-half month old baby. Then he walked out the door.

I felt wonderful. Reassured. I wasn't even angry that he had put me down. I thought, there's nothing wrong with her! He knows. *I called my husband and told him that the doctor had said everything was fine.*

We went on vacation for two weeks, leaving Emily with my in-laws, and when we came back I noticed a marked difference. She should have been exploding with growth, but she wasn't. Again the pediatrician said her developmental milestones were fine with him, and we kept buying this reassurance of his, even though all the symptoms were there: She was terribly constipated; her hair was coarse and dry; her muscle tone was floppy; and she was very overweight. She didn't look right to me. She didn't feel right to me. Nothing was right.

She was definitely slow, but the baby books (and I read them all) said there are fast babies, and slow babies, and it doesn't make any difference, so I kept kidding myself into believing that she was okay.

When she was seven-and-a-half months old I took her to the pediatrician again, and this time it was different. He looked at her for all of about sixty seconds and immediately the man's color changed, he literally blanched when he picked her up. It was as if all of a sudden a light went off in his head—"Something is amiss here."

They ran tests on Emily over a period of three days and it came out that she had a low thyroid, how low I did not know at the time, and the pediatrician never really discussed with us what was wrong with her. He said he would have to put her on thyroid replacement, so he did that and within ten days she was a different child. She sat up; her muscle tone improved; she was no longer constipated; she was smiling and happy. There was a really dramatic difference in her behavior.

The pediatrician called the house a couple of times to ask how she was doing, and we reported to him and everyone seemed happy. The only hitch was that he failed to tell us the disease was threatening her brain development. Essentially, it was presented as if it were a vitamin deficiency; if you don't have it you don't grow right, so we'll give her some and she'll grow right. He never once mentioned that she might be brain damaged, retarded, screwed up—never once.

Then I started reading medical books, and I began to get hysterical. The very first one said that the prognosis for an infant with hypothyroidism is very grave, that the chances of the child achieving normal development are poor if the disease isn't caught in time. It stressed how important the dosage of the thyroid was, and how if the disease were caught soon enough it could be reversed and the child left without much damage. And I, of course, hung on to that like crazy. I didn't know that we had already run out of time.

I began pestering the doctor and begging him, and he got very turned off by us. He did refer us to a neurologist, after I insisted, but he never got us to any endocrine people to regulate the kind of medication she was on, or the dosage, until she was seventeen months old.

We've learned since that all the damage that can be done is done before eighteen months; after that point the disease is not so threatening. It's only in those first months when the brain development is very explosive.

So we started trucking Emily around to different pediatricians and we discovered a very interesting thing: no one in our medical community would dispute anything that our pediatrician had done. Finally we felt we had to get her out of this medical community for an honest opinion, so when my husband was in Los Angeles, where he does a lot of business, he walked into the University of California at Los Angeles Medical Center, which he knew was one of the best, and asked to see a neurologist. He made an appointment and we took her out there.

In the interim she had been in all kinds of infant programming. The local neurologist had told us to get her into a program, so we did. She was in out-patient therapy at one hospital and in various other zero-to-three programs, and the experience was just horrible because no one would tell us anything, not the teachers or the speech therapists or anyone else. We literally walked around in limbo for eighteen months.

Emily was really too young to be tested, or for anyone to make a prognosis, but at that time I needed desperately for someone to tell me, "Yes, she's retarded," or "No, she isn't retarded," or "Hey, she's really retarded," or, "Yes, she's just a little bit retarded." Anything would have been helpful at that point, because here was this pediatrician still telling us, "Hey, what a cute little girl," and never mentioning the fact that she was permanently damaged.

When she was twelve months old Emily tested out at nine months, which meant that she was still what they considered a little delayed; no one would put a label on it. When she was tested at UCLA she was almost twenty-four months old and she tested out at thirteen months. So there had been a tremendous loss in that year.

The doctor who tested her at UCLA was the first one who

looked at us straight, eye to eye, and said, "She is retarded." But given the range she was functioning in then he was willing to say that she was mildly retarded. And he could see that we really needed to know what that meant, so he told us that as an adult she would probably be able to function alone with supervision, and I remember sitting there with tears streaming down my face and asking the stupid question, "Do you think anybody will ever marry her?"

We left the doctor's office and got as far as the parking lot. We couldn't make it any further. We sat down on a park bench, with Emily, and cried our eyes out. Then we went back to the hotel and cried all night, and we decided to leave Los Angeles and come home. We had all kinds of social things on our calendar, but we couldn't do them. In a way we felt better because someone had labeled her; someone had finally been straight with us. At least we had something definitive to come home to and face.

Emily was the victim of medical malpractice. Her parents sued the pediatrician who had failed to diagnose her condition until it was too late. The case was settled out of court and they won a settlement sufficient to provide financially for Emily and the special care she needs for the rest of her life. They won the case, but they couldn't win back her normality. The fact remains that a little girl who should have been normal is now severely retarded. After living at home for seven years, Emily will most likely spend the rest of her days in a residential home for children like herself.

Emily's retardation was preventable. An estimated fifty percent of all cases of retardation that occur in the United States are classified by the national Association for Retarded Citizens as preventable.

getting the facts: the parents' right to know

Emily is a proven instance of how a child who is born normal can become retarded as a result of outside circumstances. There are other cases which are not so extreme but which offer evidence that lack of information from sources that should be competent, and willing, to provide it seriously hampers a parent's ability to cope. Even when there's no indication of actual wrongdoing on the part of any person involved in the birth or treatment of a handicapped child, the way some professionals handle (or mishandle) parents can cause a tremendous amount of grief and pain that might otherwise have been avoided.

A case in point is that of Richard, now (like Victoria) eighteen years old, whose mother Ilene still questions the circumstances of his birth and the treatment she received at the hands of the professionals involved. Ilene says:

Richard was born when I was twenty-six. Before I became pregnant I had been taking birth control pills for at least six years, originally, I suspect, in very high dosages. I had had recurring infections for which I was taking many medications, and the infections were having such a bad effect on my mental state that I was also taking tranquilizers even while I was trying to get pregnant. My doctors assured me that all these drugs had been taken safely by pregnant women. (I am not an habitual user of tranquilizers; when I am in decent mental health I find them obnoxious.)

My pregnancy seemed normal except for some bleeding in the third month. I was told that this was not serious. When the time of birth approached I asked my gynecologist about anesthetics. I knew nothing about anesthetics, certainly not that they might have any potential for harm, and I was interested in not feeling any pain during the delivery.

The gynecologist said, "What about twilight sleep?"

Twilight sleep sounded nice and restful so, without asking any questions, I said, "That sounds fine."

I did not know then that twilight sleep is actually a mind-altering drug. You do not remember consciously any of the events of your delivery, but I am told by nurses that you scream and you struggle and you act very much like an animal under the veterinarian's hands. When I came up out of it after Richard was born I had a feeling that something horrible had happened, but I could not remember what it was.

When I was at the hospital, in labor, they told me, "These first-time mothers are very antsy," and that it would be many hours before the baby was born. In the labor room I was feeling more and more pain, and the nurses and interns assured me they could do nothing for me until I was dilated a certain number of centimeters.

I said, "Humor me, and measure."

So they did, and they started to run around, scurrying like ants and sticking things in my arm. The doctor came and said, "This is twilight sleep; is it okay?"

I said, "Okay," because I felt I was losing track of my pain-controlling mechanism and was about to start screaming. I never consciously saw the delivery room; I never saw the child; I never knew what had happened. Somewhere along the line I was told that it was a boy and that the weight was normal.

It seems fairly obvious to me now that whatever happened to Richard happened sometime in the period after conception and through delivery. I went back to my obstetrician when I'd gotten a final diagnosis that the child was mentally impaired and, being very naive about what his reactions might be, I wanted to know whether anything abnormal had happened during the delivery. He gave me a very hostile "no" without even looking at the records. Later, of course, I realized that if he had said "yes" he might have let himself in for all kinds of lawsuits.

So I felt very much that people were denying me information, and I have never found out yet any definitive cause for Richard's problems—whether they were hereditary, or caused by a medication I was taking or a disease I had, or by circumstances of the delivery. It's a moot point, really, because I can't go back and do anything about his delivery.

The experiences of both Emily's mother and Richard's give credence to the assumption that the mother is frequently the first to suspect that something is not right with the child. Given that the mother is still usually the primary care-giver for a very young child, it follows that she will be the one who observes the child closely, day by day. Even first-time mothers seem to have that innate knowledge of what's normal and what isn't. Some avoid that knowledge longer than others and I, for whatever reasons, avoided it for longer than many mothers I've met since. With Victoria, however, the signs were—at the beginning—very tenuous, tiny clues to the pattern that her life would follow, easy enough to miss. Richard's mother says:

> It seemed to me that there was something odd about the child, but I couldn't put my finger on it; I hadn't had any experience with infants. When I asked my pediatrician, he told me I was a nervous Nellie. Now I believe it must have been obvious to him from certain unnatural movements my son made, waving his hands and his head and going through repeated ritual motions. But I suspect that this very paternalistic older pediatrician did not want to make me upset any sooner than he thought I needed to be upset.
>
> I took books out of the library on assisting your child to speak, and I discovered that Richard was not making the pre-speech sounds—the syllables—that babies are supposed to make. I had been suspicious for a long time and I suspected deafness, because it runs in my husband's family. Also, Richard did not appear to have any wide interest in toys. His motor development, crawling and walking, was very close to normal. His feeding was not; he rejected food with lumps in it and gagged and vomited if I tried to force him. He was not interested in self-feeding. He was extremely hungry. When he ate I had to use two spoons and shovel the food right into him.
>
> Because I suspected deafness I took Richard to a hearing clinic. His hearing was normal, but the people at the clinic sent me to a neurologist. The neurologist examined Richard and told me that Richard was "globally retarded." When I asked what "globally" meant he told me that rather than being retarded in a specific area Richard was totally, in all areas, retarded. The neurologist was very cold and nonsupportive in giving me this information. The only comfort he offered consisted of telling me that I was young and could have more children.
>
> He also said, "Don't let anyone tell you he is autistic; he's not autistic." I didn't know what autism was, so that didn't help too much. The neurologist said that it had something to do with being affectionate. He took the child, and Richard reached out for me, obviously in preference to him. He said that an autistic child would not do that. I still don't know whether that's true.
>
> The electroencephalogram showed spikes in the side that has to do with speech; but I was told that perfectly normal people can show that same response in an electroencephalogram, so it didn't prove anything. We also had some genetic work done, and checked our genealogy, but it wasn't conclusive. It just showed that he didn't have any chromosomal abnormalities or anything

they could detect at that time. We did find out that I had a retarded uncle, but it seemed unlikely that the retardation was hereditary.

I received pressure from family members who considered that there was nothing really wrong with Richard, or that if there was some little thing wrong with him then certainly working with him twenty-four hours a day would improve it. If I would only work with him properly and teach him properly, and not be such a lazy good-for-nothing mother, he would be feeding himself and getting toilet trained. That was the implication. He also turned out to have allergies and he got rashes which made him less than becoming to look at and required extra treatment and care.

After Richard was diagnosed I took him for a while to a research institute where they were really much more interested in him as a subject for research than as a patient to be helped. He was accepted on the basis that he was not a conventional retarded child, not typical of some well-recognized syndrome. The cause of his retardation was not known, and he had what they called "bizarre behaviors," which was a description I was going to hear very frequently in the future.

At the institute I saw a psychiatrist who gave me a very brutal interview during which I started shaking uncontrollably. It reminded me of articles that I've read in which a lot of guilt is tossed onto the mother: "Why do you want this? Why do you think that? Why do you think he's hyperactive? Is there some way you want him to behave that he's not fulfilling?"

I had told him I suspected the child was hyperactive because of all the movement he made. I didn't know what the technical definition of hyperactive was, but Richard was more active than other children. Although the psychiatrist must have seen that I was very distressed, he did nothing whatever to help me.

He prescribed a couple of medications for Richard which drove the child right up the wall and made him scream all night. When I called the psychiatrist about this reaction he said, essentially, "Well, if you don't want to use medications, that's your decision." I stopped giving Richard medications.

I knew that some drugs could have paradoxical effects on children, but what he was giving Richard did not have a paradoxical reaction. It was an "upper" and it had the reaction it was supposed to have—it drove him up the wall. I myself experimented by taking the same dose that he was given as a small child. It drove me right up the wall, and I weighed considerably more than Richard did, so it's quite understandable that he screamed all night.

The other medication Richard was given was a tranquilizer that simply made him like a zombie. His teachers said that he wasn't doing his bad behaviors at school, but he wasn't doing anything else either. He just sat there in a stupor. No one ever suggested giving him lower doses of anything. And nobody ever told me that there were side effects to these drugs.

Now I'm older and wiser, and with any drug I ask about side effects.

Katherine—"an error of judgment"

Katherine, Carol's first child, was normal at birth, but she contracted spinal meningitis in the hospital nursery. Carol says:

Evidently they waited too long to give her medication and to start treating her as a child with a very serious illness. And by the time she was on medication, she was going into convulsions.

It was an error of judgment. The doctor said, "I don't think this fever is a big deal. I think this kid is going to outgrow it in a day or two." So he didn't take any precautions. And she did not outgrow it. I know now that with a newborn infant they should have started her on antibiotics right away, as soon as she started running a temperature.

I realized early that something was going wrong. I had questions and concerns right at the beginning. Even in the first few days she didn't cry right and she didn't nurse right.

Then, while I was still in the hospital, she was isolated on the pediatric floor. They moved her down there on Saturday, and on the following Monday I was released. That day I went to see her, and that was one of the most horrifying experiences I've ever been through. She had been this perfect and very beautiful newborn. I know every mother says that about her own baby, but with Katherine it really was true. She was the baby the nurses and the other mothers came to look at. They'd say, "Goodness, isn't she pretty!" When I went down to see her she was in an incubator, which was upsetting in itself. Worse was that they do intravenous

*feedings in newborns in their skulls (which I did not know), and
the feeding had not gone right but no one had bothered to check
it. Her head was swollen to ten times its normal size, and the side
that had been lying on the mat was totally flattened out. So what
I saw was this totally grotesque . . . thing . . . that had been my
beautiful baby.*

*The nurse was a lot of help. She said, "Oh, isn't she doing
wonderfully?" Which was hardly the way it looked to me. But
apparently they had thought that she was going to die on Sunday,
and they were so surprised that she was still alive on Monday
morning that to them she was doing wonderfully. They didn't see
her quite the way I did.*

*Then the nurse picked her up in the incubator and her swollen
head rolled over and around and it was awful, just awful. I had
to get out of there.*

*They don't know how they saved Katherine. She was so crit-
ically ill that medical science still can't account for why she lived.*

Carol left her daughter in the hospital and went home and
"cried a lot." Her husband, who had been granted leave from
the Army for the birth, had to return to his unit, so Carol was
alone.

*I was left, basically, to deal with it alone. Katherine came home
when she was ten days old, and she was still a critically ill child
who needed a lot of care. She probably shouldn't have been sent
home so soon, because the infection hadn't localized, which it did
two days after she was home.*

*I spent many long nights just sitting with her. I put her up
against me, her little naked body up against my body, and I
wrapped a big terrycloth bathrobe that was my husband's—Tom's
a large man—around the two of us. I would sit and rock and
that was the only thing that would get her to quit crying. Otherwise, she cried constantly.*

*Recently, I talked to a doctor and found out the reason for the
crying. He said that she was in pain—she had constant pain in
her intestines. I also found out recently that her head had been
thrown way back from the spinal meningitis, which I hadn't
realized, so she was never comfortable. Her head had always hurt
for the first three months. I'd put her in the buggy and she'd be
fine for about five minutes, then she'd start crying. So she was
comfortable only when she was up on my shoulder with her head
pushed forward. I look at her baby pictures now and I can see
how her head was pushed back, but I didn't know it then. I didn't
know about all that pain she had gone through.*

The way Carol found out about Katherine's early days was through taking legal action. When her daughter was sixteen, Carol filed a medical malpractice suit which has not yet been resolved.

I'd wanted for a long time to look into the legal side of it, but Katherine's father couldn't face the fact that she was retarded— even though the retardation became more and more apparent as time went on. If you're going to start on a major malpractice suit because your child is handicapped, first you've got to say, "Yes, my child is handicapped." But he couldn't do that.

When we divorced, Katherine was twelve; I asked my lawyer about a malpractice suit and he said, "One thing at a time; let's get this divorce handled first." So that's why it's been delayed as long as it has.

One of my main reasons for taking legal action was to get questions answered about her birth. Because I've had a lot of them and they've never been answered—they've never even been addressed—and she's now going on eighteen. It's been interesting, because certain questions have been answered, not only the ones I had but ones I didn't even think of asking. I'm really getting my eyes opened.

I always assumed that the doctor who delivered her was basically at fault. In my mind his ethics and his approach to delivery were very questionable. But that's not the basis for a lawsuit—that I was induced for a doctor's convenience before my due date, nor that she was exposed to spinal meningitis staph infection in the hospital nursery, which is what evidently happened and which isn't the sort of thing that should happen. The basis for the lawsuit is that they waited too long to give medication to a sick baby, and that was not accepted medical practice at the time.

So that's the basis of the lawsuit, and it has been a long, painful process. I've been dredging up a lot of stuff. I'm learning about what was going on at the time she was born, and it's helpful to me because I wanted to find out what happened. Looking back, it's very upsetting, very perturbing. I wish that I had known it all at the time.

Katherine has cerebral palsy, moderate to minimal, or moderate to severe, in different parts of her body, and she is severely brain-damaged. Extensively brain-damaged. Every area of learning is damaged. Kathy does not have an undamaged area of learning, and why she functions as well as she does nobody knows. Even the neurologist who examined her most recently said to me, "Don't listen to any of the doctors and don't listen to what any of the schools say to you, because you and she evidently have more answers. But I can't tell you why she can do eighty percent of the things she does. She shouldn't be able to."

"does he look like anyone in your family?"

Emily and Katherine are children who should be normal today; they fall in the estimated fifty percent of retardation in the United States that is classified as preventable. Not all the stories, however, are horror stories, and not all of them involve delayed diagnosis, confusion, or withholding of information.

Chris, who is now twelve, was born with Down syndrome, and his mother, Sheila, describes the circumstances of her son's birth in more positive terms than the parents who have already spoken in these pages. She says:

We are a good example, I think, of how the birth of a handicapped baby does not have to be devastating. It's difficult. I'm not saying it's not difficult. The shock takes your breath away. You can't believe it.

I first saw Chris when he was five hours old, and it wasn't a nurse who brought him to me, it was our personal pediatrician. I didn't know if this was typical procedure because I'd never had a baby before.

So I was holding the baby and the pediatrician asked, "Does he look like anyone in your family?" My response was that, well, babies are babies and they all look pretty much alike to me, so no, I couldn't really say he looked like anyone in the family. Then all of a sudden I realized that the doctor was trying to tell me something.

My aunt has a boy with Down syndrome. I don't know him very well because they live in England and I haven't really watched him grow up, but the experience with my aunt's child meant that when I looked at my own son I could recognize that he had Down syndrome.

Nobody said anything, but when I recognized the physical characteristics of Down syndrome it was a flash in my mind and I said to myself, "My God, I know what the doctor is trying to tell me. Chris is going to be retarded."

So I said to the doctor, "I think I know what you are trying to tell me." He was a little surprised, I think, that I had recognized it myself.

He had the sense to tell me when Peter, my husband, was with me. It is a very critical thing, as far as I'm concerned, that when a doctor tells new parents that they have a handicapped child they should be told together, so that they can support each other and nobody gets this disastrous news alone.

The doctor treated us in a very sensitive way, which I think at that time was quite unusual for a pediatrician dealing with parents of a handicapped newborn. He explained what Down syndrome is, how it is caused by an extra chromosome, and he said that the diagnosis wasn't definite but that some of the physical characteristics would indicate it, and he showed us what they were. Then he told us they would do a blood test and a chromosome study, and it would take four to six weeks before we got the results.

So there was that length of time when we didn't know for sure, although in my own mind I knew, and that period of uncertainty was helpful because you seem to need that space before the reality is actually grasped. It's good to be able to say, "Maybe there's a slight possibility that they are wrong; they've been wrong before." It buys you time for buffering the shock. Some days you can say, "Yes, he does have Down syndrome and I am going to cope with that"; and other days you say, "Today I can't cope with it; he doesn't have Down syndrome."

I remember very clearly saying to the doctor, "Well, I guess I'm going to have some good days and some bad days," and he replied, "I think you're right." And that's probably a realistic way of approaching it.

The next thing I did was ask for information. I asked where I could get some facts on Down syndrome. There wasn't a whole lot to read that was positive. You'd never want to read books about it from the public library, or look in the dictionary or encyclopedia for a definition. The things parents learn that way are devastating.

However, one of the books that friends brought me was actually written by a young man who had Down syndrome, an Englishman named Nigel Hunt who traveled very widely with *his parents and then wrote his own book,* The Story of Nigel Hunt. *That was what I wr* *reading the day after Chris was born, and it was very helpful.*

We've been lucky. Not that it doesn't hurt at first. I remember so clearly the moment of shock when I realized that the doctor was trying to tell me that Chris would be retarded. But nobody said anything like, "You ought to institutionalize this child." Nobody came in and told me, "Your child is probably going to be a vegetable," or "Don't take this baby home." I didn't have to recover from the kind of negative garbage that a lot of parents get dumped on them. I just had to recover from the shock, the breathtaking shock of recognition that, my God, my baby is mentally retarded. And that was just in my mind. Nobody said a negative word. We didn't have to undo a lot of unnecessary hurt as some parents have to.

I learned very early in my son's life that as soon as a child is labeled Down syndrome people start making assumptions, most of them negative.

When the nurse brought me Chris to breastfeed he wouldn't nurse, and she said, "Oh, these babies don't know how to suck." It turned out that he wouldn't eat because he wasn't hungry. They had made the assumption that I wouldn't be able to breastfeed him and they'd been giving him formula in the nursery. I called the pediatrician and told him, "This is my baby, and I intend to breastfeed him, so please instruct the nursery to stop giving him formula." I breastfed him until he was a year old.

That incident showed me right away that people in the world make predictions and assumptions about kids with Down syndrome from the day they open their eyes, mostly about what they can't do.

Part of the problem has to do with something I've found out over the years: many doctors have no concept of who children with Down syndrome are. Also, doctors often place education very high in their personal value systems, and the first thing you know about a child with Down syndrome is that he won't be going to Harvard. That affects the worth they see in the child—they feel that if he won't be able to achieve academically he won't be able to achieve at all. Such doctors impose their own value systems upon parents, and I object to that very strongly.

This attitude seems to be more prevalent in the United States than elsewhere, because here many parents also place education so high on their priority list that they have their children enrolled in college almost before they are born. If you've been raised to place a high value on education, or if you live in a big university city, it has to be more difficult for your mentally retarded child to be accepted and assimilated into society. But if you live in a small village where all the children play together and probably all go to the same school, or if you live on a farm, then it's possible that your retarded child may be as valuable as your other children, or more so, even though he won't ever go to college.

In my family in England college wasn't a top priority. We took Chris to England for the first time when he was a year old; my Dad just said, "Well, he's one of ours." Not being able to drive a car, or pass examinations, or do those things that are expected by parents in America—to my dad they were not important. He couldn't relate to them.

He said, "Well, my brother has never married, and he's never driven a car, and he's never been to college. I bet you that Chris will probably do better than him." His point was that Chris will have a lot more opportunities than my dad's brother had, even though he wasn't mentally retarded.

When Chris was born it certainly helped that neither Peter nor I came from families who presupposed great things for Chris academically. We wanted a healthy child, but I don't really believe I ever looked so far into the future as to wonder what particular school he would go to.

I do know one mother, though, who told me that before their first baby was born they were choosing names, and her husband wanted a real impressive name because his son was going to be a member of the Supreme Court one day. Then the baby was born with Down syndrome. When you've been daydreaming like that before the birth, and then you're told that your child is mentally retarded, it means you've got a long way to come back to get to square one.

Sheila's experiences as Chris's mother led her to become active in the field of rights for handicapped children. Many parents find themselves inevitably, sometimes reluctantly, drawn into active participation in causes and campaigns related to their child's disability. Few of them, though, take their involvement as far as Sheila did: she became executive director of a major organization concerned with Down syndrome. In this capacity she has had more than enough opportunity to discover that, even though the situation is improving, not all parents of children who have a recognizable disability such as Down syndrome receive the civilized treatment that she and her husband received at the time of their son's birth. She says:

When I say we were lucky in not having any negative garbage to recover from I'm thinking in particular of one family who did not take their baby home. They did not initiate the circumstances that led to that decision; it wasn't their idea.

After the baby was born, the hospital staff immediately moved the mother out of the maternity unit. She never saw her child. They told her she would never want to see this baby. She was made to feel that the child, a little girl, was grotesque, that she had all kinds of blood disorders and was a total disaster. And so the mother left the hospital with this horrible vision of a baby she had brought into the world and hadn't even seen but that wasn't worth seeing.

The infant was placed in a foster home, and the obstetrician told the father, "I can get you a baby. If you want a normal baby why don't we put out some feelers for you?" But after a few weeks the mother decided that she wanted to see her own child, and the parents went to see the baby and they brought her home.

That mother had a very difficult time. Her friends stopped calling. One set of grandparents had a hard time accepting the baby. The mother had suffered terribly, and she had a lot to recover from. And this baby they'd told her she would never want to see was as cute as a button. You couldn't believe it; she was a beautiful child. But a great deal of pain had been inflicted on that mother, and the worst of it was that it had been unnecessary pain.

"I'll give you a quarter
if you can make John smile"

John is the youngest of Millie and Bill's six children. The eldest son, David, was adopted after their first child died of leukemia at the age of four because, Millie says, the couple wanted "to turn something bad into something good." John's mother believes that experiencing the death of a child made it easier for her and her husband to accept John's handicap. She says:

I think that the death of a child makes life itself more valuable and material things less important, so that you live each day the best way you can and you're grateful for life itself. It's certain that it gives you an appreciation of life, of being alive, that other people who have not dealt with a child dying simply do not have.

We knew for a year that Billy was going to die, and we had to deal with it one day at a time, trying not to be too protective, to support the child but be matter-of-fact about it, and to take care of the rest of the family. So for my husband and myself, having gone through that together, finding out that John was retarded was just one more thing.

John, who is now nineteen, is the last of our six children; there are four girls between David and John. I first suspected that something was not right when he was three months old and still wasn't smiling. I mentioned this to the pediatrician, who said, "He'll smile when he's got something to smile about."

I can remember bribing the other kids: "I'll give you a quarter [later it got to be a dollar] if you can make John smile." Now I don't even remember when he did smile, but I know that was the first sign. Then by the time he was two and wasn't talking very much I was really concerned. Also, he had trouble sucking as a baby, and he ate baby food until he was three or four because somehow he couldn't chew, which I'm sure is related to his problem with speaking.

Finally, when John was four, I got the name of a pediatric neurologist, who did an electroencephalogram which showed long sleep spindles usually associated with mental retardation. That was all. There was nothing else specific that they could give us, so they called it "an underdeveloped nervous system with aphasia," expressive aphasia, because he wasn't talking.

For three or four years he had speech therapy which didn't really accomplish very much, and he started school in a regular classroom. He couldn't sing, he couldn't hop on one foot or skip like the other kids could, but he didn't bother anyone so they kept him there for two years. Then, after that, they suggested either a class for educable mentally handicapped children in a regular school, or special schooling.

Bill visited both options, and everyone thought John could function in the EMH class, so that's where we sent him. I knew he wasn't really happy because of the stigma of being in a special class. John was smart enough to know that he was not like the other children, and of course he got very frustrated because he couldn't talk.

When he was nine we took him to an adolescent center at our local hospital for testing, and they told us the tests indicated he would be better off in a special school. One of the tests was a palm print, and they told me it showed that the retardation, or whatever it was, occurred during the first three months in embryo. I remembered one of the children's friends coming down with German measles while I was pregnant with John, and thinking at the time about what I would do if I caught it, whether I would have an abortion. But we've never really known the cause.

At the time of that testing the speech therapist wanted to start signing with John as a means of getting him to express himself, but the head of speech pathology at the clinic said, "No, take him back and try babbling." So they spent three months trying to teach him to babble as a way to get the speech going. Then they gave up on that and he did start to learn signing.

John's problem is expressive; he can't talk much. His receptive language has always been fine, and so has his hearing. He understands what you say, but he used to get really frustrated at not being able to express what he was feeling or what he wanted to say. He knew a few words, and he could point and make his needs known, but he didn't have enough speech even for the EMH class, and that's why he was moved to a special school for mentally handicapped children.

He did learn to sign there, but he doesn't sign much. However, it was a stimulus for speech, and he can talk much more now. He came in this morning and told me that Foote was gone—Barry Foote from the Cubs baseball team had been traded. He can say "John" now, which he had trouble with because of the j. He knows all the kids' names and can communicate in school, and when somebody does something he doesn't like he'll say, "That's not nice," or "Leave me alone."

why kids in our house
don't call each other "dummy"

Victoria's maternal great-grandmother was a convert to Roman Catholicism whose conspicuous religiosity was matched by her contempt for all who did not share her views. Once she had seen the light she expected everyone else to see it too, and when they did not she dismissed them as "MD," which was short for "mentally defective." She died long before Victoria was born, thereby missing her chance to welcome a mental defective into her family.

My grandmother was the first in my experience to use insultingly a term that would later turn out to be a technically accurate description of my daughter. She certainly never stopped to consider that mental deficiency, which is no fault of the individual's, is not at all the same as the willful bloody-mindedness that she attributed to all who did not choose to convert to her religion. Or that mental deficiency is frequently present from birth, which means that the God whose cause she had embraced had been responsible for each person's allotment and it was His judgment she was calling in question.

Well, of course she did not think of those things. She wanted a nice handy insult and "MD" did the job just fine. No offense meant. And none taken. Until one is actually personally involved with someone who is mentally defective.

Having a retarded child, in fact, severely limits one's vocabulary of derogatory terms. Cretin, moron, imbecile, half-wit, idiot—such words do not come trippingly from the tongue of a person who has a retarded child. Nor are they easy to listen to. In our house the children aren't even allowed to call each other dummy or stupid, and if I'm inhibiting their freedom of speech that's just fine with me.

There have been times in the past when any of those terms

would have been considered appropriate labels for Victoria, classifying her without hope of reprieve as one of society's rejects. There have also been times when she would have been hailed as one of God's innocents or, very possibly, hanged as a witch. It is not much fun to dwell on such matters.

Sometimes I feel, though, that she might have been better off in a simpler age or a different setting. There are places even today where nobody would require her to read or write or look both ways before crossing the busy highway. She could sit in the village square and play with the children and watch the world go by and nobody would scorn her lack of learning.

But here she is with us, and she has to make the best of us. And we, being afflicted with literacy, squirm and suffer when others refer to people like Victoria as "retards." It is not, at least I don't think it is, that we are avoiding the reality. Literally speaking, we are enforcing the reality. Our children are retarded people, not "retards." They're not things, rejects from a human assembly line. They are persons, individuals, and they are entitled to respect. Rejects of any kind get put in boxes on a back shelf, or thrown out, or sold off cheap because they're not much good. Of course I mind when I hear a child of mine referred to in that way; I'd be inhuman not to mind.

I was at a meeting where a father stood up and described his son as learning disabled. "That kid is not learning disabled," whispered the mother who sat next to me. "He's in the same group as my child, and it's a group of retarded children. If he were learning disabled he'd be somewhere else." It bothered her a lot that the father seemed not to be able to use the accurate term for his son's disability. "I don't mind saying that my son is retarded," she went on, "because that is what he is. I could go around describing him as learning disabled, but it wouldn't make him any the less retarded."

If there must be a label, she was saying, at least let us use the right one. Or, as my mother used to tell me, "Always say what you mean—call a spade a spade and not a bloody shovel."

We all have our special areas of sensitivity, and parents who have retarded children react differently to different words.

Sheila, Chris's mother, also has a lot of trouble with labels.

Especially because she has a child who is easily labeled. Chris's disability is a chromosomal abnormality that has a name in the medical textbooks. The very fact that the disorder is medically known can have its disadvantages, and one of them, Sheila says, is that many people can't look beyond the syndrome and see the child. She says:

I get very mad at people who see my son as a syndrome. He's not a syndrome. He's an individual. But the name, the label that can be put on him, can present a real problem.

Down syndrome is shrouded in all sorts of myths. People with Down syndrome used to be called 'mongoloids' because J. Langdon Down, an English physician in the last century, thought that people with Down syndrome resembled Mongolians, and so he called them "mongoloids" or "mongols." It's a totally erroneous name, but it's still being used.

My sister-in-law wrote to a newspaper that used the term. She pointed out that it happened to be the International Year of the Disabled Person and she asked, "Why do we insist on using an inaccurate term for a medical condition?"

The editor wrote back, "Nicknames can sometimes be used in fondness, and we're sure this is what happened in this case."

Well, that is so much baloney. "Mongoloid" is not a nickname. It is a totally inaccurate term which carries a very derogatory connotation and there's no excuse for using it. If I hear anyone refer to Chris as "mongoloid" it sends me right through the roof and I have to correct the person who said it, no matter who it is.

Another myth exists about functioning levels, and there's a simple reason for this. Most studies used to be done on Down syndrome people who had lived all their lives in institutions, and the results of those studies led researchers to assume that all persons with Down syndrome were low-functioning. But if you put a perfectly normal person in the sort of institution that existed when those studies were made, that person would deteriorate. Now that studies are being carried out on children who have been raised at home, researchers are finding much higher functioning levels and much wider acceptance in society.

Times are changing, but the old assumptions die hard. Like that all people with Down syndrome are placid and easy-going, happy-go-lucky, pliable, fat, short. . . . Of the kids I know with Down syndrome, the younger children who have been raised at home and who have been in early intervention programs have had good educational opportunities and are fairly well-adjusted into their families and their families' life-styles. That doesn't mean that they're pliable and easy-going. It means that their degree of retardation allows them to function in a normal environment.

Another myth is that all people with Down syndrome like music. So if one's son with Down syndrome happens to have a talent for music one is hesitant to mention it because the response will be, "Oh, that's because he has Down syndrome." And heaven forbid that he should have a talent a normal person might have.

I also resent the assumption that all people with Down syndrome are trainable, not educable. I don't think we should use these labels any more. It irritates me that the educational profession assumes that a child with Down syndrome is going to function at a certain predictable level. I am always reminding educators that every child has a right to be treated as an individual. I see it as a challenge to get that message across.

pity: the gift that nobody wants

After the diagnosis—major crisis number one—comes the never-ending process of trying to establish where the mentally retarded child fits into the structure of the family in particular and society in general. The child's parent engenders in others all sorts of uncomfortable feelings—fear, anxiety, embarrassment, pity. People think, and say, "Oh, poor you, what a burden!" From there it's a series of short steps, from, "How can you possibly cope?" to "I know I couldn't cope," to "I won't think about you because then I might have to consider that what has happened to you could happen to me. And I don't want to think about that."

The presence of a mentally handicapped child does some very interesting things to the family's existing social environment. The changes that develop may be positive or negative or, most likely, a mixture of both. But the one thing you can be absolutely sure of is that changes will occur. Life will not be the same.

The other thing you can be absolutely sure of is that you will become an object of pity, and pity is the one reaction that you can do without. Pity is of no practical use to parents of handicapped children. There's not a thing we can do with it.

One afternoon I was watching Victoria roller-skate and a neighbor started talking about how pitiful it was that she was retarded and what a terrible burden I had to bear. It is not easy to decide how to react to that kind of comment. One solution is to let it pass because the speaker means well. Another is to try to explain that when a child with Victoria's faulty gross motor coordination learns to roller-skate it is a cause for rejoicing, not for pity.

One of the particular joys we experience with our handicapped children is the triumph of seeing them succeed. For somebody like my daughter, learning to roller-skate or swim or ride a bicycle is as great an achievement as someone else's conquest of Everest. Victoria has worked very hard, and so have we, to acquire the accomplishments she now has. So when Emma asked her sister to demonstrate a particular roller-skating technique that Victoria had mastered and Emma had not, it made me dizzy with delight. For once Victoria was in the heady position of being the teacher, not the pupil. But my neighbor did not see the incident through my eyes. How could she? In that case I did not try to explain, but often I do: I point out that parents whose children are normal experience all sorts of pleasures, but there are some moments which are special to us.

That is one of the reasons why parents of retarded children often, even without having to be close friends, share a special bond. Not having to explain is a healing experience. We don't have to be told what a particular satisfaction it is when a child finally ties his own shoelace at the age of nine. We know, because we've waited so long ourselves. And we see our kids, when they succeed, not as objects of pity because they are doing it later than other children, but as objects of profound gratification to themselves and to their families.

We do not care, therefore, to be pitied for the burdens our children's handicaps lay upon us. We do not all see their condition as a burden (although assuredly we do all feel very heavily burdened at times) but rather as a circumstance to be dealt with as effectively as possible. Among ourselves, however, we may well complain. Most of us, on occasion, find ourselves sinking in the sludge of self pity; if there's any pity needed, we'll supply our own.

Personally, I do plenty of complaining. I have a low tolerance for frustration, so I need to let off steam. I do not, however, perceive myself as a pitiful creature. I'm just a parent, doing my best with whatever the cards turn up. Parenting is an unpredictable profession.

I don't believe people would be so nervous around those of us who have exceptional children if they realized just how unexceptional we are. We'd like to be accepted, with our children, but we don't need—or want—any special treatment. It would be nice if people understood that they don't have to avoid us or pussyfoot around us. And they don't have to feel sorry for us. So, our children are mentally retarded. Other parents have children who are on drugs, or on the streets, or on probation. If it came to the crunch, it might be expected that we should be sorry for them.

Anyway, I've never heard anyone who knew anything about it claim that being a parent is ever a piece of cake.

"first of all, he's a person"

Chris's mother, who has said that she and Peter, her husband, constitute a good example of how the birth of a mentally handicapped child does not have to be devastating, believes that people are often given a totally unrealistic picture of what life is like with a handicapped child, so that the parents' predicament is made to seem far worse than it actually is. She says:

The hardest part for me was telling everybody. Nobody would wish a person to be handicapped. Life is tough enough when you don't have any mental or physical handicaps. When I see how hard Chris has to work to accomplish what he does—one would never wish anyone to have to work that hard. So it's understandable that people feel bad when you tell them, because they know how hard it's going to be, too.

When we sent out the birth announcements we did not include mention of Chris's handicap. Our whole attitude has been that first of all, he's a person. He has a right to be announced to this world as a person—his name is Christopher and this is when he was born and how much he weighed—just like any other child. In our perspective the fact that he has Down syndrome is secondary; we try not to allow that to take over his whole person or our whole lives. So I do not feel that we were being deceptive or withholding information.

After the announcements went out we did let everybody know, in a letter or by a phone call, and we've always tried to encourage questions and to deal with it very openly. Once everybody knew, it seemed that we could go on with living and dealing with Chris as a person.

We were luckier with our friends and family than a lot of new parents, although there were some difficult moments. Often people don't realize what they are saying; I don't think they mean to be cruel, but they just don't know how they would handle it themselves, and they don't know the questions to ask. They don't know what to say to make you feel good, and they don't want to make you feel bad, so they don't say anything and that makes you feel bad. And everything that happens right then is important because the kind of support you get at the beginning is critical.

Sometimes you think that people feel sorry for you, and by this time you love your baby, so your feelings get very mixed. There I was, holding my child and nursing him and seeing him respond, and I was thinking, "It's one thing that he's mentally handicapped, but he's my baby." And then I had to pick up the phone and tell my family, "Chris has Down syndrome."

I am the youngest of five children, so I knew my older siblings were going to feel bad for me; and my parents live far away so they felt they couldn't help us. I won't say I felt guilty about telling them, but I did have some problems because then they went into a tailspin and I had to deal with that as well.

We had just moved into the neighborhood when Chris was born, so telling the neighbors wasn't easy either. One person came over and said, "Oh, what a burden!" That bothered me. You know there's no hurt intended, but it doesn't make you feel good when society views your child, whom you just brought into the world, as a burden. When our neighbor said, "Oh, what a burden," I replied, "I'm sorry, but we don't view him that way." When people make such statements to me I tend to deal with them straight on and contradict the ones I don't agree with. I don't feel

I have to go into a lengthy explanation of Down syndrome for a perfect stranger in the supermarket—unless someone asks me. But when the occasion arises I do have to put matters straight.

Chris was a healthy baby. He didn't have any heart problems or any serious physical conditions that we had to worry about, and that is not always true of children with Down syndrome. We came home from the hospital when he was four days old, and right away he was accepted by everyone, which made it easier for us, too. Pete's parents came to stay, and I'll always remember them coming in and saying, "Well, where is he? Where's our grandson?" There was total acceptance of him as a person. Everybody acknowledged that he was handicapped but that he was a person, and I think that really gave us a lot of strength to deal with the reality of raising a kid that's mentally retarded.

It was fortunate that Pete and I were mature and had a good relationship, which we still do. That makes a tremendous difference. My son has a father who participates actively in his life, who has always taken him places and done things with him, has never been ashamed of him or embarrassed by him—maybe embarrassed by him occasionally, as any parents are with their child's behavior, but not embarrassed by him because he's handicapped. I've had a lot of support; I've never had to go it alone, and that has made a great difference in how I feel.

If you have good support, and good medical information, and you don't have all sorts of negative garbage to recover from, then your chances of dealing with the reality are that much better. To me it's horrible that so many people are given such a dreadful picture of what life is like with a handicapped child that their perspective is warped right from the beginning. They don't recognize that the reality is not nearly as bad as the picture they've been given. There's no excuse for giving people such false expectations. They're bad in themselves, and extremely hard to recover from.

the runaways, the miracle workers, and the deniers

Emily's parents, who had spent eighteen months "in limbo" trying to find out just what had gone wrong with their child, were a lot less fortunate than Chris's parents. When Chris was born, Sheila and Pete had three important things in their favor: they had a diagnosis; they had caring and informed professional advice; and they had strong family support.

Lacking those immediate aids, and having waited so long to learn why their once-normal daughter was now retarded, Donna and Gary were already at the end of their emotional tether and found the time after the diagnosis "a period of incredible frustration." It was also a period during which their social network fell apart. Donna says:

During the time after the diagnosis we lost a lot of our friends because we were obsessed with this child. We were obsessed by what we were going through, and we had a tremendous need to dump it on everybody. We did have friends who stuck by us and who put up with us, and God knows, I don't understand how they did it. But we also had friendships of ten or fifteen years standing that went by the wayside.

Then, after a few years had passed, there were the Christmas cards: "We're still alive, are you still alive?" In effect they were asking, "Are you better now? Can we be friends now that you've got your act together?" And my answer to that is, forget it. That's not friendship. I wanted to ask, "Where were you when I needed you?"

I was aware that I was dumping on my friends, and that they were having trouble handling it, but I think all I ever wanted was for somebody to put their arms around me and say, "Yes, this is really a piece of shit, and I'm sorry it happened to you." And nobody ever had the courage to do that.

Gary and I labeled our friends. We divided them into categories. There were the runaways, who could no more touch our

50

pain than fly; they couldn't cope with our pain and so they disappeared.

Then we had the miracle-story group, who would say, "Well, my sister's kid was just like that when he was three and you should see him today. . . ." These people would have their friends and relatives write to me—anyone who knew someone who knew someone who had a miracle story to tell. I even started getting letters from people all across the country telling me that if I prayed, God would save this child; or that they had a kid who never talked until he was six and now he's a genius.

I was disgusted, absolutely disgusted. Because I'm a realist; I know. Once I realized that her brain cells were dead I knew that there was no miracle cure for this child. I was not deeply religious, so I did not contemplate a trip to Lourdes. I did a lot of reading about damaged brains and I came to understand the finality of it, which helped me. What's gone is gone.

The other group of friends were the deniers. They would come and play with Emily and say, "You know, she's not so bad." It was always, "It could be worse." "How?" I wanted to ask. "Tell me, you with your nice whole children, how exactly could it be worse?"

In retrospect I think I expected too much of people. I don't think anyone could have given me as much as I needed. It would have been impossible.

Donna has worked hard on her attitudes towards other people and her response to their attitudes towards her daughter. Having realized that no one could have given her as much support as she needed in the months following Emily's diagnosis, she has tried to develop a working understanding of how society views her child. One of the things that makes it harder is that Emily is very pretty and does not—unless the observer knows what to look for—immediately present herself as handicapped. I have the same problem with Victoria (if you want to call a child's beauty a problem), and it has become more difficult over the years. As the child grows, people's expectations change. What's acceptable in a four-year-old is no longer acceptable when the child is fourteen.

Of Emily, who is now ten, her mother says:

It's certainly harder to accept the way Emily has been damaged because she is so beautiful. You look at her and think, "This is just not right." Even when she was younger people used to come up to her in the supermarket and say, "Hi, little girl, what's your name?" And all Emily said was "Hi. . . ." Now the same thing happens and Emily stills says, "Hi. . . ." First she'll say, "Hi," and then she'll say, "Hi, hi . . . hi, hi. . . ." And by this time I'd be looking at the person and thinking, "Isn't it dawning on you that something is not right?" But I've learned to accept other people's incredible lack of awareness and I don't want to embarrass them. I know that if I said, "She's retarded; she can't talk," they'd be aghast that they had made such a faux pas. And it isn't worth the embarrassment it would cause them. I guess I try to spare them that.

Many times, though, I have become extremely angry and I have wanted to say something; maybe I lack courage and that's a part of me that needs to grow more. Sometimes when people have stared at us in restaurants or elsewhere I have wanted to stand up and yell, "Yes, she is retarded, and she's making a terrible mess but she's doing the best she can." Because she appears normal, people look at her as if to say, "Is there something wrong with her, or is she really a pig? Are her parents just sitting there, letting her throw food over the side of the dish and not paying any attention to her?"

I don't believe in spoonfeeding her. I let her go at it and do the best she can, and she does seem to sense that when she's in a restaurant she's supposed to behave a little differently. She knows she's in a different environment and to me it shows in her behavior. But to the rest of the world she's still a barbarian, ten years old and absolutely uncivilized. I could leave her at home, of course. I could, and most of the time my gut feeling is that I want to, but I don't. One reason why I don't is that I believe I have her so that I can help the rest of the world to know her.

I am still less comfortable with Emily in public than Gary is. My husband is one of these people who has no qualms whatsoever; he will take her anywhere. He sort of marvels at his own ability to cope with her. I marvel at it, too.

I remember an occasion when he took her out shopping. I would never take Emily into Marshall Field's or anywhere like that because she won't stay still. She's into running away now, which is one of those "good news, bad news" situations. It drives us crazy because she doesn't have any ID on her, so if she disappears she can't do anything but tap at someone and say "Hi, hi, hi. . . ." But usually she can't move that fast. It's good news because we're glad that suddenly she has become independent enough to want to run away. She's showing curiosity—"I want to go over there and look at that," or just, "I don't want to be with you; I want to be free." That's progress, so we should be happy about it.

Anyway, Gary came back from a shopping trip to Marshall Field's, very proud of himself.

He said, "I've finally figured it out."
I said, "Figured what out?"
"How to keep her from running away."
I said, "How?"
And he said, "Stand on her foot."
I didn't know whether to laugh or scream at him. In many respects that may seem really barbaric—a hundred-and-fifty-pound man standing there with his foot on a little kid's tennis shoe. But it's restraining her, not hurting her. I've seen him do it, and Emily looks at him quizzically, "What is this?" But it's a real problem-solving technique and it's not barbaric at all, because the whole time the message is very slowly sinking into her mind. A message that a normal child would get in two seconds is going to take Emily five years of having her foot stood on in Marshall Field's to get—that you don't run away from Mom or Dad in a store.

"the doctors can repair anything, except the mind"

Meg is the last of six children, three boys and three girls. Peg, her mother, manages a telephone answering service. David, Peg's husband, was an electrician. He died three years ago. The couple had been through a great deal of anxiety with their third child, also named David, who was born with a hole in his heart and other physical problems which required years of intermittent hospital treatment. Peg says:

I remember one of the nuns at the hospital where he was born telling me, "Look, don't worry, because the doctors can repair anything, except the mind." And there was nothing wrong with David's mind. She was trying to tell me that physical things can be repaired, but when they're born retarded, that's it. Which I found out.

Down syndrome, the condition which caused Meg's retardation, is commonly, although erroneously, believed to occur only in children born to older mothers. Meg's mother was forty-two when she was pregnant with Meg, and one of her cousins had a daughter with Down syndrome. But it never entered Peg's head that there might be anything wrong with her own child. She says:

You don't think about it. You think, well, it's just one more baby. Then, when she was born, they knew as soon as she was delivered—at least they had a good idea. The doctor said she had all the outward signs: a larger space than usual, a web, between her thumbs and her first fingers; a fat pad at the back of the neck; a short neck; and slanty eyes. Those are all signs of Down syndrome. But they still did tests, just to make sure.

When I found out, I called her Margaret, because it's my name. When I knew that she would be handicapped I wanted to give her my name. I told my husband the diagnosis, but we decided not to say anything to the children because we wanted them to know her first. I thought if they had a chance to see her just as a baby I could tell them later that she was going to have a handicap. But I thought if I told them right away they'd immediately start looking on her as something different. So in time, within the first week, I told them all separately, and I don't know if waiting made any difference, but Meg's handicap has never bothered them one way or another. Never. She's spent many weekends with the older children at college where roommates come in and out and they've always just said, "This is my sister," and it's never bothered them.

David used to get temper tantrums a lot, partly because he was in and out of the hospital all the time, and I used to tell the other kids, "Now, David has problems. Just ignore him and he'll get out of it." And he would, after a bit. Once Kathy was out visiting and there was a little Down syndrome girl there. I guess they gave her a bowl of potato chips to take out to the rest of the kids, and she sat and ate them and wouldn't let anyone else touch them. When Kathy came home she said, "Mom, there was a little girl there and you know, she must have had a problem. . . ." And it didn't strike me until years later that she never said anything about the child's looks; she meant she must have had problems like David's because she ate all the potato chips and wouldn't share. Her manners bothered Kathy more than her looks.

Maybe because David had so many physical problems, or maybe because of Meg, our kids are very understanding and kind toward people. I think it's made them more sensitive. I don't think they'd be as good if they hadn't had those experiences.

It was hardest for Karen. When Meg was born Karen was five, so first of all Karen was no longer the baby of the family. And she was always a little wiseacre and to this day she and Meg fight worst. If we'd had any trouble it would have been with Karen, but she's never turned her back. Another thing, so many times the kids have come home from college or high school and told me how a friend of theirs has a brother or sister who's retarded. The kids talk about it, they talk to their friends. They're much better than we were. They're not the least bit ashamed to say that this is in their family.

When I first told my mother that Meg would be handicapped she said, "Everybody gets a cross. . . ." I said, "Well, I got mine in David and this is a goof. I don't need another one." But you accept it; you feel there's got to be a good reason somewhere.

There's a famous poem, where they're talking about how the angels are getting ready to send a baby down, and it's going to be a special baby that needs a lot of love. Maybe they figured that in our family we could accommodate one, that there were enough of us.

We've been lucky. Sometimes when I'm listening to people who have autistic children, or kids with bad behavioral problems, or kids who aren't socially acceptable so that they can't take them wherever they go, I think, well, we don't have those problems, or I think that I couldn't survive having a child like that.

I took Meg to an orthopedic doctor once and the nurse said to me, "Oh, I sympathize with you so much." She knew someone with a Down syndrome child who ran away all the time, and it was terrible for the parents. But I thought what she was saying was terrible. First of all, I didn't feel that I had a problem. And then you can never compare two kids, no matter what they are. I mean, it's ridiculous.

I really believe we've been lucky. I can't pick one of the other kids who I could say is hampered at all by Meg or who would rather she wasn't here. It's all been good experiences. So I think she's been very blessed.

the look that says, "you poor other person"

Peg has always been grateful that she has been able to take Meg with her anywhere without hassle or difficulty. For Peg, the fact that her daughter is socially acceptable is an advantage that far outweighs many of the disadvantages, such as Meg's lack of academic skills.

Richard's mother, Ilene understands how Peg feels. She says:

When Richard was small he was very difficult to take places. He would run away, often with hazard to his own safety—like into the street. He would stage incredible scenes in public places and embarrass me. Since he had three or four bowel movements a day, it was inevitable that he would have one while I was out with him, and they were very smelly and could not be ignored. This problem was partly due to my giving him a lot of baby and junior foods because he could only tolerate things that were puréed. When I started to purée our own food for him the situation improved somewhat.

Of course, he was still not toilet trained, and when he was four I became very angry about this and tried to force him to become trained. There was a lot of screaming and torment, so I concluded that he was not ready. He was actually trained at about six. Accidents persisted until well into his teens, and he had a regression into bedwetting between the ages of ten and twelve. But that was not my main concern. My main concern was that he would have an accident in public and I would have difficulty finding a place to clean him. He was already old enough that it looked very strange for me to take him into the ladies' room, and since my husband lost his temper with him violently when he had toilet accidents I never wanted to ask Paul to clean him, because I was quite sure Richard would get spanked in the process.

Frequently I lost my temper with him myself, because I didn't learn for quite a while that his smiling at me when he had loaded up his pants was fear, and not thinking that it was funny. And he'd smile at me while I had the shitty pants to take care of, and

I'd pound him. Then I found out that he's just one of those people who smile nervously when they're upset.

I hunted up some special pants for people who can't control their urine, that were triple thick, because he got too big to use diapers on. The special pants helped enormously, especially with the wetting problem. Of course, I had problems with baby-sitters, so I tried to arrange to go out after he had been put to bed, because once he was asleep he did not usually have accidents.

But all those things I could live with. It was not being able to go anywhere with him that was really hard; to have to make elaborate plans just to go to the store; to take him to a friend's house and spend my entire time chasing him around to keep him from breaking things or dirtying something; or having him make a bowel movement in his pants when he was five years old and having people—even people I knew—give me funny looks. I didn't even like the looks I got from people who were understanding. I don't like to be looked at with a look of sympathy or pity, the look that says, "You poor other person; how glad I am I don't have your problems."

The public image that a retarded child projects changes as the child gets older. Behavior that passes easily enough in a three-year-old draws a lot of negative attention when exhibited by a teenager. Ilene says:

Richard loves to ice-skate, and we take him as often as we take our other child. He loves movies and we take him to the movies. The only thing that bothers me is that he tends to fall asleep at eight-thirty in the evening, even at the movie. Also, while he's waiting for the show to begin he may do quite a bit of head-flopping that I can't seem to constrain, and if we are unfortunate enough to have young children in front of us they will turn round and goggle at him. And it must disturb the person in back of him. Richard doesn't seem to mind being stared or laughed at. People can actually come up to him and make an ugly face at him, or push him or shove him or tell him to go away. It's Mom who's hurt when people do that.

Pamela's too friendly, and that's a problem

Don, a biochemist, is the father of Pamela, a multiply handi-capped teenager. One of his major concerns about Pamela also involves social behavior, but on a different level—Pamela is too friendly. Don says:

> Pamela is hearing impaired and mentally retarded, and she has behavioral problems which may be due to her lack of hearing, to her retardation, or to family experiences early in her life. Her mother was mentally ill, and Pamela and her younger brother went through quite a lot of misery before I got a divorce and took over as custodial parent.
>
> The behavioral problems constitute Pamela's biggest deficit, and the major one that I would identify is her friendliness. Now you may say, why should that be a behavior problem? Shouldn't we have more friendly people in the world? Pamela is overly friendly. She does not appreciate that people may be anything other than good friends or loving each other very much. There-fore she will talk to anybody at all, to complete strangers on the street or in the store, without any fear or apprehension what-soever. Nothing we do at home or at school seems to be able to alter this trend; she is simply not aware that people are not always friendly and this is a big cause of concern to me as she is growing up.
>
> The other week, for example, she was out in the front yard when a car pulled up to the stoplight on our street corner. While the driver was waiting for the light to change Pamela saw children in the car and went over to talk to them; they were Oriental, and she was fascinated by the fact that they had narrow eyes. So first she talked to them, and then she opened the door and got in the car. And this has happened before. Fortunately I was there, and I apologized and gave her a lecture about not getting in people's cars. It is a serious concern for a parent, having a kid who thinks it's quite acceptable to get into strangers' cars.
>
> This kind of behavior is very difficult to control because most people think it's delightful. When Pamela goes up to strangers

and gives them a hug, they think it's terrific. Nobody does this to them, and they enjoy it. But the drawback is that their approval encourages Pamela to do it again; she thinks this is the way to behave. Of course, when I punish her or talk to her harshly they immediately look at me as if thinking, "What a terrible father; how could he treat such a beautiful kid that way?" So it's very difficult to correct her and the potential for danger is very great; it would be easy to take advantage of a child like Pamela.

Part of the problem is that many people try to be nice because they see Pamela's hearing aid and it tells them immediately that she has a handicap. They may not know that she's retarded, but they know that she is hearing impaired and probably cannot speak as well as other people, so they make allowances, they try to be kind and pleasant to the child. In the circumstances, kind and pleasant is not what I want them to be.

Pamela is very fond of little babies, and once she saw a lady across the road with a child in her arms. Pamela cried, "Ooooh, baby!" and dashed across the road, straight in front of a car, to say hello. And there I was, trying to get across the road, fit to be tied. When I did reach her, I started to give Pamela a lecture, and the baby's mother looked at me as though I were a monster. Then it finally clicked in her brain and she said, "Is this what you really want to do?" And I said, "Yes, it is. She has a problem and I want to discourage her from this kind of behavior." And she said, "Oh, I understand." But she was the first and only person who ever said that.

Normally I don't come on very severely in front of other people. I suppose I don't like the idea of people thinking, "Oh my God, the child's done nothing wrong. Why is he talking to her like that?" I feel they will think badly of me, or of Pamela. I feel also that I might embarrass the people involved, and I don't particularly want to put them on the spot.

I paint people as being pleasant, and most are. I encounter a few who react unpleasantly and start giving me a hard time about why I don't keep my child under better control. I say, "Well, I can see that you've got a handicap, too, haven't you?" And they usually walk off. Often people don't realize that she has a handicap, and once they find out they bend over backwards to be friendly.

Occasionally there's one who knows the situation and still doesn't change. I had a next-door neighbor like this and it was a very difficult relationship. At one time Pamela used to enter not only strange cars, but strange houses as well. On a summer's day when people had their front doors open, she'd just walk into a house and play with the dog or look in the refrigerator for something good to eat. Of course, it sounds funny, but at the time *it was very embarrassing because there'd be no way to get her out. If I was lucky, I'd see her go into the house and go in after her— that was the only way to get her out. So there I would be, running around with my kid in the middle of someone else's house, while maybe the owner who was outside sunbathing on the patio would suddenly hear all this commotion inside and wonder what the devil was going on. It could get quite difficult.*

These neighbors had basically never spoken to us for the three years that they lived there, and I was never sure why. At first my wife was also living there, and she had a habit of ostracizing people, so that was probably part of it. But even when she moved out, it never seemed to occur to them that I might be a decent guy on my own account.

Anyway, at that time Pamela's behavior was worse than it is now, and I remember one time this neighbor came over and said he wanted me to keep my child under better control. Our driveways were open, there were no gates on them, and he said, "I don't want her playing with my dog in the driveway." I said, "May I suggest you keep your dog locked up, because I'm not going to keep my daughter chained to the wall."

I explained to him that Pamela was handicapped and his reply was, "Oh well, we all have problems and we all have to live with them. You live with yours," he said, "and I'll live with mine." Those were the only dealings I ever had with him. I did my best to keep the child out of the driveway, and I think I succeeded.

"that's Emma's sister—she's retarded"

We are collecting Emma from a neighbor's house where a Brownie meeting, of which she is not a part, is about to begin. Five or six little girls mill around. As Victoria and I walk in they quiet down and one nudges another and says audibly, "Hey, that's Emma's sister. She's retarded." And they all stare. The mother of the resident Brownie appears to be minimally aware that the situation is not entirely comfortable, but makes no comment. (Later I wonder at this, because I know that this parent herself has a retarded sibling.) Nor do I say anything to the gaggle of little girls; it does not seem to be the time to embark upon a discussion about retardation. Victoria, Emma, and I take our leave.

At home, Emma is furious. "How dare they?" she shouts. "How dare they hurt her feelings? She's my sister and she can't help being retarded."

I praise her lavishly for her defense of a family member and point out, as I have had cause to do many times before and since, that the offending children offend out of ignorance, not malice. Nobody has ever taught them to be courteous, or sensitive, or accepting towards someone who is different. Perhaps they assume that Victoria, being retarded, cannot understand or have her feelings hurt by what they say. I tell Emma, as I have told her before, that she is in a special (though sometimes uncomfortable) position because she can explain to her friends about retarded people and help them understand that it's okay to be different.

Now I can see how well Emma has learned that hard lesson. I've watched her help her friends accept her sister, and I've seen some of those children develop a particular tenderness toward Victoria. I've also seen Emma choose to reject one young friend who consistently failed to display toward Victoria the kind of respect that Emma expected from her. Hard lessons.

It *has* been hard for Emma. And for Victoria. Everything was fine (or better, anyway) when Emma was a baby whom Victoria could mother, and the situation continued to be manageable while the two of them were still both definitely little children. Even when Emma was six or seven and Victoria eleven or twelve they were pretty much able to enjoy the same toys and games and activities and friends. After that it began to change. It gradually became clear to both of them that Victoria was out of place with the "little kids," except when she could play the role of mother, baby sitter, or nurse. And even then they had to simplify the structure of their make-believe to her level.

The transition period was also hard for me as I tried inappropriately to pressure the younger children into accepting and including Victoria so that she didn't feel left out.

What I was actually doing was both reinforcing her differentness and forcing on her sister an unwarranted degree of social responsibility. With the best intentions in the world I prepared a situation absolutely guaranteed to foster resentment in both the girls. Retarded children are a lot less different from other children than even their parents give them credit for. They may be retarded, but they're not dumb. And exceptional parents are quite unexceptional enough to make the same mistakes as other parents.

The Brownie meeting incident occurred when Victoria was twelve or thirteen. I didn't know if Victoria understood that she was retarded, but at that point she was certainly aware of being somehow different. She recognized that she was out of kilter in some situations. To this day she has never used the word "retarded" to me, or "handicapped," or even "different." She has never asked questions beyond wanting to know why a certain behavior is no longer permitted. When I stopped allowing her to take her doll to the little park which adjoins the alley behind our house, she wanted to know why. She used to enjoy swinging the doll on the baby swings and bouncing her on the rocking horse. It was painful for both of us that she wasn't allowed to do that anymore.

"Why can't I take my doll?" she wanted to know.

And I told her, in the language that the school uses to train their youngsters, "Because you're getting too big. It is not young adult behavior."

Beyond such questions Victoria has questioned very little. I don't know to this day how much she knows. It's very disconcerting and very frustrating. Because she cannot express her feelings clearly in words, I have to guess at what she's feeling. There are times when I want to shake her and plead and yell at her to let me into her mind. "What are you thinking?" I want to scream. "Just tell me, tell me what's going on in your head!"

But she can't, or doesn't want to, and all these years I've muddled along on a combination of intuition and guesswork, wondering how many times I'm way off target. Perhaps when she was younger I tried to shield her from imaginary ills. Or shield myself. Perhaps she doesn't care or get hurt if people stare or talk behind their hands. Perhaps she cares, but not as much as I think she does. Perhaps I am the one who cares.

Be that as it may, I instructed Emma early not to use the word "retarded" or get into heavy discussions about handicaps in Victoria's presence. There was a reason for this. When Emma was younger, any time she got mad at her sister she seemed to make a point of initiating such topics, trying to manipulate me into discussions which indirectly concerned Victoria but in which Victoria took no part. Emma was smart enough to do this while the three of us were in the car, a captive audience, and it was up to me to make an issue of changing the course of the conversation.

I had qualms, however, about setting these limits. Was it really a courtesy to Victoria, or just another way of trying to push the truth a bit further under the table? Victoria herself has always been quick to draw attention to someone in a wheelchair, or with a hearing aid or a seeing-eye dog. These are the people she's used to. People who are different are the ordinary people of her world; she's comfortable with them and singles them out.

Most of us choose our friends from among those who are in some way most like ourselves.

Although I still don't know how much Victoria understands about her handicap—or even if the term "handicap" is part of her vocabulary—it has become clearer as she has gotten older that she knows and has always known that her world is somehow separate, and that it is rejected and scorned by many people.

Gradually, she ceased to be part of Emma's social group, and she made the decision herself. She seldom attempts any more to play with Emma's young friends or to initiate an activity with them. Sometimes, if they initiate a game, she'll go along with it for a while. But she's no longer comfortable in that setting. She is, however, a lot more comfortable with me. In many ways we now relate on the level that a mother and an ordinary teenager relate, once they've got over the mutual hatred stage.

Socially, too, I've come to accept the situations that Victoria can and cannot handle. I don't fight it any more—or not so much as I used to. Depending on how I happen to feel at the moment, I attribute my acceptance either to true resignation or to deep fatigue. There's only so much fighting anyone can do.

Emma, too, has changed. She's become more independent

and I've encouraged the attitude that although Victoria's needs may sometimes inconvenience her, Victoria is not her responsibility. I hope she's got the message. And Emma surely knows that she's not alone in having a retarded sibling. There are some thirty kids in her class and three of them, including Emma, have a retarded sibling. A nice, neat ten percent. So Emma has already learned what most parents of retarded children learn at some point—that sometimes it's nice not to have to explain.

Meg's mother also found that her perception of her daughter's handicap and her own reaction to it changed as Meg got older. She says:

> When Meg was little I could accept the young kids who were in school with her, but I found the older ones heartbreaking. Now that Meg's older, I've gotten to know them better and I find it's easier to visit and talk with the older kids than with the young ones. But when she was little I had no connection with the older kids and had a hard time accepting them.
>
> One thing I find is that any normal kid who sees someone with a physical handicap can be kind, because they can see what's wrong. I've never seen children being cruel to a physically handicapped person where there's something to see. If there's a kid in the classroom with a broken arm or leg, everyone's out to help them. But it's these unseen handicaps. . . .
>
> With children, if you don't behave within a certain category, you've had it. That's why, with Meg, the reading and writing didn't bother me, but I felt we had to be able to take her with us anywhere we went. I've always felt, since Meg was a baby, that if she were socially acceptable anywhere we went I wouldn't care about anything else.

PART TWO

holding on

a rose that would never bloom

When a child is diagnosed as mentally retarded, whether the diagnosis is made at birth or years later, a goodly proportion of the parents' expectations for that child go straight out the window. The higher the expectations, the more devastating the loss.

The fact that Victoria was an unplanned baby was probably a major advantage for me. We hadn't planned to have a child right then, and I had not spent any considerable length of time dreaming of how or what my child would be or projecting my own hopes and desires into the future of a person as yet unborn. I'm convinced now that the unexpectedness of Victoria's conception helped keep my expectations of her within reasonable limits.

When I was pregnant with Victoria I visited a friend of mine, an earth-mother type with three young of her own, and we discussed motherhood and its myriad implications. She did not, she told me, consider her children to be attached to her. She considered them to be people whom it was her temporary task to cherish and protect, but that was it. I was shocked. To me this seemed an unsuitably casual attitude toward child-rearing. Later I came to realize that it was one of the smartest things about kids anyone had ever said to me up to that time.

Years later I read the words of Kahlil Gibran in *The Prophet:*

> *Your children are not your children.*
> *They are the sons and daughters of Life's longing for itself.*
> *They come through you but not from you,*
> *And though they are with you yet they belong not to you.*
>
> *You may give them your love but not your thoughts,*
> *For they have their own thoughts.*
> *You may house their bodies but not their souls,*

For their souls dwell in the house of tomorrow, which you cannot visit, not even in your dreams.

. . . You are the bows from which your children as living arrows are sent forth.

The archer sees the mark upon the path of the infinite and He bends you with His might that His arrows may go swift and far.

Let your bending in the archer's hand be for gladness;

For even as he loves the arrow that flies, so He loves also the bow that is stable.

Since I first read those words it has seemed to me that they are particularly valuable to the parent of a handicapped child. Inaccessible as the soul of an ordinary child may be to the parent, the soul of the mentally retarded child is even more so—and I have tried very hard, in my dreams, to visit that distant place where part of Victoria lives.

Perhaps the analogy of the bow and arrow is especially comforting because the parent is involved with the handicapped child beyond the point when a normal one breaks away. Separating from the mentally retarded child, emotionally or in any other way, can be a real mind bender. It's not easy to "let your bending in the archer's hand be for gladness." But that is part of major crisis number three—letting go.

To get back to my earlier thought: what *did* I want for Victoria? What were the expectations I had for her, and of her, during the months while I waited for her to be born? I wanted her to be healthy, I suppose, although it never crossed my mind that she would be otherwise. I wanted her to be beautiful. I wanted her to have a lot of things that I never had. What I wanted most for her was a secure, loving home with two full-time parents who would raise her to be capable of building a secure, loving home of her own with someone who would, in turn, provide her children—my grandchildren—with the same security and love.

I wanted to give her the opportunity to do things and go places—do things that I had done and that I'd never had a chance to do, go places I had been and places I'd like to go to. I wanted to give her, as my parents had gone to great lengths to give me, the sort of education that would allow her to make choices about what to do with her life.

Simple enough expectations, I would say.

I never wanted Victoria to be me, or even to be particularly like me. I never wanted a baby as an extension of myself. I didn't consider myself a very promising model although, thanks in part to Victoria, I have a more generous opinion of myself these days.

So when Victoria was born I was not, unless I am lying royally to myself, encumbered with grandiose expectations of her glorious future. I had wanted her to be healthy and, as far as I could see, she was. And she was beautiful, a beautiful baby. A rose unfolding. A cliché, but so what? That's the sort of baby she was. In our more sentimental moments, the girls and I still talk about how, when they were babies, they were just like flowers: Victoria a pink rose, Emma a pale yellow rosebud.

And there I was, a brand new mother, pathetically inexperienced, handed this flower-like child and petrified that she would fall to pieces in my hands. She didn't; the rose petals began to open and the beautiful baby became a beautiful child. I had no way of knowing, then, that this rose would never reach full bloom. The flower of her mind had been damaged in the bud.

The most basic hopes I had for Victoria—that she should be healthy and beautiful—have been realized. She has no major physical problems; technically she's a healthy kid. For the rest. . . .

Although she has the love of two natural parents and two step-parents, she does not have that secure, loving, two-parent home that I wanted so badly for her—not right now, anyway. That situation is, to a significant degree, a result of the stress her condition imposed on our family. It's not her fault. It's just a fact.

She will never, or so I believe, be able to marry and create a secure, loving home for herself and someone she cares for. She won't have children to make a home for. Even such simple expectations cannot be fulfilled. I mourn for them still.

letting go of the dreams

One reason that parents of handicapped children are sensitive to the reactions of other people is that those reactions frequently remind us of the expectations we have been forced to forgo. When a stranger in the shoe store looks on curiously as Victoria (whose behavior in stores is, at best, unpredictable) kicks up holy hell about trying on new sneakers, I am forced to see Victoria through that stranger's eyes. And I see this large, leggy, almost adult person who is my daughter acting like a five-year-old. I do not need that extra reminder of reality.

When I'm with Victoria and I see pity in someone's eyes I still resent it, even though I'm aware that what I'm interpreting as pity may be genuine empathy and concern. I've said before that if there's any pity needed around here I'll supply it for myself.

The pitying people don't see the other side of the story. They don't know how desperately hard we have worked—Victoria, myself, Emma, the children's stepfather, all the others who have been involved in Victoria's development—and how many dramatic victories we have achieved. Pity is not the emotion that's appropriate here. We are to be admired. When a child is mentally handicapped, success is measured in terms quite different from those employed in other circumstances.

I want to tell people, "What you're seeing here is the tip of the iceberg. Don't be too quick to jump to conclusions."

All the same, it still hurts when other people reinforce, intentionally or unintentionally, the differentness that has meant the death of some of my hopes for my child.

Expectations color a parent's attitude toward a mentally handicapped child to widely varying degrees. Looking back, Meg's mother wonders at the very simplicity of her reaction to her daughter's diagnosis. Peg says:

When my cousin's baby was born with Down syndrome I had no idea about differences—I mean, if someone was retarded he was retarded, that's all I knew. And the only thing that hurt me when Meg was born—because I was thinking of my cousin's girl—was that she wouldn't be pretty. I didn't care that she couldn't learn, but I thought, "Oh, they're not pretty children." Now I've grown up with her and she suits me fine. Since she was very little she was like a doll to her sisters. Kathy and Karen loved to dress her up and take her out, and we've always told her she looks very pretty. And now when she puts on a dress she thinks she's just gorgeous, and she wants you to tell her so.

When I got out of the hospital with Meg a friend arranged for someone to visit me from the National Association for Down Syndrome. It was a mother whose daughter also had Down syndrome and she told me, "You know, I cried because mine would never take dancing lessons." It's funny the things that hit you. (And now that girl is taking dancing lessons.) So then I said to her that all I cared about was that Meg wouldn't be pretty, and she told me to go into the supermarket and look at the people there. "They're not so hot-looking, anyway," she said. It's true, too.

For Donna, whose daughter was born perfectly normal and who waited over eighteen months for a final diagnosis, the process of giving up her expectations for her child was much harder than it was for Peg. Donna had had a chance to believe that her fantasies would come true. She says:

The fact that Emily was normal for even as little as five months of her life allowed me to have every normal fantasy. I had the prom fantasy, the high school graduation fantasy, the Easter Bunny fantasy, the Christmas fantasy. I had them all, and then someone came and snatched them from me.

It took listening to a psychologist who works with parents of handicapped children for me to grasp the idea that it was my dream that had been snatched from me, not Emily's. It was Gary's and my right to be average Mr. and Mrs. America and have kids.

We waited eight years to have children, and when I opted to stop working and start a family it was because I was into the Koolade-and-brownies-after-school fantasy; I just wanted to be Mom, and being Mom to a kid who didn't walk until she was three was not part of the scenario.

My biggest response to the whole thing, which no one seemed to recognize, was that it was my life that was screwed up. Here's

Emily—is she ever going to know the difference? I don't know. I still can't answer that question. But I can answer for myself. I had a lot of dreams that died, and nobody seemed to be able to understand what that meant to me.

With Ilene, Richard's mother, the question of expectations and hopes destroyed took on a significance that complicates the lives of many parents who place a high value on academic achievement. Richard's father Paul, a scientist, is one such parent. Says Ilene:

Once it had been established that Richard was mentally retarded, my husband more or less withdrew. Retardation is the one disability that could be guaranteed to strike him to the heart because he values intellectual development above anything else. He just didn't know how to cope. He flapped at the mouth about having Richard put away in an institution, on which subject I was just about homicidal. I couldn't bear even to discuss it, with him or with any professional persons or psychologists.

As far as I was concerned they were saying, essentially, that because Richard was defective he was garbage and should be thrown away. They were denying the basic bond of loyalty between a parent and a child, saying that if the child doesn't measure up to certain standards the parent has the right to discard him. Which, of course, if it applies to the mother-child relationship applies to any relationship. I regard child abandonment as one of the most horrible of human sins, and I always have. Besides, he was a baby. Who would care for him?

Ilene developed her own defense pattern, but it was one that did not, she found out, work for very long:

After I began to realize that something was wrong with Richard, I avoided acquiring any new knowledge about child development, and I blocked or ignored the knowledge I already had because it was extremely painful to me. An experience such as following a school bus and seeing the normal kindergarten kids dropped off at their homes and running into their houses was so unbelievably painful to me that I would go home and cry for hours. I developed an imaginary life in which my child was growing normally, until the discrepancy between the imaginary child and the real one made it so unbearably painful that when he was about five I gave up that fantasy altogether. Now I am totally incapable of imagining him as a normal child. He is what he is, and he is nothing else.

It took time for Richard's mother to be able to say of her son, "He is what he is, and he is nothing else." Until that point she, like Emily's mother, had run the gamut of people who supposedly wanted to help but only succeeded in increasing her feelings of inadequacy. Incidentally, such feelings come very naturally to parents of handicapped children and need no reinforcement, however well-intentioned or professionally motivated. Ilene says:

When I was younger, I was approached by people who knew various saviors of the retarded. One suggested a program that required four hours of intensive manipulation daily, for which you needed teams of volunteers manipulating the child through various crawling patterns. I could not face that. Later I was told that if your child didn't improve, these folks laid the blame on you—you must not have done it right.

I did not choose to accept that suggestion. I did not go for vitamin injections. I did not pray. I did not do any of the things that various persons recommended, and I got very tired of having things recommended to me.

I even had disagreeable experiences with other mothers of retarded children who insinuated that I was abnormal for having hostile feelings towards my retarded child. I could not understand how they could possibly not have hostile feelings. They were probably very traditional, putting away from themselves any notion that you could have hostile feelings about this poor, dependent, utterly defenseless handicapped child.

When I had a normal child and felt the same hostile feelings toward her, I found I could say, "I'd really love to break her neck," and other mothers would agree that they felt exactly the same way about their children. So it wasn't abnormal at all; it just wasn't acceptable to voice those feelings about a retarded child.

Millie, John's mother, found that her loss of expectations for her son took on a keener edge when the "label" put upon him was changed. She says:

There have been two difficult times for me. The first was coming home after seeing the pediatric neurologist who said, "He will not lead a normal life; he will not go to college or fulfill any of those expectations that you will have for your other children, and it is really unknown where he will go or what he will do."

The other real blow was the recommendation that John go to a special school instead of staying in the EMH class. "Educable mentally handicapped" is a higher level, one I could deal with. When you've gotten used to thinking that your child is educable and they tell you all of a sudden, "No, he's not; he's trainable," that's very hard to take.

We went and visited the school. I had never before seen "mongoloid" children, or kids on crutches, or kids who had seizures or any of that, and it really *shook me. I knew John had been unhappy in the EMH class and he'd be better off in this school, but he didn't look like most of the kids and I didn't know what his reaction to them was going to be. I figured he'd be happier, though, and he has been. He loves the school. He absolutely loves it. It was my shock, it wasn't his.*

Bill had already been to the school and was much more accepting. It did not upset him the way it upset me. I don't know why that was. Maybe he had given up, and I was still hoping; I suspect that I still had expectations.

The school has a gym show once a year and every kid in the school takes part, the ones in wheelchairs, or on crutches, or with hearing aids or whatever, and some of them have to be helped to walk or do the movements. The first time I went to the gym show I just sat there in tears. I had never seen the whole school together before. They all came in, about fifty of them, waving their flags and smiling. I can still cry, just thinking about it.

Pamela's program: "a real significant chore"

An exceptional parent's constant striving to do right by a mentally handicapped child resembles a rambling path with all sorts of little tracks, not one of them signposted, running off to the sides. There are thickets and potholes and unexpected puddles (in which to sink when one is already wallowing in self-pity). There are a lot of people to meet along the way: friends, would-be friends, do-gooders, and more professionals in more areas than you can count on the fingers of both hands. You could, I suppose, call it a pilgrim's progress, but I believe that the description has already been pre-empted by someone else.

As must be clear by this point, it is important to walk the rambling path with extreme caution and to be very careful about whom you talk to along the way. As the mothers of both Emily and Richard have pointed out, there are innumerable people out there who want to tell you what to do with your child.

Pamela's father, Don, also found this out when he tried to set up a contingency plan against the time when his mother, who has looked after Pamela and her brother since their parents' divorce, would become less able to carry out such extensive care-taking duties. Don says:

I was searching out day care possibilities for Pamela, and at one point I naively approached the state department of mental health. I told them that right now I didn't have a problem, but wanted a contingency plan for the future. It took close to five months before I got the courtesy of a reply. After seven months a lady came out to the house. She seemed to be sympathetic but quite unaware of the problems of living with a handicapped child. She suggested that it might be possible to develop some residential arrangements for Pamela. That was the last I heard of that.

Three months or so later, after I'd made call after call, a girl got in touch with me who said she was a behavioral social worker or something. She was going to assist me in modifying Pamela's behavior so that she would be easier for Grandma to manage. There was nothing wrong with this approach—it was something that needed to be done anyway—although it was not really answering my question. So this lady came out every other Saturday for two or three months and we sat down and we developed a behavioral program, and it got to be a real significant chore.

We had a chart on the wall, a big chart with a very structured program: at certain times Pamela was to do certain things. It was great; it was just what she needed, but the problem was that somebody had to enforce that structure. The behavioral program required a lot of time, a lot of consistency, and, I think, a lot more effort than either my mother or myself could give. I wasn't always there, Grandma wouldn't always listen, the other child needed things, and sometimes the easiest way to get Pamela out of our hair was to let her sit in front of the TV. She enjoys watching TV. While she is watching TV she is not getting in anybody's hair. And there are times when I look at the chart and see that now she's supposed to stop watching TV and do this or that, but that means doing it with her. Unless you enforce the program consistently, every single day, the same time, the same operation, you've lost it. I think there are limits to the amount of time you can devote to this kind of activity. Sometimes I don't have the time, and sometimes I just don't feel like it. So if I want to take a nap or something, I let her watch TV.

The only thing that's really worked is "telephone time." From six-thirty to seven in the evening was defined as telephone time, and Pamela thinks it's the greatest thing since sliced bread. We use it a little bit as a reward system to get things done: "There'll be no telephone time today unless. . . ." However, enforcing "no telephone time" is horrendous. When six-thirty comes, Pamela doesn't understand why she is not getting telephone time. It is very difficult to get through to her that it is because of something she has or has not done. She does not appreciate that. So come telephone time all hell breaks loose, and the only way to enforce it is to unplug the telephones and hide them. We have a little extra bell that rings even if the telephone is unplugged, so you have to go around hunting for a telephone to plug back in before you can answer, and by that time the caller has usually hung up.

The behavioral plan also calls for TV time, and that is being abused. We bought locks that we put on the TV, but we are one of these affluent families with no fewer than three TVs in our house, so in order to enforce TV time you have to go around locking up three TVs. Just to stay with a consistent behavioral program after I get home from work is a real chore, a real headache, and I have a lot of concerns about it.

The plan that everyone believes is the best sort of thing for Pamela calls for a lot of structure. In some ways Pamela structures herself, but hers is an entirely different kind of structure. Pamela's structure is totally inflexible. It doesn't allow for the sort of give-and-take that you've got to have in a family. For instance, at twelve o'clock Pamela will say, "Lunchtime, Daddy, eat lunch now." I say, "Let's wait until twelve-thirty and we'll go to McDonald's." "No, eat lunch now." She has a watch and she can tell time, and she points to her watch and twelve o'clock it is and twelve o'clock is lunchtime. To get her to wait until twelve-thirty or one o'clock is nearly impossible. It's pretty hard to reconcile Pamela's program with an ordinary family routine.

The way I see it is this: school is very structured, with a bunch of professionals all pulling together in a very clearly defined program, and it is their job, and that is what they do. If my job was to work on something with the same employee at ten-thirty each morning and then at eleven o'clock finish and do something else, I'd do it, too. I would follow the structure of the job. Home, though, is a very unstructured environment. I've had all my appointments and schedules, and I'm tired. Nobody wants to get home and have to start all over with another series of appointments and schedules, and that's what Pamela's behavioral plan demands—to know that at seven o'clock telephone time ends and it's time to play games, so everyone has to fish out a game. I can't do it every day. I can't work to a schedule at home. I guess that's my problem.

The behavior thing with Pamela affects a lot of different areas of our lives. My mother is well into her seventies; she takes wonderful physical care of the children, but she has difficulty understanding what is, in my judgment, best for Pamela. She feels sorry for her and thinks we should bend over backwards to take care of her needs. She thinks we should be very forgiving toward the child because "she can't help it." Grandma is over-permissive, and she doesn't think we should scold Pamela or send her to her room if she does something wrong.

This is a problem, and what is most disturbing is that she will find any excuse she can for Pamela's behavior. If there's a fight between the two kids, as there often is, then it has to be Tom's fault because he tantalized Pamela. If there are shenanigans at the meal table, then Tom is to blame because if he wasn't laughing Pamela wouldn't be behaving badly. When children start laughing Pamela gets excited, and then the thing snowballs and pandemonium begins.

It causes me a certain amount of grief that my mother has difficulty being objective about Pamela's problem and does not expect enough of her. Personally, I expect Pamela to take responsibility like anyone else in the family and to live up to certain standards. I do not expect her to fool around when there's work to be done, although getting this across is very difficult. If Tom objects to something and refuses to do it I say, "Fine, don't do it and tomorrow you don't get to go to McDonald's." It gets done. With Pamela it won't get done. She has to be told over and over, and eventually she'll get the message and do what is needed to get what she wants.

We just had an instance of this. She rides the school bus, and if a kid misbehaves on the bus they issue a citation. After the third citation they stop the kid from riding the bus. After Pamela's second citation her teacher called me and I went down to the school and we all talked to her, the teacher, the principal, myself. I've never seen her so serious. It was the first time I've ever really seen the smile wiped off her face. I don't know how they got through to her, but she knew she was in big trouble.

The net result was that they developed a star system of rewards. If Pamela behaves herself she gets two stars and if she doesn't she gets no stars. On Thursdays they have pizza for lunch at school, and Pamela really loves pizza. If she collects ten stars over five school days she gets to have pizza for lunch on Thursday, and if she collects nine stars she gets no pizza. It really hasn't taken long for her to catch on to that, and I think we have only had three weeks in six months when she didn't get pizza.

Now we've seen the star system work I guess we should apply it to other things, except that I don't quite know how. I'd like to apply it to her behavior in the street; the difficulty is that the people she meets do not interpret this as bad behavior, so they don't yell at her. The bus driver yells.

Pamela loves to do things. She loves to achieve. It's always a challenge to her to do things other people are doing. She can roller skate and ice skate. She loves to play games. She taught herself to swim. She can ride a bike, which is actually a big problem because it gives her mobility—she can take off. At least she is now very good in traffic, and I do take credit for teaching her that myself. She can poach an egg or make toast, and she can make cupcakes or pizza out of a package. She uses a sewing machine, and she can latch-hook; she's making herself a rug.

It's very important to her that she does things herself, and she tends to be a little bit too arrogant in that respect. She says, "No, you go away; do it by myself." "By myself" is her favorite expression. The latest thing is that she knows how to drive a car. "Key, put foot down, pull down." I ask her, "How do you stop?" "Put foot down, that one." So I have to keep my eyes on where the keys are because I'm sure she'd take off if she got the chance. And of course she's driven bumper cars at the fairground, which she believes are just one step removed from Daddy's car. So I've managed to convince her that she is too young and cannot drive a car until she is twenty-one. All I have to do now is think up another story before she is twenty-one.

The hardest part about having a handicapped child is that you are physically and mentally incapable of putting in as much time as you would like. I get home after a day at work and I'm bushed. By the time the children are ready to go to bed, so am I. It's tough. It's very frustrating to have to recognize your own limits.

I haven't really thought what I will do when the children leave home, when Pamela goes, as I anticipate that she will, to a community living facility of some kind. I'll have so much time on my hands that I won't know which way to turn. That may sound like a wonderful prospect but I am not sure whether it is or not. It will be almost like losing your job and not being able to find another one.

the primrose path of academia

"Reality testing" is a technique that her teachers use constantly, and have taught me to use, with Victoria. "Did so-and-so really steal your lunch today, or is that a story you made up in your head?" Or, "Don't you remember that it's not tomorrow that you're going to do such-and-such? Remember we said that we were going to do that next week, after the weekend's over and you're back at school?"

Reality testing is also a process that parents of mentally retarded children must put themselves through. Somewhere along the line one's expectations must be stashed away in the back of the mind. There's no room for them anywhere else because reality shoves them aside and plants itself firmly in their place. When you've waited nine years for a child to tie her shoelaces, you tend to find it difficult to persist in the fantasy that she might become a dentist. When it takes until age seventeen for your son to learn to make change for a dollar, it's time to let go of any plans you might have had for him to go into the family accounting business.

Steve, the principal of Victoria's school for mentally handicapped children, deplores the way some educators lead parents down what he calls "the primrose path of academia." When parents have some kind of grandiose goal in mind for a child who will never read, write, or ride the subway without supervision it is, says Steve, the teacher's job to help those parents get their heads straight. He reiterates the views of Sheila, Chris's mother, who talked about the father who wanted to choose a splendid name for his son because the boy was going to be a member of the Supreme Court one day—when you've been dealing on that level, and the child is born retarded, you've got an awful long journey back to get to square one. Steve says:

My son is twelve years old and he's a perfectly normal kid in the sense that he has no handicapping condition. But academically he is not really very proficient, and I'm not confident that college will be right for him. I mentioned this recently when we were at dinner with my in-laws and other members of our fairly extended family. I said that there are a lot of things that my son can do well, but basically he is not academically inclined. You should have seen their faces. They were horrified.

It made me think: here he is, twelve years old, and already we're talking about college. What we're implying is that how he does in school is more important than what he's like as a person— whether he's a sensitive person, whether he can do other things well.

I keep saying to my wife that I hope we do not let anyone squelch his enthusiasm by judging him only in academic terms: that if he does well in school, he's good; that if he fails academically, he's bad. It's a trap that parents fall into, especially in an affluent, middle-class area like the one we live in. It's a college environment; the expectations are ready-made. And it can be devastating to a normal child, let alone one who is mentally handicapped.

What dead-end street do we push handicapped children into if the academic area is the only one we're trying to develop? Where are they going to go? They're going to wind up untrained for anything that lies within their capabilities. They will be programmed for dependence. They're going to be minimally functioning human beings and society is going to have to take care of them.

We as educators have to get parents to realize that there are plenty of things their children can do, and that they can help their children to develop those areas and become people they can be proud of. Some of the graduates from this school who are mentally handicapped have accomplished a tremendous amount. Their parents can look at those kids and take a lot of pride in their accomplishments.

Vocational training is an important part of the curriculum at Steve's school, and an impressive number of the young graduates work not in sheltered workshops but in the community. One young man works at the public library, another at a local recreation center. Several former students work in the cafeteria on the campus of the university. Another works in a laundry, and a number of others in department stores. The school's vocational coordinator is constantly seeking job openings for students in the community, and it is the school's policy to seek such work situations for all the students who are able to maintain them.

Steve believes that teachers in the field of special education have a particular obligation to be straight with parents, a task that is sometimes much harder than it sounds. He says:

It's much easier to go along with parents than to say, "Wait a minute, I don't agree with you." For instance, with a parent who wants a child to succeed academically, who is really interested in the academic program, we have to get it across that this is not the area that is important to the child. It may be something that the parents want for the child, but from the child's point of view it is not a priority. That's not saying that we don't need to teach functional academics—to read signs, fill in a job application, tell time. If we took a child who was blind and said we'd teach him through writing large and using lots of bright colors—visual aids—everyone would think we were crazy. But trying to teach a retarded child purely academic skills is just like that—we'd be using the wrong teaching tools. Yet in the area of mental retardation educators and parents have been going along for years insisting, "What I want for this child is an academic program." It's the one damned area we know we can't compete in.

What's going to matter for somebody who is mentally retarded is independence skills—being able to cope, make decisions, act independently within the environment. That's a big part of it. The other part is how the retarded person feels about himself or herself and how he or she gets along with people. That's very important and it has to be trained; it doesn't just happen.

Schools have a certain structure. Our school is right next door to an ordinary elementary school, and you can watch those children line up to go to gym; they form lines exactly the way kids did when I was at school. Their structure is to pull in; they can't let the kids roam, exploit their environment, interact freely. In a regular school that would only lead to problems, so they survive by pulling in.

For our children, though, that would be the worst thing. They need independence in their environment. They need interaction on an independent basis. The very things that you can't allow in a regular school are the things that our kids need more than anything else.

There's a lot of pressure being put on educators to eliminate facilities like ours, to put our children back into the regular elementary schools. That's fine. I don't see any problem in that. The problem comes when you try to combine programs and environments.

Unless handicapped children can be trained in areas in which they can function on an appropriate basis, no amount of interaction on a social level can help them. If they don't have the skills that are necessary to enable them to interact, they're not going to learn just from being in the same school or the same hall or whatever. The regular school program is, by definition, academic, the very area that most of our children can't compete in. From the time the child is three until the time he leaves school this is the area that is being stressed. There is limited, if any, vocational training, limited home living skills training, limited mobility training. All the same, parents are led down this primrose path of academia, led into thinking that it is the most important thing for their children, when in fact if those children don't get proper training in nonacademic or functional areas they are not going to make it when they leave school.

In the school that my son and daughter attend there is a special education class, and recently the whole school, including the special education class, took part in a song festival. The parents of the handicapped children wanted them in that festival. They wanted it very badly. But they did their kids a disservice because the kids couldn't handle it. They stood out from the group. Being on display like that just accentuated their handicaps.

Being an administrator myself, I was interested in why the principal of the school allowed that to happen. He told me that the parents had insisted, because it was such an important issue for them to have their children involved in an activity with nonhandicapped peers. He said, "Since when is the regular school in the business of providing social interaction? That's not what we're here for." But to him that seems to be all the parents of those retarded children are interested in.

Mentally handicapped children can be manipulated more easily than other children. The song festival showed that very clearly. The special education students were dressed differently and they looked different. Try to get a normal fourth or fifth grader into a suit and tie, even for a presentation, and you know how far you'll get.

They want to wear jeans and gym shoes, and that's what most of them did wear. Not the special education kids—all the girls were in skirts, most of them out of style, either too long or too short, and their hair was cut in a way that drew attention to them, not that let them blend in. Those are subtle ways in which parents have the power to manipulate mentally handicapped children. If you've got a mentally retarded fourteen-year-old, and you have to choose his clothes, at least you can be aware of what other teenagers are wearing. It's sometimes better to buy jeans and gym shoes and let the child blend in with the other kids than to dress the child up and show him off, even though you have the power to do so. If you use that power, you reinforce the handicap instead of diminishing it.

Often, too, it is easier to do things for the child than to let the child try something and fail. Having the child take responsibility for doing things in the home can be much more difficult than doing things for him—cleaning his room, setting the table, doing his laundry. But look at it on a long-term basis. Unless retarded children are given the opportunity, they'll never become independent or semi-independent in those areas. When the normal child leaves home he has to make it or break it. The retarded child also has to be prepared for leaving home.

When I went away to college I made the classic mistakes. Once I wanted to cook rice for four people, so I put in four cups of rice. I had rice coming out of everywhere. I only did it once because I learned from that first experience. I learned to read the directions or to ask someone to do it. With a handicapped person it's all got to be taught—how to turn on the stove, how to deal with these things.

It's hard for a parent to allow that to happen. It's hard to sort your own laundry and separate out the child's laundry and have him do it himself. It's hard, it's time-consuming, and its frustrating. It's easier to do it for him. But it's very important that the child have the chance to do it himself, and this is where the school has to cooperate. The parent sits down with the teacher at the beginning of the school year and says, "This year I want her to learn to make a sack lunch." And if that is a realistic goal we'll teach her, and the parent has to hold us accountable. At the beginning we'll buy the food for her, then we'll keep building the skills until maybe by the end of the year she'll be going to the grocery store, buying her own food, and making her own lunch. It's hard. But what's important is that the parent and the teacher must go hand in hand.

When it seems like a really tough job, being the parent of a retarded child, it's good to remember that a few years ago retarded children not only couldn't achieve but weren't even expected to. They had no chance of living up to whatever potential they had because there was no one there to teach them the skills or to train them to survive. Now, when a baby is born with Down syndrome there are still physicians who say, "Put him away. Get him out of here. Go put him in an institution. He'll be better off and you will be better off." But who are we to presume to suggest what other people should or shouldn't do with their lives and with their families?

As an educator, Steve believes that parents are entitled to make their own decisions about the path their retarded children will follow, free from inappropriate pressure from outsiders. He also believes, however, that parents—in order to do what is best for the child—must be realistic, and that those involved in the education of mentally handicapped children must respond to the parents in a realistic manner. Steve says:

Parents must always keep an open mind about what the future holds for their child. That means that they must be open with the school system and insist that the school system be open with them. It can't be a one-way street. This may sound simple, but it's very difficult to achieve. For one thing, accepting that a child is handicapped involves grief and pain and mourning for the parents. What makes it harder for the child's teachers is that some parents never get through the mourning process, or get through it only to start all over again because the child has reached another stage of development.

Developmentally, children go through different stages, and just when parents believe they've dealt with all the feelings they find that they're back to square one—the feelings come back and swamp them all over again. It happens first in infancy, then at adolescence, and then when the child becomes an adult. I think once you get past the guilt and understand that you, as a parent, didn't do anything to cause the child to be retarded, you can deal more clearly with the situation. It would be convenient if it always happened that way—that parents came to accept that they weren't personally responsible for a child's handicap—but it's not always that clear cut.

There are parents who turn their backs and are totally rejecting. There are parents who don't reject the child but reject the handicap. Here at school we've had parents who said, "My child is different from all the other children in this school. He's not like the rest." Some can deal with it on certain levels and not on others. Like the parent who says, "Yes, yes, I can deal with my child being here. I understand that he has learning problems. When are you going to teach him to drive a car?"

My advice to parents looking for the best educational possibilities for their handicapped children is this: go into it with your eyes open; keep holding me responsible, because I am principal of this school and your child's future is in my hands to a certain extent. Hold me and the rest of the people here in the school accountable for what your child learns or does not learn while he's with us. We are not here to provide lip service, to tell you that you can do your thing and we will do ours and never the twain shall meet. That's when both the parents and the teachers really wind up spinning their wheels. Each can be doing positive things—parents at home and teachers in school—but it's a whole lot more effective when you combine these two efforts. The end result is more than if the two parts operate separately.

the dignity of risk

Part of the philosophy that Steve has developed over his years as an educator and administrator in the field of special education is that a natural tendency to overprotect a mentally retarded child can put a stranglehold on that child's chance of achieving his or her highest functioning level in society. Overprotectiveness further retards a retarded child. Steve says, "With a handicapped child there's a tendency not to allow that child the dignity of risk. Normal children risk on their own, but the handicapped child has to be encouraged to risk and to be presented with the opportunities for taking risks. The natural tendency of parents and, often, educators, is to close in even more and create even greater dependency. It's a temptation, especially for parents, because if the child isn't allowed to risk, the parent doesn't have to risk either. The parent can avoid having to risk, but it is at the expense of the child."

From the parent's point of view, allowing the mentally handicapped child the dignity of risk is, indeed, a risky business. It's risky emotionally, because by the time your retarded child is technically old enough to take risks you have begun to believe that you are the only person competent enough to protect this at-risk child from a potentially hostile and exploitative world. It's very hard to let go of that kind of control. It is, in a way, a blow to your ego, and even the most sophisticated parent of a retarded child finds self-doubt and self-distrust making unsuspected inroads into a meticulously nurtured sense of self-worth. You may even fail to rejoice at some evidence of progress in your child, because it means that your child is doing something without your support or intervention. And if your retarded kid doesn't need you, who does? Everyone's ego has its moments of irrationality.

More rational, certainly, are the practical doubts about

letting a child who is unversed in the ways of the world face the real dangers that exist outside the safe confines of home or school. When you have a mentally retarded child who has some freedom of movement, you have a child who is particularly susceptible to danger. You have a child who is particularly easy prey for the muggers, rapists, and child abusers whose deeds are so regularly chronicled in the newspapers and on TV. When your handicapped child is out on the streets enjoying, perhaps, the maximum degree of freedom that will ever be her lot, certain news stories can unhinge you for days.

Take, for instance, the story of Stevie, an eighteen-year-old with Down syndrome, who was beaten up on the street just around the time that Victoria was being mobility trained to walk to school by herself. Stevie was on his way to visit a friend, another retarded boy who lived a few blocks away. It had taken him seven years to develop the independence and social competence to undertake this small adventure alone. Stevie, a good-natured young man, still doesn't understand why anyone would want to hurt him. There was no apparent motive for the attack, which happened within shouting distance of Stevie's home. The attackers did not take the two dollars he had in his pocket; if someone had asked him for the money he'd have handed it over without question.

It is the sort of story that scores a direct hit in the heart of every parent who has a retarded child. Children who lack a reasonably well-developed instinct for self-preservation are singularly at risk, and parents are torn between the necessity of letting the child be independent and the temptation of protecting him from the dangers they know only too well are out there.

Independence training, as the principal of Victoria's school has so insistently explained, is vital if young people like Stevie and Victoria are going to make it in the real world—and that is what we want for them. We want that training for them because we want them to live as normal a life as possible with as many of life's rewards as possible. We want it also because we, unlike our handicapped kids, are street-wise: we know that the proverbial jungle didn't get its name for nothing.

For seven years Stevie's parents had labored to give their son some small measure of autonomy. When he was brought

At the time of the Stevie incident Victoria, a few months home, beaten and bleeding, seven years went out the window. How long will it be before he overcomes the fear of such a senseless, confusing thing happening again? How long before his parents get up the courage to let him go out alone and again take his chances on the street?

shy of her fourteenth birthday, had just learned to walk the six blocks to school by herself. The mobility training had paid off. The achievement had been the occasion of enormous rejoicing (on her part and on ours) and was doing wonders for her shaky adolescent self-esteem. She had never had any road sense and I was beginning to despair of her ever learning any. But her teachers put her through a minutely detailed and painstaking program that trains retarded children in those skills of self-preservation that most kids acquire naturally and with rudimentary parental guidance— like observing traffic signals and looking both ways before crossing the street.

There were three crossing guards on the route, and they kept their eyes open for Victoria and her friends as they walked to school. So every morning I reminded myself that Victoria was as safe as any other kid. But despite all precautions any kid can get knocked down by some driver who's drugged or half asleep or speeding to get to work on time.

In fact, Victoria and her friends may be safer than some. They have been so rigorously trained that they do stop at the curb and look for oncoming cars. Despite their higher functioning levels and instinctive awareness of danger, some normal kids take terrible chances on the street. I've watched Victoria follow her program, stopping and looking both ways, while kids from the neighboring regular school charged straight across the road, blinkered and unconcerned.

And what of other dangers? Any kid can be approached by a stranger whose intentions are far from friendly. How well do mentally handicapped children assimilate their "stranger-danger" training? How deep do the warnings sink in? How much do they really grasp about what accepting a ride from a stranger can mean? Not much, by all accounts.

Not so long ago Victoria's teachers staged a "stranger-danger" demonstration and watched in utter frustration as one child after another—all of them previously drilled to the point of exhaustion—was persuaded to go off with the stranger. Victoria was one of them. And she would still do it. Like Pamela, whose friendliness causes her father such concern, Victoria will talk to absolutely anyone, anywhere. Victoria, however, does have some notion that this is something she's not supposed to do.

"Hi," she will say to a total stranger, "my name's Victoria; what's your name?" Then she'll say, "You're a stranger. I mustn't talk to you." Or she'll greet someone in the store with cheerful familiarity, then turn to me and say, "I don't know that man. He's a stranger. I mustn't talk to strangers."

"Then why do you talk to strangers, when you know some people aren't nice?" I demand.

"I don't know!" replies Victoria. And she giggles.

For me it's no laughing matter. Victoria is a pretty girl—a tall, leggy, striking teenager with a beautiful young body. And not an atom of street sense. In my blackest moments I inform myself that my delightful daughter is just the sort of girl who, lacking the appropriate supervision that I provide for her, might wind up raped, murdered, and dumped in a ditch. It is not productive to dwell on such possibilities, but it's very important to be aware of them.

Very many retarded youngsters have an imperfect sense of danger. Their reactions are slow. Many, like Victoria and Pamela, can't grasp the practical drawbacks of assuming that everyone they meet is a nice person. Clearly such children are extraordinarily vulnerable, and a story like Stevie's is a chilling reminder that the world is full not only of rotten drivers but of people who are genuinely rotten.

There's another turn of the screw, too. Retarded children are subject to more authority figures than other children. Retarded children must submit to control by parents, educators, and administrators to a degree which does not apply to other children. So to many of them *any* adult is an authority figure to be trusted and obeyed without demur. That is an issue which poses grave concerns to parents whose handicapped children are ready to leave home for some other supervised setting.

With any child, however, the parent is faced with the problem of how far to let the fledgling spread his wings, how far to let her hop from the nest. Growing up involves taking risks, and this applies as much to handicapped kids as to their nonhandicapped siblings.

What Victoria learned at nearly fourteen, her sister learned at half that age. But when Emma walked to school alone I had exactly the same fears I still have for Victoria. It just happened at a different stage of development. After the Stevie incident Victoria continued to walk to school, and we're still trying to extend her mobility. Her pride and delight in her progress outweigh the risks and give her (and me) a sense of possibility: today, six blocks; tomorrow, who knows? For a child whose successes are hard won and rare, each one is proportionately more significant.

As Steve so often reminds his students' parents, over-protectiveness only further handicaps a child whose limitations are already the cause of all too much frustration. Smother love is the coward's way out. If I never ask Victoria to achieve, I can't blame her for failing. And no one can blame *me* for her failure. Well, what did you expect? The child's retarded.

It's the coward's way out. It's tempting, but it's cowardly just the same.

mobility: a mixed blessing

One parent for whom mobility has been a mixed blessing is Lynne, the mother of Laura.* Laura, now in her early twenties, is mildly retarded and has had a hard time accepting herself as retarded. Although she attended a special school for seven years she does not associate, if she can help it, with others whom she knows are mentally handicapped. This has been a problem for Lynne because Laura's reluctance to acknowledge her handicap has meant that she could not be

---

*In this family's story, names have been changed in order to protect the family's privacy.

persuaded to take advantage of social activities for young-sters like herself. Instead, she sought companions among the normal population, and some of the companions she found were totally unacceptable to her mother.

Laura's mobility has been a source of anxiety since she was in her early teens, and she has been running away since she was fourteen. Lynne says:

Laura had just entered the local high school, and she ran away from there in the first week of school. It was too much for her to handle—too much stimulus, hundreds of kids in the halls. It was a bad placement. I should have sent her from junior high to the special school, but I didn't. I did what I thought was appropriate at the time.

Laura never had any friends in the school community. When she was small she had schoolmates who lived in the neighborhood, but the older she got the wider the gap became. That's why I have reservations now about mainstreaming retarded youngsters in the regular schools. I feel differently about it now than I did when Laura went to high school. I was glad when the school district people told me that they tried to keep the children as much with the regular population as possible. But my experience has taught me that the regular population is not accepting. As a parent I suffered many hurts for my child and children like her. To see them belittled, devalued, was incredibly painful.

My experiences with mainstreaming have led me to believe that if Laura had had the chance to be in the same school from kindergarten onward she would have been a lot more stable. I don't think she would have had a problem with running away. As it was, she didn't get into a special school until she was fourteen, and I think that had a lot to do with it. Until then she didn't fit in anywhere. So she attached herself to losers, girls who dropped out of school and hung around on the street. Some of them would start out for school but not go. In a lot of cases their parents worked, so they could go home and no one was any the wiser. When I found out about this I would walk Laura to school, but it didn't solve anything. Once, she got all the way into the city—about five miles away—and a policeman brought her back. That scared me. She didn't actually disappear; she knew exactly where she was going. She wanted to know how the bus got to Howard Street, so she just stayed on it until Howard Street, the end of the line. It was quite chaotic.

Laura still doesn't accept her handicap, and she won't go to a special program because she doesn't want to be with "those retardeds," so she makes all sorts of wrong friends. And she's learned what rejection means. We talk about it often, and I have to be careful that I don't cry. I have to put myself in a tough matron mode and say, "You know, Laura, you know what it's like out there. These people are just using you, and they are not becoming your friends. They are using you for reasons of their own and you know that most of it is not healthy."

Nobody can click in with Laura. She's difficult for a normal person to talk to for any length of time. What can she talk about to another person her age? Records, because music is a big thing. The weather. What kind of makeup the kids wear. That's about it. Now maybe this is what they do talk about, I don't know. But I can't see how she can develop an ongoing relationship through that.

So Laura has found the seamy side of the neighborhood. A man she knows is a pervert. The police have their eye on him. He recruits young girls to "model," as he calls it. It's a little prostitution ring. Laura used to call this guy up and I wondered why he would spend so much time on the phone with her. He has a bunch of young teenage boys, pimp types; one smile at Laura and she'd fall all over them. And that place exists and the police can't get the goods on the guy. It's hard to protect Laura because she's mobile; she does have that much independence. And she's not obviously handicapped, she can pass very easily, until she starts to talk.

We have tried to help Laura understand her handicap, and the school has helped with that. We've seen television shows about handicaps and discussed them afterwards. All of this did not come about overnight; it is a very slow process. First we had to get her to the point where she could admit she had a handicap, and admit it to herself. Then she could say, "Yes, but there are other people who also have handicaps." She found that she wasn't alone, just as we parents find that we're not alone in having a handicapped child. This came about when she was around seventeen. It helped that she was accepted by her stepsister, Anne. (My husband died when Laura was ten, and I remarried eight years later.) Anne is now living out of state, but when she was home she let Laura know, "You're okay. I like you. I know you have a problem, but I still like you."

That was important, and it accomplished something I couldn't have done by verbalizing abstractions. They have to find out, they have to go through it themselves. At school she was presented with situations that were real, and the same thing happened at home.

All her life, though, Laura has been surrounded by people who are not handicapped. She has even had dates with nonhandicapped boys, and that scares me. I don't like it, and I don't want it. In each instance I have suspected that the boy had *a problem too; otherwise why would he select someone like Laura with whom, as soon as you get beyond "hello" and "how are you?" you must start to think that maybe something isn't quite right.*

I think her level of freedom would be easier for me to deal with if I knew that there were structured times of the day when she was positively engaged in activity. At the moment I don't see this. There's no job, and I don't know if there will be one. That is clearly something that I'm going to have to start taking seriously now, finding a job for Laura. The other thing I have to do is look at where she will live, because I can't see that it's going to be good for her or for anybody else to have her live at home indefinitely.

a not so merry merry-go-round

Don't believe that all parents of mentally handicapped children huddle together for comfort. "I have a mentally retarded child and so do you, and therefore we are one." Many parents, myself included, sometimes find enormous support in the company of others who are in the same boat; as I've said before, it's nice not to have to explain. But the situation is not that simple.

For one thing, it appears that for parents the grass is always greener on the other side of the fence—not the fence that separates mentally retarded children from other children, but the fence that separates children with one kind of handicap from those with another kind of handicap. Time and again I hear parents say, "I think I would find it easier to deal with, if he (or she) were more (or less) retarded."

Each type or level of retardation requires something a bit different from the parent, and there are times when, long after one has ceased to indulge in fantasies about the child being normal, one simply wishes that the child's handicap were different. It's possible, as the parent of a mentally impaired child, actually to become envious of another parent of a child whose impairment is a bit different. It's a strange trick your emotions pull on you.

Lynne tells me, "It would be easier if Laura weren't so mobile. At least you can keep your eye on Victoria."

I counter, "Yes, but you can explain things to Laura; you can try to help her understand about her handicap."

And Lynne comes back with, "But you don't have the pain of hearing Victoria ask, 'Why am I retarded?'"

Peg, who mourned because Meg would never be pretty, envies me because Victoria is so beautiful. I tell her, "It's not so great, actually, because the fact that she looks so normal means people expect much more of her than they do of Meg. Perhaps Meg has an easier time because her handicap is visible and people make allowances."

Donna, whose once-normal daughter is now more seriously retarded than Victoria, feels that she can deal with Emily's retardation just because it is severe and that she would be less able to cope with a child like Victoria, of whom she says, "Being that close to real, that close to passing the test the way society looks at it—I couldn't handle that; I'd be crazy."

Which is more or less what I say to Lynne. A merry-go-round. Not so merry, though.

Another mother of a child in Emily's functioning area says of her daughter, "It makes it worse that she's cute and pretty. If she were deformed and ugly and lay around and made bizarre noises, or if she were comatose like Karen Ann Quinlan was all those years, I think I could handle it. That kind of nursing care might bring out the Florence Nightingale in me."

So, many of us believe we'd perform better if the task with which we're confronted were just that bit different. . . .

Sheila, who can put a medical "label" on her son's handicap, views the issue from yet another perspective. She says:

When Chris was very young I met a woman who had a mentally retarded child who had no label, no identifiable cause of the retardation that they knew of. She said to me, "You're very lucky to have a child with Down syndrome." My eyebrows went a peculiar shape and I thought, "What's the matter with this lady?" She said, "Let me explain. You're lucky because you know what you're dealing with. Everybody knows what you're dealing with."

Now that's true up to a point, but it's not the whole story. For one thing, we don't always know what we're dealing with because all individuals with Down syndrome are different in terms of how they function. So it's not that clear cut.

The advantage lies in having a diagnosis. We know why Chris is retarded; we know it's because he's got an extra chromosome. Knowledge is very consoling, and it helps to get rid of some of the old myths that still hang over the subject of mental retardation. We know now what Down syndrome is, and there are other things we know about it too. For one thing, we know that it doesn't always happen when older women get pregnant, and that's a long-standing myth. Now we know that the age of the mother is not necessarily the deciding factor. Although the risk increases as a woman gets older, the average age of women having babies with Down syndrome is twenty-eight. There's also a higher risk factor in early teen pregnancies; I know of a thirteen-year-old mother whose baby was born with Down syndrome.

We know too that Down syndrome is not always attributable to the mother: in twenty-five percent of the cases the extra chromosome is derived from the father. This is very comforting news for mothers who have been told that Down syndrome always comes from the mother's side, and therefore feel guilty. One mother said to me, "Do you have that in writing? I've got to show my husband." Her husband had obviously been making her feel responsible for their child's condition.

We also know that Down syndrome occurs right at conception, so if a mother is feeling guilty about smoking or whatever during pregnancy we can give her facts to help her get rid of those bad feelings.

Another advantage is knowing that a child who is diagnosed at birth can go, even at one week old, into an early intervention program. That means the parents get the good feeling of helping their child, of doing all they can do. Most programs now have fairly sensitive professionals, accustomed to working with parents of retarded children, who can help counteract any negative input that the parents have received from doctors or hospital staff.

Early intervention programs also offer support from other parents, and that's really important for people who feel that they are the only ones in the world this has ever happened to. If they're in the right network they can get this support right away, and once the baby starts doing things they begin to feel good.

If you don't know that a child is retarded and his developmental milestones don't occur, it's very discouraging. It's almost the opposite when you have a child with Down syndrome: you know he's retarded, so his milestones are great; you celebrate them.

Then, when he's older, how you deal with it depends on your attitudes, your philosophy, and the kind of community you live in.

Attitudes matter a lot when you take your child to a restaurant or to the park. How do you deal with the reactions you get from other people? When your child is two years old and isn't walking, and someone asks you how old he is, what do you say? Mothers often ask me, "Do you tell the truth?"

One of my friends had a child who was very small at two-and-a-half, so she would tell people that the baby was a year old, because she didn't want to have to explain to everyone, "Well, she's two-and-a-half but she's not walking because she's got Down syndrome." So those are things that you learn to deal with—what to tell people in the park.

And how do you answer other children's questions? When some kid looks at Chris and asks me, "Is he retarded?" I always answer, "Yes, he is; do you know what that means?" I never just say, "Yes." I always try to talk about it because it's important for that other child to understand.

As a parent, I believe that children with handicapping conditions belong in society, and it's only logical to start by teaching kids about one another. I believe it's vitally important to start with handicapped and nonhandicapped children growing up together and being sensitized all the way along in a structured program.

To me it should be as much a part of a child's school curriculum to learn about children who are different as to learn about dollars and cents. Normal children, in a normal school environment, need to be taught in a systematic and sensitive way that we are not all the same.

Donna believes that the nature of a child's handicap significantly affects the parent's emotional adjustment to the situation. She says:

Something I've come to realize, that I didn't realize early in the game, is that your own emotional state—where you are emotionally with your own handicapped child—depends a great deal on what your child's handicap is. I used to think we were all one big happy family, each with a broken kid, so therefore we should band together and hold hands and everything would be fine. Very early on, though, I started having some difficulties relating to other mothers. I had trouble dealing with the ones who operated on denial, and there are many who do. They have a kid lying there who has no functions at all, and they're telling you miracle stories about how they know their kid is going to get up and walk. That is a real killer. I stayed away from those women.

I also had trouble with the ones who were so depressed that they became nonfunctional themselves. I wanted to pinch them and say, "Look, you have to get up in the morning and put one foot in front of the other and get moving, because if you don't your whole life is going to go down the drain."

I found that I would make instantaneous judgments about where parents were and what their problem was. I can't imagine how I must have seemed to them. It's funny, but I have very little sense of what I must have been like to other people. It may have been one of the few times in my life when I was not concerned about what impression I was making.

There can be great areas of disagreement among parents of retarded children, because their children's life situations are different. In general, other people don't understand that.

I get a great kick out of what I call "socially acceptable" handicaps. It seems that lately it's okay to be blind, deaf, or in a wheelchair. I am not minimizing the tremendous impact of a handicap like blindness, deafness, or paraplegia or whatever—God knows I would not want to be in those shoes. But the point is, when you live with a child whose brain doesn't work right you realize that what constitutes wholeness is not whether a person can see or hear or walk, it's being intellectually intact and functional.

It's relatively easy for people to look at a blind person, or a deaf person who is using sign language or wearing a hearing aid; that's comfortable, they can relate to that. So it's okay, it's an okay handicap. But I do not feel that same sense of being okay when society starts talking about the retarded. There is still a tremendous amount of discomfort there, and a lot of fear. Even retarded children are not too bad, but retarded adults are definitely out, definitely not okay; they're threatening, they're weird.

In the seven years preceding Victoria's final diagnosis of retardation I had known, on a personal level, only one family that was dealing with anything like the situation that confronted me. Moreover I had no family network to shore up my damaged defenses. I had not seen my parents since I went to Argentina when Victoria was three. My mother had died a year later, before Emma was born. I had close friends in England—or as close as you can be across half a world. My only close family member was my father, who simply did not deal in terms like retardation. Not, at least, where Victoria was concerned. Being an Irishman and a dreamer (and, of course, half a world away from the reality in which we were living), he considered Victoria a dreamer like himself—and who is to say that there's no truth in that? My then mother-in-law invariably referred to Victoria as "poor, dear Victoria," which drove me crazy.

So when I discovered a whole school hall full of parents just like me I was amazed, astounded. I had had no idea that there were so many of me. It was a revelation, and it was enormously reinforcing. For a while thereafter I had no time for anyone who *didn't* have a retarded child: I was too heavily involved in the cleansing knowledge that I was not alone. From there it was a short mental progression to, "It wasn't my fault." Because there couldn't be that many people who had single-handedly wrecked their children's lives and made them retarded, the chances were that I hadn't, either.

Today I can think a little more clearly, my head is straighter. Although there are experiences I can share only with other parents like myself, I can see too that a lot of what goes on with a handicapped child goes on with any child, and it can be a lot healthier to deal with the similarities than to dwell on the differences.

Moreover, in the different stages through which one progresses as the parent of a mentally handicapped child, the support or society of others who are experiencing the same emotions and making the same adjustments may or may not help. In fact it can be dangerous, when you're already wounded, to associate with others who are similarly hurt. It can retard rather than encourage the healing processes.

It can, therefore, be a very strange relationship that exists between parents of children who are mentally handicapped. We alternately clutch at each other for comfort or avoid each other like the plague because we are remorseless reminders to each other of the reality that we sometimes want to stuff out of sight.

A few of my close friends are parents of handicapped children. Many other parents whose kids are handicapped play no part in my social life, although sometimes I feel closer to them than I do to other friends who don't have personal experience of retardation. There is a kinship. That is not to say, however, that the kinship is always welcome. Enough is enough. Living with the reality of one's own child's retardation can be quite sufficient in the way of emotional taxation. Associating with others who live with the same reality can be overkill.

A certain amount of wallowing is permissible when you're

trying to come to terms with having a mentally retarded child. Then you have to get up, wash off the tears, and get on with the job. The natural follow-up is to "do something useful": you join the PTA, or write your congressperson about special education, or volunteer to man the lunchroom at school once a week, or bake cookies for school functions. As a writer, I inevitably found myself editing the school newsletter.

It was when I became part of the parent board at Victoria's school that all those people who had become instantly kin to me simply by having a handicapped child of their own began to emerge as real people who also existed outside the context of their child's handicap and had homes, and families, and other children, and even other problems that had nothing to do with having a retarded kid. I'd lost sight of the fact that there could be other kinds of problems. The one I was dealing with at the time was so overwhelming.

Don, Pamela's father, feels that the hardest part of having a handicapped child is not being able to put as much time and energy as he would like into the child and the issues that surround her. Other parents can be a source of comfort because they help him understand that everyone has limited endurance; he says, "I get satisfaction out of talking to other parents who have similar experiences. First of all you think, here are all these people doing wonderful things for their children, and look at the crummy job I'm doing. It's very consoling to find that everyone feels that way. Parent group support is very important. We don't do it enough."

And once, when I wrote a newspaper article about community-living facilities for the mentally handicapped, a father telephoned me in great frustration to say that he felt the "exceptional" parents in his area didn't provide much support for each other. "We should be more together," he said.

The kinship—be it welcome or unwelcome—that seems to exist among parents of mentally handicapped children is characterized by a special kind of awareness. Donna says:

Another thing that happens when you have a retarded child is that you start to recognize problem signs in other people's children. You can go up to an eighteen-month-old baby with some developmental problem that you have not been told about, and you know, you don't need to be told. It's like being a member of a secret club, except it's not the sort of club you'd want to extend an invitation to.

It puts you on the spot if it happens to be the child of a friend, and you feel there's something wrong and the parents obviously have no suspicion. Do you tell them, and scare them to death? You could be wrong. But if you're not wrong, you have knowledge that they really need to have too. It is not a comfortable situation.

Basically, I have found many of my relationships with other parents of handicapped children rather trying. Many other parents find them very supportive and I can see how they would be. I could wish in some respects that my daughter had a different handicap, a more ordinary form of retardation, so that I could get a feeling of communal support and togetherness with people who are all in the same boat. As it is, I'd rather hang out with people who don't have a handicapped child.

The secret club that Donna talks about is one that we all belong to, like it or not. For years I've been able to go into a playground or a classroom full of kids and spot the one that probably needs some kind of special help. I can do it in a supermarket. I can do it at church. And so can Emma. At age twelve she's been around handicapped people long enough to recognize when something is not quite right. It's frightening.

What's even more frightening (and I found this out very recently) is that even when you belong to the club you can react to a retarded person in exactly the same way some people react to your own handicapped family member, with embarrassment and a sense of not knowing what to do.

"Mom," said Emma one evening, "there's this lady outside and I think she's coming to our door and I think she's handicapped."

Sure enough, on the doorstep was an obese woman, about forty years old, wearing an orange T-shirt with the name of a community shelter across the front and clutching a scrap of paper in her hand. She asked directions to an address on our street, but was so confused that I suggested she come in and sit down while I tried to figure out where she was trying to get to. The woman's speech was slurred. I thought perhaps she'd been drinking.

I told her that if she'd give me the phone number of the person she was trying to locate—she said it was her brother—

we could call and get directions to the house. The woman felt around in her purse, produced an address book, and pointed to a phone number. I showed her where the phone was, and she indicated that I should make the call. A man answered the phone, but he sounded as confused as she did so I didn't pursue the conversation.

Emma asked the woman if she'd like a soft drink, and when she said yes went into the kitchen and got her one. The woman then asked to go to the bathroom, and we showed her where it was. Emma, apprehensive, waited at the bottom of the stairs. Meanwhile, I called directory assistance and got the number of the shelter named on the woman's T-shirt. I called the number, but there was no response. As I put down the phone the woman came downstairs and lowered herself heavily into an armchair. I noticed that her shorts were wet. And finally I got it into my head, "This woman is retarded."

"I can't get hold of your brother," I told her, "so I think I'd better call the police and see if they can help you get where you want to go."

She didn't seem too bothered about this. She was more interested in one of our cats, who was circling her with the haughty suspicion he usually accords to strangers. So I called the police and told them I had someone in my home who seemed lost and needed help, and a few minutes later a surly cop took the woman out and drove her off in a squad car.

Emma, familiar for many years with Victoria's tendency to wet her pants when under stress, went up to check on the state of the bathroom. She reported that the bathroom was okay but the armchair where the woman had been sitting was a bit wet.

"Emma," I said, "at first I thought that lady was drunk, but she's retarded."

"Well, yes," my daughter answered. "I knew that right away."

I did not, as I had planned to do, call the police station the following day to find out if the woman in the orange T-shirt had been safely delivered to wherever she was going. Instead, I spent some uncomfortable moments with the realization that, first, I had managed to avoid recognition of the woman's handicap even though I am a bona fide member of that select "club," and that, second, twenty years from now it could be my own retarded daughter out on the street, confused, lost, dependent on the kindness, or lack of it, of strangers.

Deinstitutionalization has become a big buzz word over the past few years. It means getting retarded people, among others, out of the big institutions and into more home-like or community-based living arrangements. It's a wonderful idea; it just hasn't worked too well. Deinstitutionalization has meant that a lot of retarded and otherwise socially less-than-competent persons who should be at least in supervised settings are either out on the streets with nowhere to go or living in totally inappropriate situations. The woman who turned up on our doorstep was probably one of them. We discussed this, Emma and I, and Emma told me comfortingly that something like that could never happen to Victoria because we take good care of her.

"That's right," I told her. "That's why we do as much as we do, and that's why we have to keep on doing it even though it's so hard."

involvement: walking the extra mile

That small incident of the woman in the orange T-shirt was a potent reminder to me of why, once locked into the educational, psychological and political network that having a mentally handicapped child sets up for you, you can't get out of it. "Locked in" is an appropriate term in this context. When the services available to your child are under constant threat from well-meaning but inadequately thought-out legislation or program cutbacks, what do you do? You gather up your tattered resources and try to stagger back into the game. When you have a mentally retarded child, political consciousness is thrust upon you. I have come to feel that where

Victoria is concerned I go through life with my fists up. She has made me into a fighter. An exhausting business it is, too.

There are, however, certain factors beyond sheer necessity that keep the parent fighting for the retarded child long after burnout (a very common word among exceptional parents, special education teachers, and care-givers who work with mentally retarded children).

One factor is that you meet so many great people who are fighting hard for your child that it's virtually impossible not to fight alongside them. Victoria is not an easy person—charming and pretty and lovable, yes, but a monster when she so chooses—and I am constantly impressed that so many of her teachers and those associated with her have gone way beyond the demands of their professions on her behalf. If they are willing to walk the extra mile for her, how can I not walk it too?

Another factor that keeps you in the fight is anger. Anger is a great energizer. It gets the adrenalin going and keeps you on the move. Another parent once told me that she viewed the community of parents of retarded children as being united by their anger. "We are angry people," she said. And a lot of us are. We are angry at God. We are angry at fate. We are angry at people who have power but who will not use their power for the good of our children. We bring our anger closer to home too: we're angry with the family members, friends, and neighbors who don't understand and don't help. We have a great deal to be angry about. Any psychologist will confirm that anger is one of the stages that the parent of a retarded child has to go through if he or she is to come out of the experience whole—or even more or less whole. You get so damned mad at the people (many of them in positions of power) who seem not only to block the work you're doing for your child but actually to set it back, that you can't sleep until you've signed a petition or written a three-page letter to your congressperson. (Petitions and letters work, by the way.)

This anger, of course, can spill over into other areas of your life and become a crawling oil slick ready to ignite as soon as someone touches a lighted match to it. And it takes very little—an inopportune word from a family member or friend—to ignite the oil. Signing petitions, writing letters, or making phone calls can get the anger out so that at least some of it doesn't have to get unloaded on your nearest and dearest. Involvement helps you put the anger in the right place, to direct it toward those persons or organizations that deserve it and thus deflect it away from those who don't. A double win. Not bad, especially when you're dealing with an emotion that a lot of people have trouble expressing because they've never been allowed to. Anger is definitely a factor that keeps a parent in the inner circle.

Then there's the control issue. Control is another really suspect word in the language of mental retardation. But the fact is that when you've got a retarded child you've got a child who is subject to control by an unusually large number of people (you among them) and circumstances. All of those persons, parents included, have the opportunity to abuse their power. How do you know that others who have control are using it wisely? The only way you can have that knowledge is by being aware of what's going on, and that means attending the school meetings, asking questions, discussing issues and, if necessary, raising hell when you think something's not right.

As a retarded child gets older, the parent relinquishes more and more personal control. However, relinquishing appropriate degrees of control at the appropriate times doesn't mean you can't still know what is going on, so you go to the meetings and ask the questions and find out.

Or maybe you don't. It's a grave error to assume that every parent who has a mentally handicapped youngster spends his or her leisure hours drafting letters to legislators. A large number of parents don't deal with it that way and many don't deal with it at all; having a retarded child is something they've never accepted. Merely showing up at the school is an admission of a cold fact they're not about to acknowledge: that their child *belongs* in a school for mentally handicapped children.

Steve, the principal of Victoria's school, is of necessity resigned to the fact that some of his students' parents will never cross the threshold of his school from one annual conference to the next. (In fact, at Victoria's school conferences are held a lot oftener than once a year.) Some parents never even show up at the obligatory conferences. In extreme cases, the child's homeroom teacher will go to the child's home and talk to the parents there, just so that programming can continue. Some parents who have never gotten beyond the stage of total denial do not have the emotional resources to deal with the very emotional experience of walking into a classroom full of impaired children or talking with an administrator who deals with dozens of impaired children on a daily basis. Some parents can cope with their own child, but that's their limit. Some of them have never been able to accept the therapeutic services that might make their acceptance of their child's handicap easier. Some have never even been offered any help. Some believe that school and home are separate entities and should stay that way.

Some parents also have practical reasons for being unable to get close to a handicapped child's school or program: they've got a whole lot of other kids at home; they're working two jobs to keep food on the table; they don't have the time or the energy to expend in an effort not directly involved with their own survival or that of their family unit.

I believe that the parents who have the resources or are able to withstand the temptations—the urgent desires, maybe—to throw in the towel and leave it to the professionals are the lucky ones. I count myself among them. We are the ones who have had good support, good help, good people to give us the courage to go on. And with that kind of support, wherever from, comes a deep faith in your child and an exceptional kind of ability to extend yourself and risk.

So does it follow that the parent who doesn't join the PTA doesn't love the child? Of course it doesn't, but the question brings us to a vital point in this discussion. All this time we've never mentioned the true, gut-level reason why we stay in the fight long after we've run out of ammunition: we do it because we love our children.

The grief and pain and loss occasioned by Victoria's handicap have created an incredibly strong bond between us. These are the ties that bind. They chafe, too. If this is what the theologians and the psychologists mean when they talk about growth through pain, then I have grown. Grown enough, perhaps, to go on fighting for my daughter for as long as necessary. I'd like to believe that the worst of the fighting is over. If it's not, I guess I'll still be in there fighting. And I'm proud of myself for being able to say that. I'm proud of what I have done for my handicapped child. I'm proud that my nonhandicapped child is growing into a lovely, loving, exciting person. I'm proud that I'm not afraid—or not afraid to the point of immobilization—of what the two of them will ask of me in the future. I have not been defeated.

Donna shares some of my feelings. Discussing her experience with Emily she can say, "Many times I feel I'm just not up to snuff, and I get depressed about it and think I'm going to go over the edge because I am just not making it in life. I have to tell myself that I have made it through the toughest thing there is, and I am still here to talk about it. Nobody put me away. I have two more healthy children and I am able to take care of them. I am wounded. I am walking wounded and I always will be, but I've survived and I am proud of myself."

the social worker syndrome

In the song "Gee, Officer Krupke" from *West Side Story*, teenage gang members explain to various authority figures how they came to be so screwed up. As they go through the hierarchy from cop to social worker to judge, each authority figure gets a chance to theorize on why the kid's a punk.

I'm very fond of that song. I can, as they say, relate to it, because there exists in the life of the parent whose child is mentally handicapped a whole army of authority figures trying to figure out why the child (or the parent) is a mess.

"Gee, kindly social worker, I've got this kid who's retarded. The other kids are falling apart, dropping out, or shooting up. My husband's having a midlife crisis and my psychiatrist doesn't understand me. What are you going to do about it?"

Now maybe all the social worker, or whichever authority figure it happens to be, needs to do is pat me on the hand and say, "There, there, dear, go get yourself a new outfit or a skinful of dry martinis and you'll feel better." There are times when that is perfectly adequate advice. Most of the time, though, it isn't.

As the parent of a handicapped child you find out in a hurry that the professionals in your child's life—and therefore in yours—multiply like rabbits: pediatricians, social workers, educators, testers, re-testers, psychiatrists, neurologists, psychologists, and -ologists you've never even heard of. You're caught up in a sort of social worker syndrome. You're at the center of a veritable proliferation of professionals, all eager to tell you what to do with or about your child, most of them professing to know better than you do (which, ideally, they should), and many of them professing to know better than the others.

It can get so that the professionals in your life outnumber your friends. In any case, you're so busy dealing with the professionals that you don't have time to see your friends. Sometimes the professionals become substitutes for your friends. It's very easy to become dependent on those whose business it is to know what's wrong with your child, and what to do about it. And when each one of a number of specialists is telling you something different you can wind up with a heavy case of confusion.

Solid information is essential to meeting the needs of your retarded child. Support and encouragement are essential to handling the situation emotionally. If you're lucky you'll get some of each—solid information and supportive encouragement.

But there's another side to the coin. Frequently the useful material that the professionals are trying, quite sincerely, to give you is so heavily disguised in intimidating technical language that it's useless to you for all practical purposes. You need a translator before you can come to grips with it. And, too frequently, what you get is incomplete information, misinformation, or information colored (or discolored) by the professional's own background or bias.

It's also possible to fall into the hands of those out to convince you that you're a totally inadequate human being who is somehow responsible for the fact that this unfortunate child has a handicap, and that having gotten yourself into this mess you don't know how to handle it. The expression "God-playing doctor" did not enter the vocabulary without reason.

Beware, therefore, of so-called professionals bearing gifts of glib answers and pop psychology. Beware of those who feed on your feelings of confusion and inadequacy. Beware of those who specialize in guilt, whose message amounts to, "What do you think you did in order to make your child this way?" Be very chary of whom you trust with your child. Your child's future depends on it, and so to a significant degree does your own emotional well-being and that of the entire family.

Don't get the wrong idea. Most of the professionals out there are highly qualified and capable specialists. A gratifying number of them are also people of enormous compassion. It has been one of the special gifts permitted me in compensation for the loss of my expectations for my daughter that I have met some people of incredible goodness. But I have also met some who are insensitive and some who are small-minded, some who are actually incompetent and a few who are quite willing to exploit a child to bolster some theory or bias of their own. It's up to the parent to figure out which is which. How do you do it? There are a number of ways to make sure that you, and, your child, maintain a mutually satisfactory relationship with the professionals in your child's life.

The first step is to recognize that you have choices. The pediatrician or psychologist or neurologist you are seeing is not the only pediatrician, psychologist, or neurologist in the world, nor even in the immediate vicinity. There's such a thing as a second opinion, and a third. This is enormously important if you are the brand-new parent of a child who has been diagnosed as handicapped, or if you're brand-new to the diagnosis of an older child's handicap. Understanding that you have options means you don't have to get locked into an uneasy relationship with someone whose opinion you don't have any confidence in. It also means you don't have to stay with a professional whose qualifications are fine but whose personal approach makes you uncomfortable.

Donna, Emily's mother, had just such an experience with a school social worker. She says:

This man knew me perfectly well. He knew my first name and my last name, and everyone in the school called me by my first name.

He also knew my daughter's name because he had tested her. But in conferences he kept referring to me to my face as "the mother" and to Emily as "the child." He never once used our names and it drove me crazy. In a group of people he would always refer to me as "the mother" as though I wasn't a real person.

Then he began talking about children with Down syndrome as "mongoloids." This was when Emily was three, and most of the parents I'd met in early intervention programs had Down syndrome children, and you don't say "mongoloid" to a parent whose child has Down syndrome. I was not brave enough to tell him to stop because he was an authority figure for me, and he was making the decision about where my child was to be placed in school and I wasn't going to cross him.

At another point he referred to Emily as "spastic." This was after he'd worked with her and tested her. My daughter is not spastic. And I thought, he doesn't know one handicap from another. He calls my child a "spastic," and a Down syndrome child a "mongoloid." It really frightened me that such an ignorant man was testing children and making placements.

Donna has found that of the practical information she has needed in order to make the best arrangements for her daughter, more has come from educators than from medical specialists.

I believe that educators know more about this whole issue than medical people. Medical people are interested in diagnosing your child because it's a challenge, but once they've made the diagnosis and realize that this little kid has a permanent area of dysfunction, they say things like, "Get your child in a program and check back with me in a year." Medically, there's nothing you can do for a broken brain; you can't give it a shot of cortisone; you can't put it in traction. It's wonderful that if your child has an organic illness or a broken bone you can go to one of these medical centers and get wonderful help; that's the good news. But when you have a child who is permanently and forever broken, I think most doctors would just as soon be off the emotional hook; they would rather not be involved with the family.

Occasionally our pediatrician, when I took Emily in, would say, "How are you doing?" or "Is everything okay with you and your husband?" or "Are you making plans for the future, is there anything I can do in that area?" At least he asked. But most doctors still refer to children with handicaps as "these children." Here's a perfect example: my daughter was becoming sway-backed because her balance is so poor and her motor damage is such that in order for her to stand up and walk erect she had to lock her knees to keep from falling down. So she was getting sway-backed and the physical therapist at school said, "I think you'd better mention this to the pediatrician." I did mention it and I got the usual response: "Well, with these kinds of kids. . . ." If she were not one of "these kinds of kids" she'd probably have been in a back brace at night. It's the same with glasses or braces. The dentists or orthodontists don't want to fix their teeth because they don't want the hassle and, anyway, the kid's not going to live a normal life. Why bother fixing their teeth or straightening their backs so they look better? They'd do it for normal kids, but they don't want the bother of doing it for a retarded kid. Now why is that?

Donna learned early in Emily's life to rely on a combination of information and instinct to lead her to the professionals who were most likely to help her daughter. She has learned a great deal about how to cope with the social worker syndrome, and she has a lot of valuable information to pass on to less experienced parents. She and others like her are a tremendously rich source of information for those who are still trying to find a way through the professional jungle. Once you learn that there are alternatives, the next step is to ask other parents about their experiences: "How do you get along with so-and-so?" "Does Dr. such-and-such treat your retarded kid the same way he treats your normal kids?" "There's one teacher I can't seem to get along with. Do you have that sort of problem?" "I don't think this test report sounds like they really have a handle on my kid. What would you do if you were me?" "Is that social worker really unsympathetic, or am I being oversensitive?"

Asking questions and comparing experiences can be as useful when you're dealing with a child who is mentally handicapped as when you're dealing with a child who is nonhandicapped. You find out more because you need to find out more, and some of what you need to find out, the retarded child can't tell you. A child who is not handicapped can usually talk about a teacher who's mean or a classmate who's a problem. The tale may or may not be accurate, but at least you know that something is going on and you have an opportunity to look into it. If your teenager who is retarded but who has perfect bladder control wets the bed three nights in a row and cries when it's time to get on the school bus, you know there's something wrong. But probably the child can't tell you what it is. If you know and trust the child's teacher, you can ask the teacher what's going on and he or she should be able to tell you, or at least come up with some theories. You can also check with other parents who have kids in your child's homeroom and see if they're having problems too. Living with a mentally handicapped child is a wonderful incentive for a parent to develop a highly-tuned investigative bent. Some of us would make marvellous detectives.

how can you be jealous of a kid who's retarded?

We are in the car on our way to the Center for Enriched Living where Victoria attends weekend programs for mentally handicapped young people. At this point Victoria is fourteen and Emma is nine. The conversation is going like this:

VICTORIA: I'm going to my program and you can't come because you're too little.

EMMA: I'm having my friend Jeannette over for lunch.

VICTORIA: I'm going to see lots of friends. We make our own lunch.

EMMA: So what? Anyway, we get to make our own lunch too.

VICTORIA: We're going to make egg salad. We get pop out of the machine.

EMMA: Yuck, I hate egg salad! And I get pop after I go skating.

VICTORIA: I'm going to dance at my program. I dance with Henry. He's my boyfriend. He thinks I'm pretty.

EMMA: You're too young to have boyfriends.

VICTORIA: Greg thinks I'm pretty, too.

EMMA: Well, I'm going roller-skating with my friend after I've done ice-skating.

VICTORIA: So what?

At this point I turn the radio up loud so I don't have to listen to any more of this sisterly exchange.

We drop Victoria off and head back toward the ice rink for Emma's skating class. Emma is quiet, pouting, so I turn off the radio in order to enjoy the silence. Only parents, I am convinced, truly appreciate the wondrous beauty of pure silence. After a while Emma remarks, "I think sometimes Victoria's nicer when she's being retarded."

At this stage in her life Victoria could swim, ice-skate, and roller-skate (none of which her mother has ever learned to do worth a nickel). She played basketball and volleyball. She went to ballet class once a week until it became evident that she simply wasn't prepared to expend enough effort to make this one-on-one class worthwhile either for her or for her teacher, who still teaches both Emma and myself. At the Center for Enriched Living, Victoria attended cooking classes and played bingo and ping-pong and danced. If she didn't want to be so active she loafed around and listened to the Monkees and John Travolta. She liked John Travolta best.

Emma was jealous. She said it wasn't fair that Victoria got to do all the fun things and all *she* did was an old ballet class. She did not accept the explanation that her sister was a teenager doing teenage things that she would also do as a teenager. I told her that when she reached Victoria's age she would doubtless also have a lot more autonomy than her sister will ever have and would probably be pestering me to let her drive the car. Then we enrolled Emma in a Brownie pack and signed her up for the ice-skating classes and she felt better. Ah, sweet irony of life.

It comes as a big shock to find that a normal child can be jealous of a mentally handicapped sibling. I didn't even suspect such a thing until Emma was six. Until then I had always taken it for granted that Emma understood how I was trying to fill in Victoria's life gaps that would probably never exist in her own. Of course she didn't understand any such thing. In her young mind philanthrophy sank without trace under straightforward six-year-old logic: "You like her more than you like me."

When this situation first surfaced, it was no help that a lot of the time Emma's assumption was correct. She was a particularly willful and uncooperative six-year-old and Victoria at eleven was much easier to have around. Moreover, I had divorced the children's father and met Don, who was to become their stepfather, and Emma and Don were about to embark on a prolonged dispute about who owned Mommy. As Victoria waded deeper into the waters of adolescence Emma became less hostile and more amiable—she was growing up in an age-appropriate manner and so was her sister. Given this natural developmental pattern in both of them, their behavior balanced out a bit. Emma, accordingly, sought approval in a new way: "Who's been nicer today, me or Victoria?" The horns of the dilemma.

Once Victoria hit adolescence and began storming around her room, pounding the door with her fist and yelling about how mean we all were, it became patently obvious that Emma was nicer. However, all those years of parenthood had not been wasted on me and I was not taking anything for granted. I knew that as soon as Victoria settled down and became human again Emma would be entering adolescence and would inevitably dredge up some new behavioral horror to keep me from getting complacent.

It is, however, extremely easy to be tricked into working so hard for the retarded child that the normal one gets left out in the cold. And it is no help to tell a child who is jealous because someone else is getting all the attention: "It has to be this way; your sister is retarded." That's an open invitation to hate the intruder, as I finally learned.

Victoria's needs have always required a great deal of time and energy—mostly mine. She has needed a lot of chauffeuring. I attend two or three parent-teacher conferences at her school for every one at Emma's. I go to every happening that Victoria's school puts on, then complain about having to go to Emma's open house. I still do Victoria's school's newsletter, but the notice from Emma's school has just come around asking what I'm going to volunteer for and I'm going to have to say I just don't have the time. It certainly is not fair.

It is, however, a neat excuse for not doing other things, and it took me a long time to realize that Emma's right to equal time was going out the door. As soon as Emma could voice her own needs I asked her to do so as often and as insistently as she liked, to let me know when she was feeling neglected or left out. Her school may not need my cookies, but there are times when she needs to be able to say, "These are the ones *my* mom made."

It helps to have Emma tell me what's important to her, and I have promised to try to be available to her. But I still wonder how many times in the past she's been hurt because I've been so overconscious of her sister's needs that I've ignored or belittled her own, or demanded of her a measure of unselfishness far beyond her years. Having a child with special needs does not imply that the needs of the other children are not just as special, but it takes a while to come to grips with that fact.

Victoria, having finished her pop, asks Emma for a sip of hers and, while Emma is still considering her answer, takes silence for consent and helps herself. This, of course, is a minor instance of sibling sneakiness that the two of them should be left to resolve alone. However, with Victoria I am very hot on acceptable social behavior so I scold Victoria for having helped herself to Emma's pop without permission.

Come bedtime I take it upon myself to sermonize on the value of altruism and I have a little chat with Emma about how nice it is sometimes to do something unselfish without hoping to get any reward out of it. A little act of kindness, I tell her, is like lighting a candle in a dark place, and if we all lit lots of little candles we could brighten up the world no end. Emma is clearly not too impressed by this thought. Indeed, as my husband remarks later, altruism is out of fashion. A Northwestern University professor told me that before giving a lecture on altruistic behavior in children he had to explain to his undergraduates what the word meant.

Emma has had a hard time with the abstractions that have been thrust upon her, and on the occasion under discussion she could not relate altruism as a philosophy to having her pop snitched by her big sister. Indeed, why should Victoria get away with stealing Emma's pop, or entering her room without knocking, or playing with her toys without permission—all sins against the established domestic canon, the sort of intrusions any younger sibling (and Victoria is the younger in mind if not in body) inflicts upon an older and which should allow the victim the freedom to tell the tormentor to get the hell out. In my well-intentioned bedtime story the message I'm selling is this: you must be nice to poor Victoria because she's retarded. Even I don't believe that.

The siblings of retarded children can have a hard time of it. They suffer on emotional, social, and practical grounds. At least, most of them do. My experience has been that it takes a long time to recognize the hazards that the presence of a mentally retarded sibling pose for the other child or children, and still longer to realize that the normal child may be amassing a whole lot of emotional baggage that will be very difficult to unload later on.

Emma at twelve years old has had, I feel, more than her fair share of stress. A lot of it has had to do directly or indirectly with her sister's condition. Emma has seen my marriage to her father fail. Many times she has taken a back seat while "dealing with Victoria" has occupied all my available energy. She's been through the stress associated with my remarriage and with her adjustment to a new father figure who, initially, got along far better with Victoria than he did with the volatile little person that Emma was at the time we married. Now she has seen her stepfather walk out, giving among his reasons for leaving the fact that he felt the children's needs—essentially, Victoria's—were taking precedence over his needs.

What sorts of messages does that kind of history leave a child with? That the presence of a handicapped child is devastating to family structure and therefore she should never take a chance on letting herself get into the same position?

Emma has often told me that, observing my experience, having kids seems to be an awful lot of trouble. Unable, in conscience, to deny that her remark contains an uncomfortable deal of truth, I've told her that most things in life involve trouble and that if you don't take any trouble you are unlikely to reap any rewards. Fine as far as it goes. But Emma has had too much "trouble" for one so young, and I hope I'm right when I tell her that she's doing some suffering now that she won't have to do later. When some of her friends are struggling to become responsible people she'll be ahead of them: she's a responsible person at twelve years old.

I've told Emma time and time again that what happened to Victoria was not my fault or her father's fault. And I've insisted that it was certainly not her fault. I've tried to make her understand that although Victoria's condition played a major role in the break-up of my marriage to her father and presented a serious threat to my marriage to her stepfather, that doesn't mean that marriage is a lousy institution or that everything would have been okay in either of my marriages if Victoria had not been the way she is. Retardation is a no-fault issue for the siblings. Or it should be. Victoria can't help being retarded, and Emma can't help having a retarded sister. We all deal with Victoria's retardation as best we can—Victoria included.

One night at dinner Emma announced, "I don't think I want to have children."

"Seems a bit early to decide that, don't you think?" I responded. "If you never have kids you'll never be able to have one like you; I'd be sorry if I'd passed up the chance to have you because I think you're a good kid."

"Yeah," she said doubtfully, "But I don't think I want any."

"You'll feel differently when you meet someone you want to have children with," I said, and paused to consider whether this particular maternal platitude was quite in order considering my own shaky marital record.

"Hmmm," said my daughter, who might have been thinking the same thing.

We sat in silence for a while as awareness forced its way into my reluctant mind.

"Are you scared that your child might be handicapped like Victoria?"

"Yeah. . . ."

"But there's no reason why that should happen to you," I told her. "You know we believe that Victoria started out perfectly normal and that something happened either while I was pregnant or while she was being born to make her brain-damaged. I might have been exposed to some sort of infection and not known about it. Or something might have gone wrong while she was being born that I have no way of knowing about. It's even possible that something happened after she was born, although I don't remember her ever hitting her head or anything.

"Anyway, we've never been able to pin down any reason for Victoria being retarded, and if everything had happened the way it should I think she would be perfectly normal today."

"I didn't know that," said Emma.

"You did know it," I reminded her. "I've told you that we

115

don't believe it's anything hereditary that made your sister handicapped, so there's no reason we know of why your children shouldn't be perfectly fine. Most children are perfectly fine. Anyway, there's such a thing as genetic counseling, which means that you and your husband could talk with a specialist to see if there were anything in your family background that might affect your children. Like Down syndrome. That's genetic and can be hereditary. But on your side of the family I don't think there's anything like that."

Emma took this all in.

"Does that make you feel better?" I asked.

"Yeah," she said with a big smile, and got on with her dinner.

I have been told that it's normal for pre-adolescent children to decide they don't want children of their own. I don't know how true that is, but in this case it's irrelevant. The relevant issue is that I had been mistaken in believing that Emma had enough information about her sister's handicap to see it as something separate from herself in terms of physical and mental makeup. I had told her frequently that I believed Victoria was normal at conception, but that something went wrong. I'd told her that I didn't believe the retardation was due to any hereditary factor. I'd told her time and again that it was nobody's fault—not mine, nor her father's, and certainly not hers. Somehow, though, the piece of information that she needed at dinner that night had never got across—presumably because it wasn't until then that she had needed it.

It follows that one important way of helping siblings to deal with the fact of a child's retardation is to give them the right kind of knowledge and to understand that one-time information isn't necessarily enough. And no information at all can leave the normal child with deep confusion and anxiety. One sibling, now a special education teacher, simply wasn't told that the new baby was handicapped. She saw her mother crying a lot, but she didn't know why. Now she says, "Not knowing was the worst part."

Emma has been dealt a double whammy because she is a child of divorce. Domestic upheaval (except for the golden early years of my marriage to Don) has been her scenario for most of her life. This is the case for many children of families where there is a retarded child, and although divorce is probably the surest way of bringing about domestic upheaval, it can be created all too easily without divorce.

One of the people I talked to for this book is Leslie, another special education teacher, whose brother is retarded. We were trying to think of families where the presence of a handicapped child had not meant at least some visible degree of disturbance or damage. Out of our joint experience, which is not inconsiderable, we came up with a single name— just one—of a family where we felt all the members would have been exactly the same as they are now if the child had been normal instead of retarded. Our conclusions are probably not accurate, and I certainly wouldn't try to carry the argument much beyond general speculation. It's an interesting subject for speculation, all the same.

Of the divorced exceptional parents I know, none will deny that having a child who was mentally handicapped was a contributing factor in the break-up of the marriage. But even in families where the parents stay together there can be great, gaping rifts in the inter-family relationships. Such is the case when one parent cannot accept the child's handicap. So the normal sibling has to deal, sooner or later, with the fact that one parent holds the impaired child in disfavor or won't become involved in necessary activities concerning the child—won't go to the school open house, for example. And how long or short a step must the normal child take from the idea that Mommy or Daddy doesn't "love" the retarded sibling to the sneaky thought, "But what if it was me who was retarded: would I be rejected too?"

Oh yes, the possibilities, unfortunately, are endless. Although Emma appears to be such a well-adjusted child, I have no illusions that she will escape unscarred. There have been times when the whole family, except for Emma, has been in therapy. "It's not fair," she exploded once, "Victoria sees a shrink; Don sees a shrink; you see a shrink. How come I'm the only one who doesn't see a shrink?"

"Oh my God," I said, "Do you feel you need to see somebody? Is it getting to you?"

"No," she said, "I don't *want* to see a shrink; I just feel left out because everyone is seeing one except me."

"Consider yourself fortunate that you don't need therapy right now," I told her. "Your day will come."

I know children as young as seven who are already in therapy because of the stress occasioned by the presence of a handicapped sibling in the family and the emotional chaos thus generated. They're the lucky ones. They're getting help. Emma knows that any time she feels her situation is getting out of hand emotionally she will get help too. Any time I think it's necessary I'll have her in therapy so fast she'll think she's got wings and can fly. It's even become one of those painful family jokes. "Switch off the TV and do your homework," I tell her. "You know you're getting a good education now so that when you grow up you'll be able to get a decent job and make enough money to pay your psychiatrist."

the second child: deciding to try again

When the first child in a family is mentally handicapped, the sibling issue frequently begins with a decision about whether or not there will *be* any siblings. If you have a child who's retarded, and you don't know why, and you don't know if your future children might also be retarded, the decision to have another one can be a gesture of faith, defiance, or recklessness—or simply a gamble some families prefer not to take. Even families who have been assured that the chance of a second child being handicapped is a million to one know that the number can come up; there are two sons of such a family at Victoria's school.

If a genetic disorder can be detected before birth, by means of amniocentesis or some other test, it's possible to abort a fetus that carries the defective gene. What if you're not prepared to abort? Do you have the test and, if it's positive, consider yourself fortunate to have been warned and given the opportunity to prepare yourself for the birth of another mentally handicapped child? Do you skip the test and spend the rest of the pregnancy under a cloud of apprehension? Suppose the genetic disorder is a killer, like Tay-Sachs disease, which most frequently affects Jewish people of Eastern European origin and usually kills within three years. If you found out after the birth of your first Tay-Sachs baby that your next child would have a one in four chance of inheriting the condition, and that you might again have to watch the child slowly degenerate and die, what would you do? Become pregnant and abort if tests revealed the child to be affected? Become pregnant and carry the child to term whatever the test results? Or decide not to become pregnant?

Depending on the circumstances—if you know them—that caused the first child to be handicapped, deciding to have a second child may be the hardest thing in the world to do.

When I decided to have another child (my husband was not enthusiastic about the idea), I did not seriously believe it likely that the second child would be retarded. But I was scared. When I was pregnant with Victoria I did everything right. I did not smoke or drink. I watched my weight. I obeyed all the rules. All the same, the child was handicapped. With Emma I did everything wrong. I drank Scotch when I felt like it and I took aspirin, both of which my doctor told me were harmless, and I ate poorly because I was nauseated for most of the pregnancy. All the same, the baby was perfect.

Do not imagine that I am recommending to anyone that she go through pregnancy on aspirin and Scotch; if I had to do it over I would obey the rules to the letter and beyond. I've just always been somewhat irritated that having done everything right for Victoria, I still got it wrong. With the second child, I wanted to get it right. Not, perhaps, the ideal reason for choosing to have a second baby.

Ilene, who also believes that her first child was normal at conception and that no genetic factor contributed to his handicap, started to think about becoming pregnant again when Richard was around six. She says:

Paul was all for having more children, but he didn't want to pressure me. I was extremely nervous about it. I really felt that if I were to have another retarded child I would probably murder that child and myself too. At the time I did not give abortion a great deal of thought. However, I had heard about amniocentesis, which could identify certain abnormalities in the womb, and I decided that if I became pregnant again I would have it. I was perfectly rational. I realized that an amniocentesis probably would not have diagnosed Richard at all, but it would prevent me from having a child with Down syndrome or some other chromosomal abnormality. I knew an awful lot of children with Down syndrome living in my immediate neighborhood, and they seemed to make up about eighty percent of Richard's class at school. I looked at their mothers and thought about how all of these women could have chosen to prevent these births if they had had this diagnostic procedure.

I became pregnant again very easily, contrary to my experience with Richard when I took seven months to become pregnant. I took no medications of any kind and was determined not to take any unless they were necessary to save my life or to control a disease that might be harmful to the fetus. I found an obstetrician who delivered by the Lamaze method, and I asked him about amniocentesis. He told me that in order to qualify for amniocentesis you must either already have had a chromosome-abnormal child or you must be under or over a certain age. This meant that I did not qualify. I asked if the procedure was harmful and he thought there was nothing harmful about it. It was expensive, and I would have to be prepared to have a fourth-month abortion if necessary, because it would take four to six weeks to culture the cells and get the result. In my state of mind, I would have had a ninth-month abortion if I had known that my child would be severely retarded, so I thought it was not unreasonable to ask for the amniocentesis. But the doctor refused.

I tried a different tack. I went to a different doctor, one of a group well-known for their extremely technical view of medicine and their highly developed laboratories—very paternalistic, God-playing, super-scientific doctors. I told this doctor that I had a Down syndrome child, played hysterical lady, and got the test without any difficulty. They did not try to check that I had a child with Down syndrome. They never looked at Richard or at his records. As a result of the amniocentesis I learned that there were no chromosomal abnormalities. I also found out that my child was a girl. I asked the nurse about the baby's sex and she told me, "It didn't say on the test." I asked her what it said about the chromosomes and she said, "XX," showing that she knew less about genetics than I did.

After I got the test results I went straight back to my original obstetrician. Because I had a list of about five hundred things to feel guilty about with Richard's birth, I chose a Lamaze delivery for this second child. I was determined that I would have nothing to feel guilty about if something were wrong with this child, even though I knew that the factors that I could not control greatly outnumbered those that I could.

Carolyn, like Richard, was a back labor, but she was attractive. I got to hold her in my arms and feel that this was my child, whereas with Richard I had kept looking at him and wondering, "Is this really my baby?" I couldn't believe that he was mine.

Richard is very fond of babies, but he had mixed feelings about his sister. As they have grown up there has been the usual sibling hostility, but it has not been violent. My daughter obviously has the upper hand, though Richard is stronger than she is. He frequently tries to hit her, but his attempts are ineffectual either because he will not put enough violence into them or because he is just not skilled in the art of hitting people. He will give her a cuff, which she will elude, or he'll make a kick at her. Although there is a great disparity in their ages, he never seems to hurt her.

He does complain about her and, in fact, she has usually instigated the incidents he complains about. For instance, in his room she will chase him off his own rocking chair when he wants to sit in it. He goes away grumbling and muttering, but he goes away. If we are being affectionate with him and she comes and obtrudes herself, he will get up and go away. He will not compete with her.

Carolyn says she dislikes her brother, but I know what true detestation is and I do not see it in her. I am sure she is embarrassed by him, but not in the same way that I would have been at her age. I would have felt humiliation. She just feels that he's weird and maybe an occasion for her to be ridiculed by other children, which has in fact happened.

We have discussed with Carolyn how she can cope with such ridicule. What I told her was simply that, in the first place, she was not responsible for how Richard behaved; and in the second place, he often could not control his behavior and was unaware of its badness in her eyes. We told her that Richard is supposed to control the things that he is able to control, and he's wrong when he doesn't; there's no excuse for him to behave badly if he knows how to improve the behavior.

We have also told her that there are some people who will use any occasion to make you miserable; if it were not her brother's weirdness it would be something else. Furthermore, people who will torment a person who is crippled in any way, mentally or physically, have something wrong in their training, or in their own brain structure, or are very much afraid. There is something wrong in themselves that they need to correct.

Carol, who knew that Katherine had been normal at birth and had become retarded as a result of spinal meningitis that was not treated early enough, had less reason to fear that a second child would be handicapped. Of her son, Christopher, who is two years younger than Katherine, she says:

I think ultimately he's going to be a very fine man, a very sensitive human being, and there aren't that many sensitive human beings around. He's very responsible, and in many ways he's very mature. He's had a lot of heavy numbers to deal with. He's had to give up a lot of his childhood. That's why I feel very strongly that as an adult he should not be burdened with the responsibility of Katherine. I have told him that how much he wants to bother with her or not bother with her will be completely up to him to decide. I hope he'll care enough to still keep in touch with her, but it's not going to be his burden. And I am trying to set it up so it won't be.

For me, it's probably been better that he was the second child. I've certainly appreciated him, his normality, a great deal. In many ways Chris is the only child, and for many years Katherine has believed that he's the older one. She's always known that he's the one in charge. But there's not that big an age difference between them and they have been together growing up, and I think that's good.

I can never forgive my former husband for the pain he forced on all of us, but especially on those kids who didn't ask for it; it wasn't their fault. I think one day the fact will hit Christopher that his father couldn't deal with his sister, and he'll have to face up to it and maybe he'll hold Katherine responsible for that first marriage falling apart. I think it takes a child a long time to forgive a handicapped sibling, even though they know that nothing that's happened is directly the sibling's fault.

Jack, Chris's stepfather, wanted Chris to go into counseling, and this really got Chris's dander up. It was a typically male response on his part, and he wouldn't go near it. I didn't push it too much, though I pushed even more than I had wanted to because everyone said I had to be the supportive wife. But I really feel that you have to come to counseling on your own terms and in your own way.

"it's no after-school tv special, you know"

Leslie is a special education teacher with a class full of young adults, Victoria currently among them. Leslie is one of seven children; her only brother, Jeffrey, one year younger than she, is mentally retarded. The cause of his retardation is still unknown. Many siblings of retarded children gravitate towards the career fields associated with special education, but Jeffrey was not the motivation behind her career choice. He was, however, a dominant issue in her family life and Leslie, being one of the girls closest in age to Jeffrey, spent a significant amount of her childhood and teen years taking care of him. She says:

> It's no after-school TV special, you know, having a sibling who's handicapped. It's not like the movies where the normal sister takes the cute retarded person with her to the beach. The one thing that sticks out in my mind about my pre-teen and teenage years is the terrible burden of having to baby-sit Jeff, to watch Jeff, to be with Jeff. It meant I couldn't stay after school to do anything; I couldn't play with friends. I had to negotiate for every afternoon off. There were a lot of us girls, but the older ones were working and the younger girls were too little, and a lot of the pressure fell on the middle children, on me and my sister Lisa. Jeff's right in the middle—I was one year up and Lisa was one year down. Lisa and I did a lot of the baby-sitting but the other girls also say they gave up a lot of time—afternoons and weekends and summers—for Jeff. As each girl got older and got a job, the responsibility for Jeff fell to the next youngest sister. At least there were a lot of us. If I had been an only child it would have been much harder. I really believe that caretaking is okay as long as it's split up equally. But if there's only one sibling, or only one that takes the responsibility, then it's far too much of a burden.
>
> When my brother was younger, there weren't the recreational opportunities for handicapped children that there are today. There were no outreach workers, no people who came to the house

and provided respite care so the family could take a break. When I was growing up, caring for a handicapped family member was the family's responsibility. Though even if those resources had been available, I don't believe my parents would have used them. They regarded Jeff as a family problem. I don't think they even liked to share their problems with the social worker at school, or the teacher. They felt there was a clear line between home and school: what happened at home was the family's problem, and we'd deal with it as a family without outside help.

My parents divorced when I was eight and Jeffrey seven. Before that time I think Jeffrey's impact on the family was negligible. He was a little kid, and there were so many of us that the differences weren't obvious. We were just a pack of little kids, playing the way little kids do. As we got older our interests changed and we matured, but Jeffrey didn't. He just got bigger, and as he got bigger having him around certainly became more difficult. All of us girls felt it. We'd have friends in to play and Jeffrey would walk through the room with his hand down his pants or his finger up his nose, and all our friends would giggle and titter. It put us in a very difficult position. I remember clearly how it felt: half of me would be mad at Jeff for being such a jerk, and half of me would want to defend him and kick those girls right out of the house.

I'd try to explain to them that he was retarded. I made countless explanations to people: "You don't understand, he's retarded and he can't help what he does. It's not funny to laugh at him, because he can't help it." I got that excuse down real pat. It didn't work, but I think it made me feel better, as if I had a better understanding of people and life. Reality imposed itself on me at an early age.

Some of my sisters wouldn't bring anybody home, and eventually that's what happened with all of us. We did not have a household where you brought friends home. We talk about that now. We look back and realize that some of our best friends have never been in our parents' house. We saw our friends when we were off duty. It got to the point where there was no question of bringing friends home or including Jeffrey in what we did. I realize now that some of my friends were curious about Jeff, and interested in him because they knew how important he was to me. But family life was one thing and friends were another thing and I didn't try to mix them. In a way I was doing the same thing my parents did in not mixing home and school.

Our family problems did not solely concern Jeff. We had to deal with my father's remarriage, and having a stepmother, and seeing the older girls move out and go back to my mother when they were eighteen. There was all this conflict in the house and it *wasn't always centered on Jeff, but it seemed that Jeff's being there heightened it so that there was constant tension. We argued about the way my parents were dealing with Jeffrey. As we got older there were things they did that seemed unreasonable to us because we didn't understand why they were doing them—things like locking Jeffrey in his room at night. To us, as young kids, that seemed barbaric. It seemed just awful, and in a way it still does. But I don't know what else they could have done.*

Jeff was a runner. He wouldn't stay in his room. He'd go downstairs to the refrigerator and eat butter or whatever he could put his hands on. He'd eat a loaf of bread. He'd wipe out an entire chocolate cake. He was a compulsive eater, and he was a compulsive roamer. He would go to the basement and turn on a power saw or drill. It wasn't safe to leave him unsupervised, and at night no one could get a good night's sleep unless Jeffrey was secure in his room. It sounds barbaric, but it was survival—not just the family's survival but Jeff's survival too.

Some evenings when I was left to baby-sit with him he wouldn't go to sleep, and if he wasn't asleep I wouldn't lock his door. I'd go against the parental mandate to lock the door, but I'd have to sit at the top of the stairs, in front of his door, and make sure he didn't leave his room. He could go into the bathroom and get out razor blades and try to shave his face. He could go in someone's room and steal their underwear or their money. He had to be watched constantly, and it was a horrendous burden.

Jeff's rages were another problem. He would throw chairs and lamps and knives and trash a room when he was angry. And he'd go after you. There's a certain amount of teasing and picking on each other that brothers and sisters do, but if you pushed Jeff too far he'd pick up whatever was handy and throw it. Sometimes it was a pillow or a lamp. Other times it was the fireplace poker. We felt that Jeff was unpredictable, to say the least. He wasn't able to check his own anger, and if you didn't check it for him the consequences could be serious. As he got older he actually started having fist fights with my dad, who was also getting older, and it was of great concern to us because Jeffrey was big. They really used to go at it. Once he gave my dad a black eye.

I never did date, not many of us girls did, but that might have been partly a function of the times. I had a lot of male and female friends and we went out together as groups; nobody really dated. I never had any special relationship with a guy until I went away to college. I probably didn't feel free to. I had very unresolved feelings about my whole family, about my place in it and my place in the world. I felt a great sense of responsibility, but at the same time I really despaired of the family taking any responsibility for their own relationships. *I was the person who ran around and tried to make sure that everybody in the family really cared about everybody else. I was the mediator. I spent a lot of time doing that when I was growing up and when I was in high school. Getting away to college was really the first opportunity I'd had to be myself, with no responsibility for anyone else. It was an exhilarating experience. To tell the truth, for four years I barely gave Jeff and the family a thought. In the summer or when I came home on vacation it was good to see them, but being free of the day-to-day burden of caring for Jeffrey was an exhilarating experience.*

When I did start dating in college I found that another interesting thing happened: the way my prospective boyfriends reacted to Jeffrey determined how much they were in the running for any permanent relationship. It's not fair, but it's what happens. You use the retarded person as a sounding board—a test of a person's better nature, to see if he can deal with it. It's not necessarily a question of whether the other person is comfortable with him—a lot of people don't have any experience with the retarded and it takes time to feel comfortable with them—but do they have any respect for him as a person even though he's retarded? Or does he nauseate them? Does he turn them off completely? That does happen. In my freshman year at college I brought a boyfriend home and he did the unforgivable: he mimicked Jeffrey and made fun of him. And he was gone. That's the last time I saw him. He was out the door. As far as I was concerned, he was dead. I told him why, and he was very surprised. He tried to make all kinds of excuses. He said, "You're being too sensitive, you know." Maybe that was the case, maybe I was being too sensitive. But he was gone.

Outside of caretaking, I didn't really have a personal relationship with Jeffrey until I was much older. I came home from college one summer and the whole family went to an outdoor concert. Jeff was sitting next to me and for some reason he was crying. I don't know whether it was the music—it was a John Denver concert and he had always loved John Denver—but he was sitting there crying. I reached over and took his hand, and I realized that it was the first time I had touched him in years. That is really a peculiar thing to say, but I remember feeling it with a jolt: my God, this is the first time that I ever reached over and took my brother's hand. This is the first time I've ever approached him as another person, not as his guardian, but as his friend. All along we'd realized he had feelings, but he was never really a person. *I couldn't remember the last time I'd ever hugged him, or kissed him, or put an arm around him. It changed a lot of things.*

My impression of Jeff as an adolescent is that he was con-stantly dirty, and as an adolescent myself I didn't go out of my way to hug him or hold his hand or anything. And so that experience at the concert was a real turning point for us—that physical reaching out and realizing that here is a person who has feelings. It is a good change; I'm starting to get to know him better, and he really appreciates gestures of affection.

My dad had always been pretty affectionate with Jeff, but that was interspersed with spells of having to discipline him and avoid getting his own eye blacked. I don't think Jeff got a lot of feminine affection—physical affection—as he was growing up. He didn't get it from us girls or from our stepmother, and he didn't get it from our mom because she wasn't around. I don't remember my stepmother ever expressing any physical affection for Jeff. Now I think she deals with him very well, as an adult. She and my father see him regularly. They take him out to play golf. They take him out to dinner. They take him on vacation with them a couple of times a year. I think all those years that Jeffrey was growing up must have been a terrible ordeal for her. She didn't know the first thing about how to raise him, and in my view she made some grave mistakes. But she'd taken on seven children, one of them retarded and all of them hostile; she had her hands full and she coped as best she could.

One of my stepmother's big crises was getting Jeffrey ready for the school bus in the morning. My father would go off to work, and the rest of us kids would be getting ready for school and going off, but there would be Jeffrey to get up. He was a slow riser. He would turn on his TV and sit there watching it for twenty minutes before he put on a piece of clothing. To get Jeffrey up and dressed, his bed made, and a bowl of cereal down his gullet before that damned school bus arrived was an ordeal for my stepmother that she probably still has nightmares about.

She'd scream up the stairs at him, "Turn off that TV and get dressed!" He learned very early to block her out; he wouldn't listen to her. The school used to be very critical because he wasn't clean. As an adolescent he had body odor and his hair was sometimes dirty. We made sure that he took a shower at least once a week, but getting Jeffrey clean and bathed—I don't think anyone understood how monumental a task that could be for the family.

I've heard staff at the school where I work criticize the parents of my students and say, "The least those parents could do is keep this child clean." I laugh and say, "I know that you never lived with a retarded child." For three or four years keeping Jeff clean was more than anyone in my family could handle. For one thing, he resisted. But also, no one had enough time. There was never enough time to do everything. We had seven kids in the family, and my stepmother went to work when the last child got into kindergarten. With seven kids, she had to work.

The school was different then. The rules were rigid about what children could and could not do. For instance, if Jeff caused a scene on the bus he was thrown out of school. My stepmother began the movement to stop that. She would say, "The hell you're going to kick him off the bus. You have that bus here tomorrow morning." The school would call her at work and say, "Come get Jeffrey because he's acting up, he's had a tantrum," and she'd say, "I'm not coming to get him. I'm at work. You keep him and send him home on the bus, and one of the girls will be home when he gets there." She told them, "I don't ask you to come and solve my problems at home, and I'm not going to come and solve your problems at school. Sorry."

Now our policy is not to send kids home. We feel that if we can't handle their behavior in school we're not doing our job. But that was not always the policy. My parents had to fight a long, hard battle to keep Jeffrey in school and on the school bus.

There are in Victoria's small special school of about seventy children at least three teachers who grew up with a mentally handicapped brother or sister. Leslie is one of them. About her career choice, Leslie says:

I had no intention of going into special education. I majored in political science with the intention of going to law school. I spent a semester in law school and really hated it, so I dropped out and went to live with my mom for six months. I had to get a job and I happened to see an ad for a teacher's aide at a home for the retarded near where my mom lived. I figured I could do that for six months until I decided what I really wanted to do instead of law. There had been problems at the school; some of the parents suspected that the children had been abused by staff members. I taught the children who remained during the last six months the facility was open, and after that I decided to go back to school, get my master's degree and a teaching certificate, and then try teaching retarded children.

I've been doing it now for six years, and frankly I'm not sure how long I intend to continue. I find that as Jeff gets older, so does the age group I'm interested in working with. So I don't know whether it's a career interest or just an extension of my interest in Jeff. Now I'm starting to look at retarded adults and to think about programming and living facilities that are designed for the over-twenty-ones. That's where my interest is focusing more and more. At the moment it's okay because I'm teaching young adults, and I am preparing them for adulthood so there's a connection there. But I don't know what the future will bring. A lot of special education teachers just burn out—the burnout rate is high—but I don't think that's going to be the case for me. I don't see myself burning out the way most people do, because you can't burn out on your family. That is, you can burn out on them, but you can't leave them, so you find a new way to deal with them. You don't go out and get a new family.

The presence of a mentally handicapped child complicates all the relationships within the family: the relationship of the parents to each other, to the handicapped child, and to the other children, and the relationship of the nonhandicapped children to their retarded sibling and to each other. Leslie says:

At times I have been extremely critical of my sisters because they didn't take more responsibility for Jeff. There were some difficult years as Jeff got older, before he was placed, when it was hard for him to be at home and hard for us to have him there. After college I came back to live at home partly to assist my folks in taking care of Jeff until they could find a placement for him, and I felt that my other sisters who lived in the area could have helped out more. They could have taken him out and done things with him and nurtured a relationship with him. They were all adults then, either at college or working, and I really resented them for not taking on some of the responsibility. I'm still not sure that I understand it. I've talked a little bit with them, but how we deal with Jeff is not a subject we talk a lot about. In a way I think my doing it saved them from having to do it. They loved him, and maybe they would have done it if I hadn't. My stepping in and filling that role made it unnecessary for anyone else to do it. Maybe if I had slacked off and decided that I was not going to take total responsibility for Jeff, one of the other girls would have done it instead.

When there are a number of siblings in the family there's usually one who takes most of the responsibility. Well, that was definitely me, and my parents acknowledge it because they intend me to be Jeffrey's guardian when they die. I will certainly assume that responsibility. I am far more qualified than anyone else in the family both by virtue of my relationship with Jeff, which is closer than that of any of the other girls, and by my knowledge of the field; I know what kinds of decisions have to be made. So I'm pretty much resigned and resolved that Jeffrey will be my responsibility for a long, long time.

Ken, my husband, and I share some of our vacations with Jeff and we have him come visit us, and we think in terms of the future and having a whole lot more responsibility for him. Ken accepts that. I wouldn't have married him if he didn't accept that. Ken is a marvellous man.

the daughter who was the "first-born son"

Pat and her sister Joanne, who has cerebral palsy, are now in their fifties. When they were children there were even fewer facilities for youngsters with handicaps than when Leslie's parents were raising their family. Pat and Joanne came from a well-to-do family, and their father was very active in efforts to provide facilities for retarded children in the 1930s and 1940s. Unfortunately, his one blind spot was his own handicapped daughter. Pat says:

My father was a corporation lawyer from an Italian ghetto, and he was one of the brightest of the bright—brilliant, totally self-made, giving, full of kindness, godfather to hundreds of people. He was extremely involved in the question of facilities for the handicapped. He wrote original legislation and introduced programming at a time when not a lot was being done for handicapped people. But he was totally unable to make the connection between his charity work and his own child. Everything he did was for other people. He would take care of his own daughter, but thought that other people didn't have either the means or the mental ability to take care of their children. Therefore he needed to get all these programs started for other people's children, but they were never appropriate for his own.

Joanne has cerebral palsy, and she has always been treated as mentally retarded. I suspect she has always been mentally retarded, but to what degree I am still uncertain. It doesn't make a whole lot of difference, anyway, because by now she's functionally retarded and her level of social functioning may be lower than her level of intellectual functioning.

My father took Joanne all over the country to be checked and to find out who was doing what in the area of handicapping conditions. One doctor said, "Institutionalize her." Well, there was no way he was going to institutionalize her. It's not in the Italian culture, which says that you cope, you adjust; God does not give you more than you can handle. You take care of your own, and the extended family and the relatives and everyone else help. According to my father's upbringing, the way you handle things is almost a test of your ability in the eyes of God. If you have a special problem, you are highly respected: you have to be a very special person to have such a burden put on you.

Because of the way my father felt, Joanne was never part of a group of handicapped people, not even as a child. She has always been with the so-called normal world, people who were either related to her, or hired to take care of her, or who would for whatever reason treat her as special. She was protected to the point that whatever she wanted, she got. She would dominate the conversation. She was the special one and that's how it always was. I was told that I wasn't to be envious; I would have my time later. That's how it was all throughout my childhood—my time was always going to be later.

I was a normal, bright child. I was given all kinds of lessons, five days a week after school, while Joanne got to sit around and play. I think I resented that; with all my God-given talents I had a very short youth. There are only two years between us, but in a sense I never had a sister, someone to play with. I knew early on that of course I would always take care of her; there wasn't any question about the fact that she would always have me. My father, and my mother too, made it quite clear that they were setting up all these arrangements and I would carry them on and be the responsible one, but I was never consulted on any decisions.

My father was very proud of my intellectual ability, which, of course, Joanne did not have. So I was the bright one and that was the role I was expected to play, while all the patience in the world went to Joanne. I really worked hard in high school and I had very few close friends. I didn't know how to make friends. It was the way I had been raised—to think that the time will come for play later on, and in these formative years you have to work and learn and, if necessary, struggle.

Of course, I never expressed any of my feelings about the inequity of this treatment. I didn't talk about it until I was already well into my forties, when I started to see a therapist.

There was no way to express those feelings in an Italian household, not when they were so kind and loving and generous in doing everything for me. What was I going to tell them? We travelled around the country. We had maids. It was a good life. I was incredibly lonely.

There was structured pleasure. We went to Florida. I played golf. I had golf clubs with blue leather handles. Now I don't play golf at all. I hate golf. But I played because that was what I was expected to do with my father and mother on Sunday afternoons, family golf. I had tennis lessons. I did all the things that would improve the body and the mind, but I wasn't ever a child.

My father had started working early—the whole newspaper boy thing—so I had to have everything he and my mother had not had. I had all the lessons, all the things that money could buy in the way of knowledge and education, and Joanne got all the love and affection. I don't remember sitting on their laps. Joanne got all the hugs and cuddles.

My father talked business with me, and called me Pal, and played golf with me and took me to the baseball game. Neither one of us liked baseball, but at the time it was the thing to do. We went to the theatre and did all kinds of things, and it was pleasant. I remember going to the circus with my mother. She really enjoyed the circus so we went to every circus that came to town, and that was fun. There was a lot of group stuff. There were a lot of Italian cousins that lived near us, and my mother had done recreation work, so she just picked right up and organized all these parties and celebrations with the cousins. But I don't know where there was time for me.

I was strong. I was their son. But I never realized it until a therapist told me, "Well, you were their first-born son."

My mother died over twenty years ago, and after her death my father spent a lot of time with Joanne. He decided that maybe she could learn more, so he got another tutor for her, and she did learn and she liked it very much. She enjoys programmed learning. But any time I talked to him about a sheltered workshop or that kind of thing the conversation just stopped. He had some very strange ideas; I think sheltered workshops were close to sweatshops in his mind. He said she couldn't possibly do anything from nine to six, and I said, "I really don't think they go for those kinds of hours." But somehow his daughter was always better than other people, and she certainly thought she was better.

My father regarded himself as special because God had given him this burden to carry and he had to prove himself. And he did prove himself, but always for other people's children. He was very active at a community living facility for retarded children. He's even got a cottage there named after him because he did so much.

He was on the board, and people have told me that he was very generous to them, but they could never talk to him about his own child. They'd try to bring the subject up and ask, "What are you planning for Joanne's future?" He'd immediately go into all the financial plans he'd made, and he had made very adequate financial plans, but they could never get him to talk about anything else.

He would never talk to me, either. Any time I said to him, "Tell me more about Joanne," his attitude was that it was all too late for her. He felt that all the programs he had worked on would help other people's children but his daughter was too old to benefit from them. I don't believe she was, but that was his attitude. It was a very convoluted protective mechanism—he would take care of his own child, but he'd get all these other things going for people who didn't have his financial or intellectual resources. That way he didn't have to admit that his daughter was handicapped just as those other people's children were.

Joanne has picked up a lot of my father's feelings. She feels she is special and does not accept herself as handicapped. To the best of my knowledge she has never been in a peer group situation in her life. A few years ago she did some work at the facility that my father was so tied up with, but it was more as a volunteer than as a participant and she resisted it terribly. There's no question that she picked up my father's feelings and she didn't want to be with those retarded people. She went, but she stood totally aside. I started taking her to a swimming class for mentally handicapped people and the same thing happened; she didn't talk to anyone.

Quite often after my mother died I tried to talk to my father about possibilities for Joanne, other things she might be doing, but he was threatened by any suggestion I made. Of course, he didn't act threatened: he was a lawyer, and everything he said was logical and rational. But he would never give a straight answer to anything I suggested, so there wasn't anything to talk about. He rationalized everything and told me very logically that everything he was doing was perfect for Joanne. In fact, what he was saying was that it was too late to make changes.

It never occurred to me to talk to my mother about it when she was alive, but now I'd really like to know how she handled a lot of it and how much of the decision-making was hers. My father always told her that she could do anything she wanted, but I think she understood very well what the limits were. Basically, she let him make all the decisions.

He wanted to help me make decisions all the time, and he used to do the kind of questioning that planted doubts in my own mind. It's devastating to deal with someone who's so accommodating, who makes you feel everything is being done for you, when you know all along it's going to come out his way. There were lots of things I didn't talk to him about; I began to back away and he was terribly hurt. He thought it was perfectly normal and natural that he would be a major part of my life, even when I married and had five daughters. When I got divorced I think it caused quite a problem for him, although when he saw that it was inevitable he became totally supportive because I was his daughter.

To a great extent I have gotten over my anger at my father. He was as he was, and he could not have done things any differently. And I don't think I could have done anything differently with Joanne if I'd wanted to until maybe ten or fifteen years ago, and I'd have had to take a huge stand and really make an issue out of it. Even then, he'd have said, "Well, I think it's too late. . . ."

Joanne, like me, is in her fifties. There's an old idea that once a woman is past forty she doesn't learn or progress very much. Well, I have done more changing since I turned fifty than I did in the whole fifty years before then. I began to think that I've got another thirty years to live, and to wonder what am I going to do with those years. That's one reason I got out of my marriage. My husband was very much like my father and I thought, "Thirty more years of that. . . ?"

Now I'm thinking that maybe Joanne has another thirty years also. She's well taken care of, but I'm not sure that a tutor and piano lessons are enough. My father practically had me sign in blood that I'd never put her in an institution—his definition of institution was anywhere out of the home. Before he died he finally admitted, "I think you're right; I don't think Joanne could live with you all the time." Before that he had assumed that she'd always live with one of the relatives. That might have been true in the old days when everyone had a great-aunt who lived with them and took care of the children, but it's not the same any more.

Once he gave up the idea that Joanne could live with me he decided she could live close to me, in a two-flat, or next door. I backed away from that but I didn't make an issue of it. I talked a little about group living facilities and his response was the same as always—that's nice for other people, but not for Joanne. Even though they named a cottage for him up at that facility where he was on the board, and a very good friend of his left the facility all his money, that was never going to be the place for my father's daughter. In any case, they would not take her now because she believes it's not for her, and to get admitted you have to want to go. I think she believes I want to put her away.

Joanne's feelings about herself are pushed very far down, because the only feelings that were acceptable at home were joy, happiness, pleasantness. Anger was unacceptable, so Joanne has pushed hers down so far that it comes out in devious and funny ways. Basically, she's mad at me for directing her life, but she can't say it. Actually, I can't express anger very well, either, although I'm doing better.

I don't know if Joanne has ever faced up to her limitations. I don't think anyone ever sat down and talked with her about them. I don't know who would have done it. It certainly wouldn't have been my father. Joanne knows she's different, but it's never been put to her in terms of limitations.

My father, I think, treated her as more retarded than she really was, with the result that she is now functionally retarded. She's programmed to do the right thing, not to break out of the mold, not to cause a scene. It's the way I was brought up too, a very ladylike upbringing, but it was accentuated in Joanne's case because my father did not want her to stand out. Heaven forbid that she should shout in public. Her clothes had to be appropriate—shorts or a skirt. For years she never wore slacks or pants because pants were for digging in the garden. When she went to church she was always one of the best dressed people there. He was trying to compensate for the handicap. She has no flexibility at all. She doesn't know how to act in any other way.

My daughters help with Joanne, but they don't share the responsibility. Nobody shares the responsibility. That belongs to me. They're really quite good, but it's not hard to help when you don't have any of the real responsibility. I can call on them for help, and I do. My father would never call on anyone. He would fume because people didn't help, but he never let them know what kind of help was needed. He never even let me know directly, although he certainly made a lot of demands indirectly. If I saw Joanne twice a week I always had the feeling that I should have gone four times a week. If I called every day, well, I should have come by instead of just calling. I'd ask them what was going on and he'd say, "Nothing," and Joanne would say, "Nothing." I'd ask, "Well, didn't you do so-and-so and such-and-such?" and they'd say, "Oh, yes. . . ." But the message was, "My life is so empty, and yours is so full."

Joanne plays that game well. She is very manipulative, which is not surprising because she had years of training from my father. She also does selective listening. The woman who lives with her thinks Joanne is hard of hearing. I don't think she's hard of hearing at all, but I'm going to have her hearing tested so there'll be one less excuse.

It's hard to know what plans to make for Joanne. I'd like to get her into more group activity. She has one friend, Nancy, who's retarded. They have been friends for years. They go to movies and Nancy comes over for supper. That's about the only friend *she has except for her companion's sister, who's a lot younger. Joanne thinks of her as "my little friend" and thinks she's taking care of her, as though she were one of my children. They have a good time together. Apart from that it's family or paid help. I'd like to get away from that, but it's going to be difficult. Social situations are hard for Joanne. She resists, and then she gets really shaky, her hands get sweaty, and she carries on because I'm trying to push her. I think it's partly because the companion likes a well-ordered life, with a little bit going on every day. The house is always immaculate; there are never papers spread around or cushions on the floor. It's not the way I'd choose to live. It's a very planned, orderly, organized life. Joanne functions pretty well in that environment but I think it's overdone. However, I don't know how much breaking out of the mold I can expect her to do.*

I would certainly like to see Joanne in some kind of group living situation eventually. I am not going to be around forever. She could easily outlive me, because I take a lot more risks than she does. I could get killed on a boat or a plane or crossing the street or whatever. Then it would be up to my daughters and I think they would take the financial responsibility very well. Joanne is not going to be a ward of the state and dumped someplace. They would probably hire a succession of housekeepers. A group home would be my choice, though, and I think her life would be enormously enriched. I believe she'd be much happier. I doubt if she could work, because I think that emotionally it's probably too late for that. I've talked about it with various people, but Joanne would probably have a hard time accepting a workshop where there were retarded people. Also, she'd be bored. So I'm not looking at that route particularly.

Although I believe she'd benefit from participation in a group, there's a long way to go to get her to feel comfortable. She was terrified of riding a Dial-a-Bus because she was afraid the driver wouldn't let her off at the right place. She is very frightened of being attacked, and I think my father instilled that fear in her. The house is double-locked to within an inch of its life. Joanne goes around and locks all the windows on the second floor. She locks the front door with a double deadbolt. She's scared to death. She can't take a taxi alone. She feels comfortable walking up and down the street and in the neighborhood, and that's about it.

Joanne and I get along okay on the surface, but it's not a great relationship. If we'd had a more normal childhood together we'd get along better today. If I had had a real opportunity to not like my sister, then I could like her now on a different level. We had a huge blow-up not so long ago. I was so mad I screamed and yelled at her and it all came out, all the frustration of years. She ended up screaming and yelling at me. It was great. I told my therapist about it and she said, "It sounds like you treated her as an equal." We haven't had a fight since; in fact Joanne is still shaken about that one. I say, "Well, it's time we had a fight about something again," but we don't fight, and I think that's hard.

Whenever I still get angry at my father and my mother about the way they raised us, I have to stop and remember that they couldn't have done anything else. I don't want to use my anger as an excuse for not doing what I have to do now. I don't like what happened, but what can I do about it? I want to use this time to get things moving in a direction which will be good for both me and Joanne, to find a way that we can both live with. And I don't want to be devious about it. I want us both to be up front and cooperative.

In view of what I went through with Joanne, I wonder how I would have dealt with the rest of my children if one of them had been handicapped. I don't think I would have done it very well. Of course, I was scared stiff during each pregnancy because my parents told me that Joanne suffered a birth injury during a high forceps delivery. I have no way of knowing if that is true, but someone in the medical field once told me that it was unlikely and that her condition was probably congenital. My parents, of course, would never have been able to accept that it could be anything in them, so it had to be the doctor's fault. But I was really scared because I didn't know how I would handle it if one of my children were like Joanne, and I had nobody to talk to about the fear I felt. My husband was like my father, so I couldn't talk to him, although I think if one of our children had been handicapped my husband would have dealt with it very well— except that he'd have done it on the same lines that my father took with Joanne. Fortunately, all our daughters were normal.

responsibility: the parent-sibling conflict

The caretaking role that is either thrust upon or—with one
or another degree of willingness—assumed by the nonhandicapped sibling interrupts the development of an ordinary
love/hate sibling relationship. Because the hating is not permissible—it is not okay to hate someone who is already burdened with disability—the loving becomes difficult or impossible.

As Pat has said, "If I had had a real opportunity to *not* like
my sister, then I could like her now on a different level."
Leslie, having spent a considerable part of her youth taking
care of Jeffrey, had never had a real person-to-person relationship with him; only when they went to a concert together
and she saw that the music made him cry was she able to
reach over, take his hand, and realize that her whole relationship with her retarded brother had done an about-face.
Responsibility dulls the perception of love.

Even now, Leslie has difficulty dealing with the implications of time passing; she views the aging process as quite
different for her and for Jeffrey. She says, "Jeff's a year
younger than I am, and he's going to be thirty. I can deal with
my getting older, but I can't deal with Jeff getting older. He's
an eternal child. It's hard to conceive of him being thirty
years old, or forty years old, or fifty, or sixty."

Whatever the relationship between the handicapped and
nonhandicapped siblings, it spills over naturally enough into
the relationships of the siblings to the parents. When there's a
handicapped child in the family and one sibling who assumes
a quasi-parental role, the relationship between that sibling
and the true parents takes on unusual subtleties. Although
the responsibility of a sibling for a mentally retarded brother
or sister never precisely matches the basic responsibility that
belongs to the parent, the two can get into all sorts of power

plays. Perhaps the nonhandicapped sibling and the parent gang up on the less responsive members of the family. Perhaps they fight for power between themselves.

As the children grow up, the demarcation line between them and the parents become less clearly defined. It also happens that the generation gap may have the effect of giving the sibling the upper hand over the parent simply in terms of knowledge of the field. Many parents whose retarded children are now teenagers or young adults remember the days when most doctors automatically recommended institutionalization of any mentally impaired child, regardless of the cause or degree of the impairment. Such parents assumed that society would reject the child. They knew that they would get little or no outside help in caring for the child, and that educational and recreational facilities would be scarce or nonexistent.

Society still expresses anxiety, fear, suspicion, and rejection of people with mental retardation. Many present-day educational and recreational facilities are threatened by lack of federal or private support. Although big and impressive words are bandied about on the subject of residential alternatives, these also are subject to the same social and financial threats. Insecurity is a state of mind for people who are responsible for the long-term well-being of a mentally retarded family member. The situation, however, has changed—not enough, but it has changed. However incomplete the services offered today to people with mental retardation, they're immeasurably ahead of the services available one, two, or three decades ago.

The sibling who has grown up in the new society may have real problems communicating with parents who remember the old way, who are unwilling to experiment with new programming, and who consider any living arrangement outside the parental home as just another version of an institution and therefore most likely a pit. The child must try to lead the parent down new and unfamiliar paths, and sometimes the parent doesn't want to be led.

Pat, whose patriarchal Italian father worked tirelessly on behalf of other people's handicapped children but refused to accept that his own daughter was in need of those same programs, found herself totally unprepared to take over his role as Joanne's care-giver. In her fifties, she had to start all over. She had missed out on whole generations of progress because her father had refused to accept that Joanne was "special" in the way the word is now used.

Leslie, the one daughter out of six who accepted primary responsibility for Jeffrey, looks back with some admiration at the way her stepmother took on seven children, "one of them retarded and all of them hostile." Although she considers that Jeffrey was, at times, treated badly, she also recognizes that her family did the best they could with a very difficult set of circumstances. Leslie believes that hers was a family that needed but never got professional help in coping with stresses aggravated by the presence of a retarded family member. She still believes strongly that most families in the same situation should consider counseling. Leslie says:

Only part of Jeff's behavior was attributable to the retardation. He was also emotionally disturbed, and I think that came from the same places all of us got our wounds: the divorce, difficulty in relating to my parents, and growing up in a large family where there was so much conflict.

Also, as Jeffrey got older it started to bother him that he couldn't keep up with the girls. He saw us coming and going, talking about leaving home, knowing people—having independence and freedom when he didn't have any independence or freedom at all. He was watched twenty-four hours a day. He had no decision-making ability. He was given no authority over his actions. He had no social outlets. When he was older we tried to put him in a special social program, but the first time he went, he stole something and was thrown out.

Jeff was also a severe behavior problem at school. They dealt with him as best they could, but nobody dealt with him well. He was a self-fulfilling prophecy. One of the disciplinary methods the school used was "time out"—temporarily separating a child who was misbehaving from the group. With Jeff they "used time" out a lot. Steve, who's now the principal, tells about the first day he came to the school to interview for a job and saw Jeffrey "timed out" in the hall, under the coat-rack. Steve says that Jeff always fulfilled that prophecy. He was always, so to speak, "timed out" under the coat-rack.

He was a behavior problem from day one, and it never stopped. Nobody ever turned him around. Not the family, not the school. Now I believe he could have been turned around. I feel very strongly that families with mentally handicapped children need some kind of counseling help. If we had gotten it we might have been able to help Jeff more, quite apart from helping ourselves. But my parents had a prejudice against social workers and psychologists telling them what they were doing wrong. We needed counseling as a family because of the divorce, but also because of Jeff, and we didn't get that help.

I started therapy when I became an adult, because I realized how much I was still dragging around with me, and I wanted to sort things out in my own mind.

I wish that every family could realize that getting counseling is not an admission of weakness or inadequacy; it's an acknowledgement of a horrendous situation that is difficult for everybody. Talking about it to someone who's not involved in it can help you. Even if your only goal for therapy is to have one day a week, or one day every two weeks, to get everything off your chest, that's a valid goal. I wish that my parents had gotten help for all of us. But at that time it wasn't the fashionable thing. It was an admission that you were crazy and that there was something wrong with you.

Because of the difficulties that arose while Jeff was growing up, Leslie now has a particular concern for sex education for mentally retarded persons, and has been instrumental in promoting awareness of the issues involved among the staff of the school where she teaches and the parents of the students who attend the school. She says:

If I had to identify the most critical current issue in the social adaptation of retarded adolescents and adults, I would name sexual awareness and sexuality, not only because it's never dealt with, but because there is no easy way to deal with it. I am very much aware of this subject because Jeffrey had a lot of sex-related problems. He was arrested twice for making sexual overtures to little girls, which sounds dreadful until you realize that it was less a case of Jeff's intent to molest a child as of Jeff's being a child in mental age and expressing childish curiosity and sexual awareness. You get someone with a five- or eight-year-old mind in a twenty-one-year-old body, who is just beginning to have sexual feelings, and you've got a miserable situation for everyone concerned.

Jeff's understanding of sex is a list of musts and must nots. It's constantly, "You can't do that. No, you cannot do that." And unfortunately there aren't too many "you cans." What can he do to express himself sexually? We all know what he can't do and we tell him about it all the time, and we medicate him so he won't do it. But what can he do? He's a physically healthy, attractive, sexual person. Where does he get to express that?

When he was growing up he wasn't even allowed to masturbate in the privacy of his own room, because the school and my parents didn't think it was healthy. The idea that masturbation is

141

healthy and acceptable is really a phenomenon of recent years. Back when Jeffrey was a youngster and masturbated in school, their way of dealing with it was to embarrass him in front of everybody and sit him under the teacher's desk. The school didn't tell him that there are places where you can masturbate and places where you can't and that public places are places where you can't. Instead they talked about Jeffrey's terrible sexual problems: "He's masturbating all the time; you've got to do something about it."

Schools didn't deal with it, and families didn't deal with it. I remember people bursting in on Jeffrey and stopping him from masturbating in his room. They used to burst in on him all the time. He had no privacy even though at night he was locked in his room. He didn't usually masturbate at night, anyway. He used to do a lot of it in the afternoon, after school. He'd use our underwear. Somewhere on TV or in a movie Jeff had made the connection between women's underwear and sex, so that's what he'd use to masturbate with. He'd steal any pair of girl's underwear he could find in the house.

My parents couldn't cope with it. My stepmother couldn't handle the fact that her underwear was being used that way. My sisters and I would go to take out some underwear and it would all be gone, and we'd say, "Damn it, Jeffrey took my underwear." It was exasperating. We'd go look under his bed or under his mattress and there'd be our underwear, in a wad. You can imagine what it was like having to keep your underwear under lock and key. We had ingenious hiding places. One of my sisters used to lock up her underwear in a little grey file box. Others hid theirs in pillowcases, because Jeff would never think to look there.

However annoying that was for us, the fact remained that Jeff had no privacy and no one respected his sexual needs. No one thought of knocking before they went into his room. They should have, but Jeff had no rights when he was growing up. He does now. I think we've all matured sufficiently to recognize that he's a person with responsibilities and rights, but then we didn't know what we were doing. We were just feeling our way along, as a family.

We had some horrendous arguments with my father as we got older and started to feel that there might be different ways of handling Jeff. We felt that he was a person, with feelings, and that he didn't always have to be treated like an animal or a great burden.

As we have seen, several of the handicapped children whose stories are told in this book have siblings who chose a career in special education. Leslie's career choice has given her the information she needs to guide Jeffrey's future and make sure he gets the best of what is available in the way of social support, programming, and living arrangements.

Meg's sister, Kathy, also became a special education teacher and worked until recently in the school that Meg attends. Their mother, Peg, appreciates Kathy's professional perspective on the way she's raising Meg. She says it doesn't always feel great to have a daughter point out the mistakes she's making as a parent, but she admits that Kathy can see Meg in a different light from her own maternal perspective, and that Kathy is usually right. Peg says:

> There are many things that I'd let Meg do without thinking twice about them if I didn't have Kathy interfering—not as a sister, but as a teacher. For instance, Meg always carried a doll around. If she was going anywhere different or strange she'd want to take either the dog or her doll. It gave her a sense of security. When she was twelve she wasn't allowed to have a doll any more, and that broke my heart. Twelve-year-old girls don't carry dolls around, so that had to go by the wayside. When she was going to camp she wanted to take the doll but Kathy said no. So Kathy got her a stuffed elephant. She said that was more appropriate: teenagers have stuffed animals on their beds. Meg took the elephant to camp and was perfectly happy. I'd have let her take the doll.
>
> There are lots of funny little things like that. Meg took some odd kind of bag to school one day and Kathy protested: "Get her a tote bag. That's what kids carry their lunch in." When you're a parent you don't think about the little things that make them look more retarded. Then there was her hat. Meg had a pull-on hat that was always on wrong, too far down in the front or pushed to one side. I had to buy her a tam. I'm not a perfectionist like Kathy, but I know she's right. You need somebody on the outside to tell you these things.
>
> I think teachers should feel a little more free to tell parents these things. We might resent it at first. I might resent it myself, because I resent it when Kathy tells me even though she's my daughter. On the other hand, it's important.

Jennifer is another special education teacher who has a mentally retarded sibling. She chose her profession because she wanted to help children like her youngest sister, Cathy, who has Down syndrome. Because Jennifer's mother had a difficult time adjusting to Cathy's handicap, Jennifer—the second of four daughters—virtually raised the two youngest girls. Her experiences with Cathy affected not only Jennifer's ca-reer choice but her personal life—she finds that she is ex-tremely ambivalent about having children of her own. Hav-ing raised two children while still in her early teens, she feels that she has already had her family.

Jennifer has also a much harder time than Peg's daughter Kathy when it comes to dealing with her parents' attitudes towards her handicapped sibling. She experiences a lot of conflict: it's hard to separate her role as her mother's daugh-ter from her role as a teacher whose classroom was, for a number of years, full of Cathys. Jennifer says:

I can see two sides to things better than most people, and that is not always a comfortable position to be in. As an educator I can sit there and say, "This is what they're supposed to be doing, getting mobility trained, getting out in the community." Then I look at my sister, who is not mobility trained because my mother always said no. We have finally gotten my mother to agree to it, so now Cathy is being mobility trained between home and a work-shop, which is a block and a half away. My parents moved just to be near the workshop.

My biggest frustration is that I know Cathy loves to be inde-pendent, and when she's with my husband, Steve, and me we allow her much more independence than my parents do. But then I look at my mother and I understand the emotional side of it. To my mother Cathy is still a child who cannot make judgments as the other children can. I understand because sometimes I get my lines crossed, too. Steve and I took Cathy camping once and we showed her where to get water, which was quite a way down the road. She wanted to go by herself, so we let her, and then she didn't come back and my heart sank. I reacted just like my mother. In fact, Cathy was having a great time with the water and she found her way back just fine.

There are many instances like that and Steve tells me, "You're getting like your mother." I'll say that she can't do something and he'll ask why she can't. He doesn't have the same emotional tie that I do. He'll say that I'm becoming overprotective, and I'll deny it, and then we'll have a fight. Then he'll say, "I'll teach her," and he does. Cathy learned a lot of things with us that she'd never been able to do before. I taught her to shower by herself, which she'd never done. Then she went home and of course lost it all.

I'm still trying to educate my parents. My dad didn't really

144

have much to do with raising the kids so he sits back most of the time, but if there's an argument about something Cathy should be doing he'll definitely side with my mother and say, "She can't do that; don't push her." I've tried sitting down with my mother, as a teacher would, to show her how to modify some of Cathy's behaviors. I tell her to pretend I'm not her daughter, and I explain what she should be doing. But she starts crying because the mother-daughter relationship gets in the way.

My mother would like Cathy to stay with her for as long as possible. I've told her I'd take Cathy into my home, but she thinks that's not fair to me. My long-range plan, if something happened to my parents, would be to take Cathy into my home for a year and train her to be more independent, because as she is now I don't think she'd make it in a community living facility. After that year, I'd place her. Not because I want to be on my own, but because I think she'd be happier. I've taught children who lived in a facility and were bussed to school. Some parents whose children were still at home got really upset at the idea of those children living in an institution, but I could see it differently. In many ways they were much better adjusted than the children who lived with their parents. The children who live in a facility go home every day to other children they can play with. That's not true of most retarded children who live at home; the gap between them and their siblings gets wider all the time.

A few years ago Cathy got very sick. She lost all her hair from stress and she started simulating seizures, which were very convincing. She had the first one at my house and I thought it was a real seizure. Part of it was that she had picked up on my mother's feelings. My mother was panic-stricken because Cathy was coming up to graduation at twenty-one and there were no plans for her future. My parents could never look to the future for Cathy.

My father is eighty and my mother is in her sixties, and there's no will. Nothing has been done to provide for Cathy. My mother still says that she would prefer Cathy to die before she does. My mother read an article in the newspaper about a boy in an institution who was stomped to death, and it upset her terribly. There was a time when I could not look at anything to do with retarded people on TV, whether it was good or bad, without crying. Now I can watch a program or read a newspaper story with a critical mind, and can recognize if it is not an accurate picture. Bad things happen in some institutions, but it doesn't mean all institutions are bad. My mother doesn't see that. She just sees the bad, and that stops her from being able to plan for Cathy. It worries me a great deal.

145

but what if it happened to my child?

It's impossible to read a week's worth of a daily newspaper, or watch a week's worth of television news, without learning of the death of a child. "Five-year-old dies in freak gun accident." "Babies die in burning home." "Missing child found dead by couple on picnic." "Child molester sought in attack on pre-teen girl." "Liver transplant baby loses battle for life."

When the stories involve an element of the unusual, the bizarre, or the violent, they make the headlines. We read, or listen, and we shudder. For a while we keep those children in our minds, or perhaps we try to forget them but can't. If we're parents, for a while we keep a closer eye on our own children, telling ourselves, "It won't happen to my child," wondering, "How are those poor parents coping?" What we are saying, essentially, is "It couldn't happen to my child because it mustn't happen to my child. I couldn't bear it."

If the child who dies has been very sick—for example, the liver transplant baby who fought for life and lost—we rationalize. We say, "Well, maybe it was for the best. Now that child need not suffer any more." We tell ourselves that now the parents can get some rest because their fight to save their child is over.

Sometimes, when a child's death makes the headlines, the grieving parents are shown on TV, affording the rest of us a vivid, voyeuristic opportunity to intrude upon a parent's experience of loss. Perhaps we watch, fascinated, as a hysterical mother is led away from the house where her children died in a fire while she was working to provide them with food and shelter. Perhaps we listen as a father explains how the gun was so well hidden he was sure the children couldn't find it. Perhaps we turn off the TV set, unwilling to pursue a line of thought that leads—if we let it—to the knowledge that it could "happen to my child." Of course it could.

Somehow the death of a child affects us as an insult to our

146

humanity, something that should not happen. But, of course, it happens all the time. Children die all the time, and only a handful of them are victims of violent crime, freak accidents, unusual or bizarre combinations of circumstances. Babies are stillborn. Toddlers drown in swimming pools. Children die of leukemia.

Parents of a child who is born with mental retardation or has become retarded after birth have already experienced, in some sense, a death associated with that child. They have experienced the death of hopes and the shattering of dreams. Somehow it puts the issues of loss and death in a different perspective and it can be very difficult to get that perspective clearly focused.

There was a time when we thought that Emma, then aged four years, had leukemia. I had taken her to the pediatrician for a routine check-up and the doctor identified a combination of symptoms that included swollen lymph nodes and an elevated white blood count. He put her in the hospital for tests, and although he tried very hard not to let me figure out what he was testing for, there can't be many parents who wouldn't jump to conclusions on that evidence. So I knew he suspected leukemia.

Emma was in the hospital for three days while the tests were run. She did not have leukemia. Emma herself has her own memories of the occasion and tends to boast about how she was only four yet it took four grown people to hold her down while they did the spinal tap. I have memories, too, because I think that whatever has happened to me before or since, those were the worst hours of my life.

While Emma was in the hospital, being tested for a potentially killing disease, she made herself something of an item in the pediatric ward. She located a tricycle and, clad in frilly green baby doll pajamas with little animals all over them, her strawberry blonde curls awry, she zipped up and down the corridors making friends.

There was one child who particularly took her fancy, but she couldn't make friends with him because that child was not and never had been capable of friendship or any other normal human relationship. He was a profoundly retarded child who was in the hospital, as he had been a number of times before, to be treated for pneumonia. His limp, malproportioned body might have been that of a three-year-old, but his head was the normal size for his age, which was twelve. This was the sort of child people call a "vegetable." He had been that way all his life. He had no control over any part of his body except for an occasional flicker of the eyes. He couldn't eat and had to be hand-fed with a dropper, like the abandoned runt from a litter of puppies. He lived with his family, and he regularly contracted pneumonia or other infections. Every time it happened his family put him back in the hospital where life was forced back into him. Then the family took him home until the next time.

Emma was most interested in this boy. She'd get off her tricycle and stand beside him to watch him being fed. She would take his hand and try to get some sort of friendly response from him. She asked a lot of questions of the nurse, who held the child gently in her lap and slowly, patiently, drop by drop, fed the life-sustaining fluids into his slack mouth. And the nurse would answer Emma's questions as best she could and tell her that yes, the boy would probably be able to leave the hospital and go home. What else could she say to a four-year-old? Emma, of course, did not have then, as she has now, sufficient experience of handicapped children to understand that this kind of child would never get well, that nothing anyone ever did for him could do more than prolong—in such comfort as he was capable of feeling— his life as a human vegetable.

Emma wasn't the only one fascinated by that child. I was, too. This was only two years after Victoria had been officially diagnosed as having mental retardation, and her handicap was in no way comparable to that of the boy. I was learning a lot about children like Victoria—children who, though mentally handicapped, could run and laugh and learn and play and have fun and throw tantrums like any other child.

This boy was something else altogether. As I watched my lovely, normal four-year-old dart about the corridors like a bright butterfly I said to myself, "She cannot have leukemia. The very thought is an obscenity." And then I looked at the profoundly retarded boy in the nurse's lap and thought, but was afraid to ask, "Why don't they let him die?" What was it in that child's life that was worth prolonging? Would it not be infinitely more merciful to allow him to die?

I did not, at that time, place Victoria somewhere in between her normal sister and the boy who was a vegetable. Nor did I ask myself, "Would I be feeling differently if it were Victoria, who is already damaged, being tested for a potentially fatal disease instead of this bright butterfly of a sister of hers? Would I feel differently? And if so, how? And why?"

Some years later, when Victoria was already a teenager, the television documentary series "60 Minutes" aired a program about a couple with a severely retarded daughter who must have been about Victoria's age. The parents insisted on keeping the girl at home even though she required around-the-clock nursing care, which they provided, more or less unaided. The girl was nonambulatory, bedridden, barely responsive to outside stimuli, and showed no signs of possible improvement.

By this time I was older, sadder, and more cynical than I had been at the time of what we now refer to as "Emma's leukemia scare." I also had one divorce behind me—in which Victoria's handicap had certainly been a major factor—and Victoria was no longer the sweet, tractable child she had been before puberty caught up with her (and us). So, as I watched this couple perform their loyal and dedicated rituals of caring for their child, I found it difficult to feel the admiration obviously due to such devotion. Instead, my primary feeling was one of exasperation. "Why don't they put that girl in a home?" I snapped. My fellow viewers were visibly shocked. They had bought the "wonderful parents" message whole and the idea that I, myself the mother of a retarded child, could be so callous was simply not in their script.

The girl in that television special might, possibly, have been getting from her parents the sort of intimacy she would not have received anywhere else. Maybe their devotion, which to me seemed, frankly, quite unnecessary, was justified. But the cost seemed too high. Those parents had no relief from this totally engrossing task that clearly consumed all the energies they possessed. It was their life. They admitted that their whole life was dedicated to this one task. To hear them talk one had to assume that she was all they had.

What would happen if the girl died and her parents had to deal with each other with no intervening medium? What if their common purpose for being together were removed and they were once again, as presumably they had been before their daughter's birth, face to face with each other as real people? Would they even know one another any more? They lived for the child. Would they have a life without her? Perhaps they would survive the loss and find a whole new life together in a real world they'd forgotten still existed. Perhaps for those parents the death of a child would be not a tragedy, but a release. But perhaps it wouldn't be like that at all. Perhaps their life together would disintegrate, like the relationship of stage partners who no longer find an audience for their act.

Inevitably, the death we hear or read about is sometimes that of a retarded child. To make the news, the child would have to die in unusual circumstances: stomped to death in a living facility, or dead in a fire, like the child whose parents had tied him to his bed to prevent his wandering. Both of these stories made the newspapers. So did the story of two youngsters who managed to get past the security gate of their living facility and were found frozen to death next morning. All those were retarded children, and those are the horror stories that leap off the page when you have a retarded child of your own.

If the death of a child always seems like something that should not happen because we see a child as a symbol of the future, a creature of unknown possibilities, is it any different when the child is mentally handicapped and certain limits have already been imposed on that child's future and certain possibilities irrevocably precluded?

Learning of the death of a mentally retarded child, especially one that you have known, however slightly, can trigger an alarmingly strong reaction. Suddenly one family's loss becomes your loss in a particularly painful way. It forces you to open your eyes to the risks involved for handicapped children, especially those whose lives are structured to allow them to be as normal as possible, to go out into the community, take buses, cross busy streets, go swimming, go on field trips. All those normal pursuits, however closely monitored and supervised, involve risk. Accidents can happen, and they do. And when they happen to someone else's child your eyes snap open both to the risks you allow your child to take, and to your own ambivalence about what you might feel if something did happen to your retarded child.

It's this ambivalence that makes it very hard to perceive the accidental death of a mentally handicapped child as an impersonal event. It tends to become a very personal experience that puts you in touch, a lot more intimately than is welcome, with feelings you do not want to feel. Specifically, it raises the very unwelcome and guilt-provoking thought that a child with a mental handicap presents emotional and practical problems that might cease to exist if the child weren't there.

I doubt if any parent who has a mentally handicapped child could, on oath, deny having considered what it would mean if the child were to die and to be there no more. I have certainly thought about it. I have thought about it many times since Emma's leukemia scare, and I thought about it often when Victoria hit puberty and my once tranquil home became the scene of daily emotional massacres. Suppose she did get hit by a car on the way to school, I used to ask myself in my darkest moments. Provided, of course, that she didn't suffer, might that not be the best thing for everyone? What, I wondered, did life really have to offer her? Independence? No. An exciting career? Not a chance. A family of her own? Not likely. So what does she have to look forward to that would make her dying such a tragedy? What about children like that little boy in the hospital? And all the children in between his level of handicap and Victoria's?

Children with mental retardation face confusion, rejection, fear, a sense of failure, the awareness of being "different" and the anger and frustration that goes along with such awareness. I know that Victoria experiences all those feelings and so, without a doubt, do most retarded people who are functioning at her level. Would it be tragic if such a person no longer had to fight those monstrous obstacles that fate had dumped in her path, or to struggle so hard to achieve simple tasks that should be child's play to a child?

Such black and pseudo-selfless thoughts, however, are only part of the picture. Given her limitations—and who among us has no limitations?—Victoria lives a pretty good life. All the same, parents of retarded children go through a significant amount of pain—from broken dreams to broken spirits and broken homes. How can we help asking what our lives would be like if we suddenly ceased to be encumbered with the responsibility for this other life, with the care-giving and the planning and the decision-making and the knowledge that none of it is going to end? Children who are mentally handicapped do not assume control, or degrees of control, over their lives at the prescribed times. There's no turning point at age sixteen, when a mentally unimpaired child may (for better or worse) drive a car; or at eighteen, when he or she may go to college or get married; or at whatever age liquor becomes officially available. Those milestones have no meaning along the road walked by a person who is mentally retarded. In an uncomfortably literal sense, retarded people stay young forever. And, being young, they need their parents. Forever.

So, if it were our child who died in an accident, would that mean freedom? Would everything that had gone bad in our lives suddenly become good again if, through some freak occurrence that was nobody's fault, our handicapped child ceased to be? Or to get to the heart of the matter, where's the parent of a mentally retarded child who can honestly deny ever having thought, "I wish this child had not lived"?

A friend of mine, the mother of a multiply handicapped teenager, and I were talking about just such a freak accident in which a retarded child, whom we both knew slightly, died. My friend said, "Well, there's one family for whom it's all over." The assumption, of course, was incomplete at best. The child's family might indeed now be free of their struggle to do right by their handicapped child, but their new struggle with grief and pain and loss and, probably, guilt had just begun. All the same, the remark demonstrated very clearly that at times "having it all over" is not an entirely unacceptable prospect. What is unacceptable, however, is voicing such feelings to those whose terms of reference are too different from your own.

The ambivalence I had felt about those parents on "60 Minutes" caused me some guilt until I heard it ratified by a number of other parents. Parents I've talked to have also admitted to moments when they thought their retarded child's death might be the easiest way out, especially in the early stages.

Peg remembers her earliest reactions to the discovery that Meg, her sixth and last child, had Down syndrome:

They knew as soon as Meg was delivered, at least they had a good idea. It was funny; there I was in the delivery room after she had been born and the doctor was telling me that he was pretty sure she had Down syndrome and I didn't realize what it was—that he was saying she was a "mongoloid" baby. Then he told me that "mongoloid" was the term they used to use for Down syndrome. He said, "We don't use it any more in the hospitals, and hopefully you won't hear it much." At first I hoped that before I left the hospital she might die, I really did. I figured that way we wouldn't have any problems.

Meg was a peaceable child, easy to live with, unlike Richard who was a problem from the word go. Ilene, who received very little emotional support during the early months of Richard's life, expresses very clearly the feelings she had towards her first-born child. For a start, she says, he was not even attractive. She says:

Apparently Richard was a back labor, and his face was somewhat skewed. He was long and thin and very unpleasant-looking, with an elongated head and mashed nose. The pediatrician, of course, examined the child and found nothing wrong with him.

Richard did not nurse well, and he screamed a lot. He seemed to me to have an odd appearance around the eyes, which I thought was just new-mother fussiness because my child did not appear to be perfect and beautiful. I did not ever think that the child might be mentally retarded because I had misconceptions about retarded children being extremely peaceable, agreeable, and nondemanding. I thought that if you didn't incite them to eat they might starve themselves. Richard, on the contrary, screamed a lot, was very demanding, and wanted a great deal of food.

After the first month or so he developed a habit of waking up at random hours of the night and screaming. It could happen six times a night, or three, or one, but it almost always happened, and I was conditioned to getting up and doing things and rocking him a lot. Sometimes a bottle quieted him, but usually he drained it, threw it down, and screamed again. I understood perfectly how mothers kill their children in the cradle. I felt a great deal of hostility towards him, which I thought was entirely normal under the circumstances.

I felt deep grief about what had happened to my child. I felt as if my child had died. But, unfortunately, he wasn't dead. I would have to live with him for the rest of my life. It was like nursing someone who was dying, but who never died and never got better.

I felt very strong love for him and very strong hatred. I had delusions of strangling or smothering him—none of this objective, scientific "I will put him out of his misery" stuff; I really sometimes thought that the most exquisite pleasure in the world would be strangling him or smothering him with a pillow.

The feelings of hostility that many parents of handicapped children feel towards their offspring are probably much the same as those felt by parents of normal children. The difference is that expressing them compounds the guilt that the parent already feels because of the child's handicap. It's not acceptable to express hostile feelings towards a handicapped child, especially one's own, and it's hard sometimes for someone who hasn't been put in the same position to understand the legitimacy of those feelings or the helplessness that, in part, triggers them.

Peg no longer wishes that Meg had died before she had to take her out of the hospital, and Ilene has come to terms with her son's handicap and can say, "He is who he is." Both Peg and Ilene, however, like the rest of us, have also had to accept the fact that the feelings of helplessness stem in part from the knowledge that a child with mental retardation does not "grow up" and become personally responsible for his or her own life in the way a nonhandicapped child can be expected to do. There's no predictable point at which the parent can cease to be responsible for the well-being of a child who is mentally handicapped. Peg says:

> *You have to be thinking ahead all the time; my head is accustomed to it. You figure, where's the end? With ordinary children you know they'll go through certain stages and all of a sudden they'll be independent. But with retarded children that is never going to come. We'll always have to be there. When Meg is seventeen, or twenty-one, I'll still be worrying about whether she has any friends or has somewhere to go. There doesn't seem to be any end to it all. That's the weariness—knowing they're not going to go off and live their own lives.*

When a parent faces that prospect of continuous responsibility for a child who is mentally handicapped, with no end in sight, it is surely not abnormal to wonder what it would be like to be without that child. I learned of the accidental death of one of Victoria's schoolmates at a time when the implications—the "would everything be all right if I didn't have this retarded child in my life?" questions—were guaranteed to hit me like a bomb. Six weeks earlier my second husband, Victoria's stepfather, had walked out. He did it, ironically enough, after Victoria had ceased to live at home, when one might expect that the worst of the pressure that we had been enduring had been eased. He also chose to do it after her weekend at home—the monthly "home visit" from the facility where she was living. I had just come back from returning

Victoria to the facility, where she had thrown a truly classic tantrum, one of her best, when Don announced that he wanted us to separate because he could no longer cope with the stress and complications occasioned by having a handicapped child in the family.

That, as far as it goes, is perfectly understandable. Frequently, very frequently, I feel that I can't stand the stress and complications either. But Don had options which I do not have and have never had. He had the option of quitting, which I have never even in my most despairing hours felt to be an option open to me, and he took it. Granted that Victoria's retardation was not the sole and only cause of his leaving, it was surely a great dumping ground for all the emotional components that went into his decision. Victoria, or any handicapped child, can be a natural scapegoat: if you don't want to pinpoint other reasons for a problem, you don't have to, because you've got a terrific reason right there.

When Don and I married he was deeply attracted to the idea of being Victoria's stepfather. But he didn't know what he was getting into. Moreover, I didn't know what he was getting into. When Don and I met, Victoria was a charmer. Her sister, on the other hand, was a six-year-old hellion. When the kids reversed roles, Victoria demonstrated that as a troublemaker Emma had been a total amateur. Victoria's early teen years were a constant and bloody battle from which none of us got away—least of all, perhaps, Victoria—unscarred.

Don and I frequently discussed his dissatisfaction with the fact that Victoria's needs deflected my attention from him; he wanted more of me than was available with Victoria in the picture. Again, a valid complaint up to a point. Time and again throughout this book parents talk of the disproportionate amount of time, energy, and emotional resources that get poured into the retarded child at the expense of other family members. In our case, by the time Victoria was placed we were, apparently, too depleted to attempt to put the pieces back together.

Victoria, especially since her volcanic eruption into puberty, had deflected my attention from my husband. And from my other child. And from myself. There are times when I'm not sure who I am any more. When I visit Victoria's school or the facility where she now lives the kids greet me with enthusiasm. Some of them know my name. Many of them greet me with, "Hi, Victoria's mother." There are times when I feel that is the only identity I have: I am Victoria's mother.

So when that child died six weeks after Don moved out I was suffering severe personal loss, and I reacted to this other mother's loss with alarming pain. It could have been my child, and because at the time the effect of my child on my life was being identified as a direct cause of what appeared to be the imminent disintegration of my second marriage, my defences were way down.

That week I went to see my therapist and I freaked out in his office. "I can understand that you're upset," he said, "but why are you *so* upset? This was not your child. This did not happen to you."

No, but it could have happened to me. And at that moment I might have had legitimate cause to wish that it had happened to me. If it had happened to me, would it make everything whole again between my husband and myself? Would things have been different if Victoria, walking to school one day, had missed her step and fallen under a car and been killed? Would things suddenly become all right if Victoria had been the child who had died in that accident?

The consequences of having a handicapped child in a family, and what happens to marriages in which that situation exists, are subjects of much interest to sociologists and psychologists. Somewhere out there somebody must be comparing the incidence of marriage break-up in families that have a mentally retarded child and families that don't. Even without statistics, professionals in the field will tell you categorically that a higher-than-average proportion of one-parent families include a mentally handicapped child.

If a marriage is solid to begin with, the presence of a child with special needs—or any other traumatic circumstance—can create a closer familial bond and make the marriage even stronger. If, for whatever reason, the marriage is already shaky, the presence of a handicapped child may shake it to its foundations. The family that includes a child with mental retardation lives astride a psychological San Andreas fault.

what happens in a marriage
when the baby's broken?

Ken is a clinical psychologist who has worked in the field of mental retardation for seventeen years and has counseled countless parents who have mentally handicapped children. Ironically, after ten years of working with such parents he became one himself. His second child, Kiel, has cerebral palsy and impaired vision. This circumstance, which he describes in view of his professional affiliations as "kind of a special kick in the ass," put him in the inescapable position of having to practice what he preached. It also validated many of his perceptions: his family went through exactly the same trauma and stress that he had seen so many other families endure.

Ken travels extensively, lecturing and giving workshops for professionals and parents. He also has a private psychotherapy practice. One way or another, he has had ample opportunity to observe the way a mentally handicapped child affects a marriage, and the dynamics that go into action when parents are confronted with a child's retardation. He says:

Women and men cope differently with having an impaired child. Sometimes it seems that women cope better than men, but it's not so. Having a child with a handicap flushes out basic sexual stereotype issues. Ultimately, they'll emerge in a marriage no matter what, but this is a situation that precipitates the process. Let's say you have a woman who defines herself primarily as a mother, secondarily as a wife, and then has some tertiary identification as a professional or worker. This would be a pretty typical structure in the majority of families today. Even after all the hoopla about sexual change, this is what you see. You hear a lot of women talk about being different from the stereotype, but when you watch what they're actually doing you'll get the pattern: primary identification, mother; secondary identification, wife; tertiary identification, some kind of worker.

For the man it's the other way around. He has a different priority system. His primary identification is with work; secondary identification, husband; tertiary identification, father. That's pretty much the way it works and that has its own inherent problems; it affects you even if you don't add the special stress of having an impaired child. The problems that are inherent in these priority differences come to the fore in a marriage and have to be worked out in one way or another. Some people work it out by subjugating a lot of feelings, maybe drifting apart but never divorcing: you go your way and I'll go mine and we'll sort of hang around together at the same address because staying together is an economically reasonable arrangement. Some people do get divorced. Others start to work the issues out and realize, "God, this is a problem. I don't know any more how important work really is to my life. I don't know how I feel about missing my kids' growing up. All these things that were clear to me aren't clear any longer and I don't know how I feel about them." That's what I mean when I say the issues are flushed out.

Then, when you have an impaired child, demands are put on the family because of the shattering of dreams that are tied to the child, both the mother's and the father's dreams. What follows is the disruption of everyday life. It's like a death, only worse. Not only do you grieve the loss of the dreams that either death or a disability destroys, but you also have to deal with the issues of everyday existence. The child is dead in the sense that he or she has shattered your dreams, but the child is very much alive and, as a matter of fact, makes many more demands than a nonimpaired child would, thereby changing your day-to-day existence in a dramatic fashion. And that generally gets worse as the kid gets older.

Three stressors thus come together at the same time. Number one is the flushing out of the priority differences in terms of sexual stereotypes. Number two is the shattering of dreams and the grieving process that goes along with that—and which men and women characteristically do in different ways. Number three is the stresses that are put on the family's everyday life and the total disruption of the way people were living before having this kid. The result is more than just grief and fatigue. It's depletion, downright depletion—empty it all out and there's nothing left for anything else.

So you're bereaved, you're confused, and you're depleted. And then you try to relate to each other. You start to blame. You start to withdraw. The acting out begins—acting out in anger, acting out in the way of, "Well, if I can't get my needs taken care of here I'll go elsewhere." It all begins to build up.

As far as the grieving differences go, again we're talking about sexual stereotyping and we have to be careful because it obviously doesn't fit all men or all women, but one of the things that I have seen fairly consistently is that men deny longer. They have more difficulty getting past denial. Men, however, have less difficulty with depression and anxiety. They switch off. It's interesting that what one does well, the other doesn't, and the way this works in terms of denial is that many men, with full support from their wives, have as a primary definition of maleness something to do with fixing things. They're problem solvers and fixers, and that's what their masculinity is all about.

Until the impaired child comes along, the whole relationship has hinged on the mutual agreement that he is the fixer. He is the male and he knows how to take care of problems and correct them. Well, what happens when the mother says, "The baby's broken"? He can't fix it. How does he deal with his image of being a man but not being able to fix it? He feels threatened. A woman's image of being a mother is not generally threatened by having a broken child. In fact, at the beginning an impaired child makes more demands of the kind she's most comfortable with: nurturing, diapering, feeding, medicating. All that a mother who's into mothering can accept. She can say, "I know this stuff." She doesn't have to fix it; she's into the process of being the mom with the baby. Dads aren't. They're into fixing things. So the father actually has to change his criteria for being a competent male—or viewing himself as a competent male—before he can acknowledge the kid's disability. The mother can acknowledge that the child is disabled without having it touch her definition of what it is to be a woman.

Later on, she runs into trouble and he doesn't. Later, he challenges her and says, "You're terrific as a mother, but you stink as a wife. You're depleting yourself with this bloody kid. You've forgotten why we got together in the first place. There's nothing left for me. What happened to the marriage? What kind of sex life do we have? What kind of play life do we have?" There's an old Southern saying that when you're up to your ass in alligators, it's hard to remember that you started out to drain the swamp.

Mothers try to compensate for the guilt, which they're more likely to feel than the fathers; they feel, irrationally, that "I was the last one to touch the kid; I must have done something wrong." Women feel more guilt than men do, but that is not to say that men do not also feel guilt. A man will ask himself, "What did I do to stress my wife when she was carrying the kid? What did my genes have to do with it?"

Men do feel guilt, but they don't get so hung up on it. For women, the guilt is two pronged. First prong is the belief, "I caused this in some fashion; I did something, or I thought

159

something, or I felt something." The "ifs" are the second prong: she thinks, "I'm the mother. I'm the primary caretaker. Mothers take care of children. I could have done it better, and if I'd done it better this child wouldn't be so impaired." Fathers usually feel only the first part—the belief that they're directly responsible, that "this happened to me because I'm a bad person." They don't generally get into the "if only" part.

In a workshop I gave recently one woman worked out her guilt before four hundred and fifty people. She had a child who was normal until age two and then developed meningitis that went out of control. The child is now profoundly retarded—no language, no toileting, nothing. Until she was two she was fine; she was cooking along. She was toilet-trained, she was talking, she was riding a trike, and then—zilch. This woman was coming at the guilt from a different perspective. She said, "I ruined my marriage because I spent two years trying to regain for my daughter what she had lost. Now I realize that I threw away my marriage, and I feel responsible for that. I threw away my marriage; I threw away my relationship with the other kids; I threw away my opportunity to have more kids, because I was too busy." So her guilt works another way: regrets and remorse not because she didn't do enough for the child but because she did too much. She threw herself wholly into trying to rehabilitate the child, and in the process she let go of everything else.

Any marriage is changed by the birth of a child. It is changed more drastically by the birth of an impaired child, and by how each parent uniquely deals with the fact of that birth. If you don't grieve together, if you don't trust each other enough to share the feelings and try and pull together, it's going to get worse. Having an impaired kid is the kind of crisis that makes things either get worse or better. The one thing you know for sure is that they're not going to stay the same. Having an impaired child puts everything in question. Though I have no statistics, I'm sure it increases the incidence of marriage break-up. An incredibly high number of single parents come to me.

What does the family do to try to arrest that process of disintegration? For one thing, you look at your natural environment and see if you can work on it, and to do that you need help. Now that is tricky, because the battle between husbands and wives can be tonight over just that issue: "I think we should get help." "I don't. It's your problem, so you go get help." One of you has to change. In some instances, when the couple isn't able to work on it together, you can predict that, for whatever reasons, the union isn't going to survive. Probably it would not have survived the first crisis, even if it had been a crisis of a different flavor.

For any couple with a handicapped child there has to be a way of opening up communication, and as far as I am concerned it has to be in some kind of a group—not necessarily in psychotherapy, but in some counseling situation where they can talk with other people who face the same kinds of issues. The problem is that the environment around families who have an impaired child does not accommodate those families. At work the father's probably around people who are still talking about getting up the corporate ladder. Everyone around the mother is still talking about whether Huggies or Pampers are better. These people are not able to incorporate what's happened and provide a societal support system, so a great feeling of alienation develops. Because when you say, "My kid is having these problems," someone's going to reply, "It's not as bad as you think," or, "Find another doctor," or "God works in strange ways." Whatever the response is, it does not work as a support system. It certainly doesn't work like the support system available to the mother who's trying to figure out what to do about diaper rash and has ten other mothers around who've dealt with diaper rash and can take it seriously.

The mother of a normal child has access to a whole support system where everyone understands everyone else's concerns and can come up with either concrete solutions or emotional support. Parents of impaired kids don't have that support system unless they get together, and they need a medium in which to get together and find out that other people are feeling the same things—the same grief, anger, or depression. In a group you find out that someone else's husband is acting out his anger the same way yours is, or someone else is having trouble with denial the way you are.

But there's no way to measure pain. Pain is pain. You can't say to the parent who has an impaired child, "On the Richter scale I think your loss is a seven, and hers is a ten, and his is a four." What's the response supposed to be? "Oh, good, I only got a four, and she's got a ten! I feel better. Thanks for letting me come to the meeting. Before I came I thought I had problems, but now that I've listened to all of you I can see that you're a lot worse off than I am." It does not work like that.

One of the big problems facing parents of a handicapped child is that the grieving is not a one-time thing. It keeps recycling. Denial, anxiety, fear, guilt, depression, and anger are all feeling states that keep recycling. Anger deals with specific issues, and one of these is a person's sense of justice. Anger is a reflection of those feelings that say on one hand that good things should happen to good people and I didn't do anything to deserve this; and on the other hand, okay, I'm not the best person in the world but I'm not the worst; there are worse persons that have gotten away with being awful and I haven't gotten away with it, and that's wrong." And all the time things happen that keep the anger and the grief and the depression recycling. Just when you think you've got it down, something happens and it's like being back at square one and that is very discouraging and hard to deal with.

I do not agree with people who claim that anyone who has a mentally retarded child needs psychological counseling, because that pathologizes the grief about having an impaired child. I think what they can use is a support group; they can use other people who come from a similar vantage point, who can listen and understand and share.

I was into this field for ten years before my wife, Renee, and myself had a handicapped child of our own. Kiel is seven now, and he's our second child. We also have a twelve-year-old daughter, Annece.

I guess Kiel's basic diagnosis would be cerebral palsy in the left hemisphere of the brain, which means it affects his right side. He is also visually impaired, and sees functionally out of only one eye. He's very well rehabilitated. He rides a trike and swims and he's working on riding a two-wheeler. He can go upstairs, alternating feet, without touching a bannister. He's doing very well, and he's integrated into a normal school classroom.

After having been in the field for ten years and now having had Kiel for seven more years, I have discovered that all of the issues I talked about previously were real. They were absolutely true for me as well. I felt very much that I had been right, and that my perceptions were correct. Our family went through hell in a handbasket, like every other family. I think now things truly have gotten better, but that's far from guaranteed. The work has been astonishing, and there has been no special dispensation for knowing what I know. It has been exactly as hard as it would have been for a plumber. How you cope with having an impaired child has nothing to do with what you know, and everything to do with how much you are willing to risk in terms of vulnerability, openness, self-examination, and the willingness to change as best you can. And most people are simply unwilling to change. Generally, you don't until you're forced to. Even then, if you can figure out a way to avoid it, you will. And that is a mistake.

the baby who brought her father home

When Joan was pregnant with her second child her physician husband, Alan, was serving in Vietnam.* When the baby, Annie, was born with a viral infection that the doctors realized would probably leave her permanently brain-damaged, it was decided that Alan should be brought home. The bureaucratic wheels were set in motion and the grounds on which permission was granted for his return were that his wife had died in childbirth and the baby with her. Thus Alan was faced with a massive fictional trauma before he ever got to face the fact of his daughter's retardation. Joan says:

They brought him back thinking that his wife and daughter were dead, that he was coming home to a four-year-old son and no one else. He did not find out until he arrived in San Francisco that we were alive. Then he came to the hospital and got hit with the real trauma—that Annie was very sick, that she might not live, and that if she did live she would probably be mentally retarded.

We never dealt with the fact that we had a child that had been transferred to another hospital so she could get the most advanced neonatal treatment available, and that the child might not live and probably was not normal. We only dealt with how wonderful it was that Alan was home from Vietnam and how we could keep him here on reassignment so that he wouldn't have to go back.

We went together to the hospital to see Annie, but I was afraid to pick her up out of the incubator. Alan reached in and said, "Well, don't be afraid. Just pick her up." But it was not like when Matthew was born and Alan wanted to hold him all the time. He never held Annie, never cuddled her. It wasn't that he was afraid of her: she just did not exist in his mind as his child. He never really accepted her as a child at all, let alone as a retarded child.

---

*In this family's story, names have been changed in order to protect the family's privacy.

He couldn't cope with it. Having been trained in the sciences, he liked to deal with things that he could see and diagnose and understand. His position was that if you can't see something, if it isn't tangible, then obviously it does not exist. And since he couldn't cure this, understand it, account for it, obviously it did not exist. So she was his obligation—he would take care of her, and that's where it ended.

The immediate issue was keeping him from having to go back to Vietnam. To get him a compassionate reassignment we needed the name of a university psychiatrist as high up as possible. The reassignment had to be based on the fact that I was too unstable to raise a four-year-old and a younger retarded child unless Alan was around. A friend of Alan's called a professor who had just taken over as head of the psychiatric division of a major university. The professor asked us in for an interview, which I will never forget as long as I live. The only thing he asked me was, "Well, how do you feel about your husband going back to Vietnam?" I said, "Extremely nervous," which was true.

On the basis of that conversation he wrote a five-page report on the neuroses of wives whose husbands are absent when they have handicapped children. Alan took this paper with him to Washington, D.C., and presented it before a board. I don't know if the board was feeling generous because it was right around Christmas, but he did get the reassignment.

The virus that caused Annie's brain damage is a very common one. Ninety percent of the population has it at one time or another, but it is very rare for a fetus to be damaged, and the damage, if it happens, can only occur in the first trimester. After Annie was born the doctors found that I had had the virus. It had infected her, and she carried it for two years, but it was an unusual case. It's possible that I had had the virus when Matthew, my first child, was born, but nothing happened to him, and we were told that there was no reason to suspect that it would affect future children that we might have. We did have two more children: Robert was born three years after Annie, and Michael two years later. They were both fine. Alan loved both of them the way he loved Matthew, but through the first twelve years of Annie's life he never accepted her.

She's fifteen now, and only recently has he begun to change. The change has come about because of psychoanalysis, which he did not go into because of Annie but because he could not cope with success. He has become a very successful physician, and when he started to get successful he couldn't handle it. He got depressed. He didn't know how to be happy. His career was going well, he was getting great boosts to his ego, but he couldn't look at himself as other people looked at him—as a success—because he

164

felt he didn't deserve it. In his depression, he dragged this family through five years of hell.

We stayed together, but it took guts, and I think it was my guts. It was a constant emotional drain. I never knew what he would do next. He could burst into the house in the middle of the afternoon and tell me that he was going to commit suicide. One time he took off and said, "I don't think I'll ever be back." Michael was then a baby, and I had the other three to take care of as well. I was really worried that he would do something to himself because he wasn't stable. Lately I found out that he would never have done anything to himself. It was just a bid for attention.

Finally, I couldn't stand it any longer and I told him so. The professor who had helped us get the compassionate reassignment was a psychoanalyst who took on selected people, and I told Alan, "Either you call this man and make an appointment with him or I walk out." I don't think he was afraid I would actually walk out; I think he knew he really needed help.

Alan is still seeing that analyst. An eight-year commitment to analysis is required, although we didn't know that at the time, and it costs a fortune, which we also didn't know. But he's coming out of it a superb person. And part of what has happened is that he has started to accept Annie.

It did not happen overnight. He was already several years into analysis and the rejection was still going on. He would kiss everybody else goodbye and not even go near Annie. Annie doesn't have much speech, so she couldn't express it in words, but she would look at him, wondering, "Don't I get a kiss, what's wrong?" She still loved her father; she followed him constantly, looking for love. Annie is autistic in some ways and one of the effects of her retardation is that she doesn't know how to reach out for love. Alan took that as rejection of him.

He rejected Annie so totally that it was difficult for me not to see it as being also a total rejection of me. I felt, "If you don't kiss Annie goodbye, you haven't kissed me goodbye." He still rejects this child in many ways, but he's coming around now, and we're moving to the point where we can sit down and talk about it.

Annie doesn't live at home any more. We've placed her. I think what Alan worked out in analysis was that Annie had to be placed, for the good of the other children, for my good, for the good of the home and the marriage, for her own good—everything.

Alan doesn't always know how to tell people these things. He doesn't have much tact when something is really bothering him. He has a lot of tact in the office, but not at home. He would come home and say, "This is the choice: either you place Annie or I leave. It's her or me." He probably would not have left, or not at that time. But we would have gone on with a very rocky marriage, and it would probably have come down to "her or me" eventually, because he couldn't take it.

One reason that it's so much easier for Alan to cope now is that he's placed Annie in a wonderful situation. She lives in a group home in a facility that has a very high reputation and is generally thought of as one of the very best available. She lives in a beautiful house with seven other girls and very loving house parents, and she has all sorts of programs and activities. And Alan did it. He is responsible for her having this marvelous life. It wasn't easy to get the placement. You had to know the right people and have the influence. He did all the paperwork, and dealt with the state mental health people to get her a grant. He had to keep after them. He's done a good thing for the other children, too, because now they don't have to cope with her. Because he accomplished that, it's easier for him to deal with Annie now. He's got something to be proud of. He did all that for his family. If it had been up to me I probably wouldn't have placed her. She'd still be living at home.

We went to an open house at the facility recently, and I could see that Alan absolutely cared about this child. He was thrilled that she was living there, and he was very happy to find out that she could probably live there as an adult. It was tremendously important to Alan that this was a good place where he had placed her, where he had put her down finally to rest.

I guess that's an odd expression to use, to talk about her being put down finally to rest, because it's an expression that's usually associated with dying. What I mean by it is that that's where we hope she'll stay for the rest of her life. When she was living at home we were always aware it was a temporary situation and we were always worrying, "What will we do with her when she grows up?"

Even now, Alan is not totally satisfied: he wants to know what we'll do twenty years from now when he retires. Alan's chances of retiring are almost zero because he's a workaholic. But what if he retires twenty years from now and we move away—will they still take care of Annie, even though his wife can't come to all the board meetings and volunteer to work the flea market at the bazaar and everything else? That's what he's worrying about now. We don't even know if the facility will exist in twenty years. These things depend on government decisions and grants and new legislation and we have no way of knowing what's going to be available for the Annies of the future.

We're still having difficulties right here and now, though. The weekends when she's home are very difficult. Alan has a lot of *trouble getting through them, even though she's happy to see him; in fact she's so tickled to see him that she spends the whole weekend laughing. He thinks she's laughing at him, when she's just laughing with pleasure at seeing him.*

The home weekends are hard on me, too. I was used to her being at home; now I'm used to her not being at home. My whole life has to change when she comes home and I get angry about it. I sometimes wonder, "Well, why do you have to come home and mess up my whole life? Why can't you just stay there?" But at the same time I can't wait to see her. So we're torn.

We went on vacation this year and while we were away Annie got sick and had to be hospitalized. When we found out about it, Alan said, "We really have to go home." Alan could not accept her being in the hospital and his not being there. I was the one who said, "I cannot go home. If I go home I have to live with her twenty-four hours a day in a hospital room, and I can't do it." I knew what was waiting for me if I went home, and I didn't want it. It was easier to push it off on other people. It wasn't disappointment about having my vacation spoiled: I just didn't want to go home and face what I knew I'd have to face.

Joan has, she says, developed her protective mechanisms to a fine degree. She can fool most of the people most of the time because she appears to be very much in control, active, participatory, involved in Annie's life both at school and in the facility where she lives. A lot of it, she says, is a facade—an impressive facade, but a facade nonetheless. In fact, she says:

I think anyone who gives birth to a retarded child, or who has a retarded brother or sister, or even grandchild, is an absolute jackass if they say, "This is wonderful, look what God has given me." We hear a lot of talk about how our special children are God's gift. Well, you can keep it. If the people who talk like that want to keep my special child, my God's gift, that's fine. They can have her. I don't think a retarded child is a gift from God. I think it's a pain. I would have given anything in this world to have a normal daughter. Giving birth to Annie was the worst thing that has ever happened to me. I hope it will always be the worst thing that has ever happened to me. Every time I see her I am reminded of the fact that I can go to Saks Fifth Avenue and I can dress her up as a china doll but she will still be a retarded, speech-impaired, fifteen-year-old little girl who acts like a four-year-old. The only way I could sum up the whole experience is that it's a bitch.

As it happens, Joan has a singular explanation for why Annie was born retarded. She says:

I've never told anyone this except my husband and the psychiatrist that I see. When Alan was in Vietnam he was stationed near the Cambodian border, and the reports I was getting from him and the reports I was hearing on TV were totally different. I was sure that any day he would be killed.

So I bargained with God. I promised God that I would be very good and I would give up this child that I was carrying, that I was seven months pregnant with, if He would bring Alan home safely. And He did. There is no way that anyone can convince me I did not pull that one off. I had a normal pregnancy, and there was no indication that anything was going to go wrong. But she was born and brought him home within forty-eight hours. One month later, his base was bombed, totally wiped out, though it wasn't even worth bombing. Because he was in the service, Alan got the reports directly. He came in one day and said, "You will not believe it. I hope to God that there was no one left on the base, that they moved them off, because that entire area has been wiped out."

I believe that if I hadn't made that deal with God, Annie would be normal and Alan would be dead. I will probably never get over the guilt I have about that. I talk about it every time I go to the shrink. I think I spend the eighty dollars every time I see her just trying to reconcile my guilt. I'll probably think about it for the rest of my life.

In the movie Sophie's Choice, *a woman in a Nazi concentration camp is told that she must give up one of her two children, a boy or a girl, to die. She gave up the girl. When I watched the scene in which she talks to the two children, I went into a sweat and had to walk out and wait in the lobby until the movie was over. That's only the second movie I've ever walked out of in my life. The other was* The Deer Hunter, *which was about Vietnam and the prisoner of war camps. Alan sat there all excited, while I remembered the fears I had when he was in Vietnam, and I had to walk out of that, too.*

I swear, among my husband, myself, and our youngest son, who has been hit worse by all these problems than the other children, what we lay out in psychiatric bills would keep another family in luxury. But if I hadn't been in therapy while Alan was going through analysis, and if the therapist hadn't been able to straighten me out and tell me exactly why Alan was doing the things he was doing and what was going on, I don't think we'd have made it through these difficult years. I've preserved my family, but I couldn't have done it without help.

Joan believes that Annie was born handicapped for a particular reason. She also thinks that Annie's birth has been a source of good in other ways. She says:

A lot of studies were done on Annie when she was an infant. A paper was written from those studies and the medical world learned a great deal about the particular virus that caused her brain damage. This virus rarely affects a fetus, so there were just a handful of Annies around that the medical people could work with. They were very excited to have another one. One researcher was crazy with excitement. I'm sure she was a sweet person, but she could hardly expect me to get excited about having a retarded child, however much the medical world could learn from her. Anyway, the medical community did learn a lot about the condition that caused Annie's retardation.

I'm also sure that somewhere down the line someone has learned better how to deal with a speech-impaired, retarded child because of Annie. As for my other children, Michael has had a lot of difficulty because of Annie and the whole marital situation. He sees a psychologist on a regular basis, which means that he's got real problems. But he's learned something, and so have the other children. They've learned to have a bit more compassion for children who aren't normal, and they've passed this on to their friends. I take their friends with them when we go visit Annie in the facility where she lives now, and those kids and the other kids in the neighborhood are not afraid of handicapped people. One of Annie's baby-sitters has learned sign language so that she can talk to Annie, because Annie has so little speech that she needs signing to help her communicate.

I remember what my father said when Annie was born. He was a delightful man; I really loved him and it was a great loss when he died eleven years ago. When Annie was born he came to the hospital and said, "Well, Annie was given to us for a reason, so now let's see if we can measure up." Of course, at the time I didn't even know what a retarded child was. But I've never forgotten what he said, and the way he said it, and I still think, "Well, my God, if my father said that, I must do it." And I've tried. But I really feel I've let her down in a lot of ways—I could have tried harder with her.

There's not a day that I don't get up in the morning and wonder what she's doing. I've gotten used to that. But I've been struggling for so long that I'm burned out. Nobody believes me, though, when I say I'm burned out because I have a very strong facade, a very strong front.

Joan and Alan preserved their marriage through some very difficult years, and both are satisfied that placing Annie was in the best interests of everyone in the family. For Donna and Gary, placing Emily did not have the effect of bringing the family closer. In fact, it precipitated another crisis.

The couple's dream of being Mr. and Mrs. Average America began to crumble with the diagnosis of Emily's retardation. It collapsed altogether seven years later. Three weeks to the day after Emily's placement in a residential facility, an event that occurred not by design but by accident on the day the couple's third child was born, Gary told his wife that he didn't want to be married any more. Donna says:

Emily was supposed to be placed before the baby was born, but the placement was delayed and Meghan came three weeks early. So while I was in the hospital with the baby, Gary took Emily to the residential facility and left her there. Later, the staff told me that in all their years of watching parents bring their handicapped children through those doors they had never seen anyone so shattered by grief as Gary was that day.

Three weeks later, after our first visit to Emily in the facility, Gary announced that he no longer wanted to be married, and a couple of months later he left. He will swear to this day that his leaving had nothing to do with Emily, that he has, as he says, "worked Emily through," but I believe it had a great deal to do with her. The pain and the powerlessness he felt about Emily triggered all the emotions that he had never dealt with, and they spilled over onto me.

His leaving was not preceded by months of argument or discontent. I was happily pregnant—having the third child was his idea, not mine. All seemed to be well with our family. But for a year we had been trying to place Emily, looking at facilities and filling out applications. Although visiting the facilities clearly wrenched Gary's heart—the rows of little beds got him every time—he seemed resolute. I thought that placing her was a mutual decision, but I was wrong.

Looking back, I can see how having a handicapped child like Emily threatened Gary's defenses. Like a lot of men, he has vulnerability inversely tied to adequacy. He had to defend himself against feeling pain, showing grief, falling apart, and to do that he had to stay on top of his emotions and be in control at all times. The diagnosis of brain damage throws all that out the window. The deficit is beyond your control and soon, as the child grows and makes demands and becomes the pivotal point of the family's functioning, your life gets beyond your control, too.

Gary had to some extent stayed in control by denying the pain of losing Emily and the dreams we had for her. But the day I was in the maternity ward and Gary had to take Emily to the facility alone was the day his denial ended. He started to feel the pain that he'd been avoiding all those years, and the only way he could stay in control was to walk away from it.

The first time we visited Emily we said goodbye to her on the playground, surrounded by a dozen or so other damaged kids, some of them not very appealing to look at. In the car Gary cried and said, "She doesn't belong there with them." And that evening he said that he wanted to leave. It seemed that all he had left was anger. All the feelings that should have immobilized him years earlier, when we learned how badly she'd been damaged, were unleashed like a tornado, and they left not a brick of our family structure standing.

There I was, with Emily's bedroom emptied of her and her belongings, and our bedroom emptied of fifteen years of intimacy. I had a stunned four-year-old at my side, and in my arms an infant who to me at that moment was a total non-entity. I was devastated. This man who had doted on Emily, changed her diapers, fed her, answered her two-in-the-morning hysterics, gone to every school conference and doctor's appointment, had removed himself from her life.

That was three years ago. Gary and I are not divorced, but we are not together. Our situation is unresolved. Gary says he is "comfortable" now. He sees all the children regularly, but where Emily is concerned he is now an observer of her struggle for growth, not a participant in that struggle.

Erin and Meghan have obviously suffered two serious set-backs—the broken sister, and the broken family. At seven and three they already have a fair understanding of the pain involved in having a retarded sibling. But there's a flip side; they also know that we have been given something most people don't get a crack at, the chance to make a difference in a handicapped child's long road to adulthood. I sometimes wonder if, down their own road, it won't be harder for them to reconcile their father's leaving Emily than his leaving them.

"I have made her my profession"

As Katherine approaches her eighteenth birthday, Carol, her mother, looks back on the effect that Katherine's handicap has had on both their lives, on Carol's marriage to Katherine's father, and on Carol's second marriage. Carol believes that her own convictions about the way she wanted to raise her children and the kind of mother she wanted to be have colored her life dramatically. When Katherine contracted spinal meningitis in the hospital nursery, she was not expected to live. But she did live, and today she can do things that the neurologists say she should not be able to do because her brain damage is so extensive. Carol believes that her daughter has achieved as much as she has for two reasons and that she herself has paid a high price for Katherine's progress. Carol says:

Part of it is Katherine's personality. She is extremely determined. She's a fighter. I believe the other part of it has been all the work I have done. I have made her my profession. It has cost me one marriage, and I can see how it could cost me my second. But I can't do it any other way because I am the kind of mother I am. I can't do mothering, for either of my children, in a slipshod way. I'm a perfectionist. I'm very hard on myself, and mothering has been incredibly important to me.

I think my first marriage would have survived if Katherine had not been handicapped. She was what they call a high-risk baby, and we needed to start facing up to the possibility that she might be brain-damaged and dealing with that as a couple, as parents, right at the beginning. If that isn't done, if you're told to go home and not worry about it and maybe it won't happen, it takes a long time to accept the realities.

When her father first found out that Katherine was seriously ill, he was very upset. He had her baptized right away. He was very young. I was twenty three; I'd been out of college and worked for a year and a half before Katherine was born. He's two

172

years younger than I am. I was young for my age, but he was even younger for his, and I think it was beyond what he would ever be able to cope with. It wasn't so bad when she was a cute little baby, a very round, cuddly baby. People would stop in the street and say, "Oh, look at her, she's so healthy." (Inwardly, I would shake my head.) But he couldn't deal with the reality that she was handicapped and that she wasn't going to outgrow it.

The grandparents were the same, on both sides. It's still really beyond their comprehension. The Irish Catholic grandparents thought along the lines of "the poor afflicted—God's chosen ones." I don't personally buy those lines, or the ones, "What are you complaining about? She could have died. Aren't you glad she's alive?" or "It could be much worse." I don't buy any of those any more.

Katherine does not fit into any clear and simple category. She has incredible deficits, but she also has incredible high points. On an IQ test she has areas in which she scores well into the normal range and other areas in which she is profoundly retarded, as well as areas in between. So for her an IQ score is a meaningless statistic. My ex-husband couldn't deal with that. Looking back, I would say that's definitely why the first marriage failed. I don't think it would have been a great marriage, but there are few great marriages. It certainly had its low points but I was able to make it function for me so that I could survive it. The better it worked for me, though, the worse it became for him. I think the crucial factor was Tom's inability to accept the realities of Katherine's handicap.

We stayed married for twelve years. We divorced when Katherine was eleven and Christopher nine. My husband was sleeping around, which I had very strongly suspected but hadn't known. He said that we didn't respect him enough as a person. It was classic. Any psychologist would say that he hadn't enough respect for himself.

He never shared the running around I did for Katherine. I could count the times he'd ever taken her to a doctor or a clinic or talked to any kind of professional. And there were years and years of running, two or three times a week sometimes. He had not shared that, although that was not the way he saw it. In his mind, he was always there and always helpful; in his mind, he thought he accepted her.

By the time Katherine was eleven Tom had started seeing other women. Katherine was rapidly approaching adolescence, no longer a round cuddly baby. That's the point when a lot of parents of retarded children freak out. It's a crisis period with any child, and when the child is handicapped it's even worse.

When I remarried, my second husband did not realize what he was taking on, and I knew it. But I felt confident about him and where he was in his life. I also felt confident about Katherine. Raising her is a horrendous job, but there are also great rewards. She's very loving, affectionate, and fun, and there's a lot of good with her. I just felt it could work. I wasn't sure; I knew marrying again was a gamble for a lot of reasons, Katherine, of course, being one of them, and Christopher another.

Then there was the fact that Jack was a fifty-year-old bachelor. He'd never been married and, as you might say, he wasn't housebroken. That had me very concerned. I knew also that he had an incredible temper, which I wasn't sure I could live with, or even wanted to live with. There were also my own restrictions. I know I'm not pliable any more. I'm worn out by life. I can't be bending and giving any more. I feel like old underwear—a pair of old pants with the elastic stretched out.

But I went ahead and married Jack, mainly because I am a risk taker, because I really feel that if you don't take risks you don't ever win. You might also lose horribly, but if you never take those risks, you never even give yourself a chance to win.

We began to have problems after Jack's mother died. She was an incredibly dynamic lady. She was an important factor in everyone's life, including mine. I've missed her greatly, too. Jack withheld his grief and became very angry, with himself and with me. He's the one who really pushed for us to go into counseling, which I considered unusual because it's not usually the husband who will initiate counseling.

Jack and I were in marriage counseling for several months. I don't know how good it was; the more I went the less good I thought it was. We're not going any more; it just petered out. I wasn't very impressed by the counselor; I didn't think she had much insight. I said all along that if Jack wanted to work things out he was perfectly welcome to go into counseling, but why was I having to be dragged into it? I suppose it has helped our relationship, although I don't know why. Other people I've known have been very euphoric and buoyed, or at least cleansed, by it, but I came out of it feeling awful. It was a terrible drain on my time and emotions.

When we started counseling I was very panicked by the idea of our marriage falling apart—second failure, and all that. But after a few months I started feeling that if it went, it went. If it worked, it had to be more on my terms than it was. So now I'm not so panicked, but I don't know if that means I don't find it as threatening anymore, either.

If this second marriage were to fail I think Katherine would be a contributing factor, but not the main one. All the same, having

174

a retarded child is always a strain on a relationship. It's also a strain on me, physically, as well as emotionally and mentally. Sometimes both Christopher and Jack are jealous of the time and energy that Katherine takes away; it certainly limits a lot of things we want to do and the way we can do them. And Jack tells me, "You're a much easier person to live with on the weekends that Katherine isn't home."

Jack understands why my first husband couldn't handle the situation. But I think because I have landed on my feet, bounced back, there's a tendency to dismiss or override what it cost me. The last series of paintings that I did was based on my experiences as the mother of a handicapped child, and they're not paintings too many people would want to hang in their home.

It's hard for me even to imagine what I would have been like if Katherine had not been handicapped. I don't think I'd be as good a person. I don't think I'd have the fortitude or the value system that I have now. I might have been very unhappy. Now, when I do have good times I really appreciate them.

I was dealing with a critically ill child when I was only twenty-three, and I had to grow up very quickly. It helped me to sort life out and to find out what is important to me personally and what isn't, and that has helped me survive. I might get muddled up sometimes, but in the end I can say, well, even if this marriage to Jack were to fall apart, it would not be the end of the world. Life would go on, and I'd know how to pick up the pieces. I know what is important to me, and that is having inner peace.

My life is in a holding pattern right now. Chris is very demanding, and we're making a final push to help Katherine reach her potential in academic terms. My personal interests have had to be put aside. I don't always like it, but I don't necessarily resent it, because I'm conscious of what I'm doing. I am making choices. I might get tired and I might get resentful at times, but basically I know that there are other choices I could be making.

the single parent: on twenty-four hour duty

When the family that includes a child with a mental handicap falls apart the inevitable happens: one parent becomes the official care-giver for the handicapped child. The qualifying "official" here is significant because in some cases the physical disintegration of the family unit doesn't actually bring about much of a change in the role of the custodial parent. For all practical purposes that mother or father may have been parenting singly for years. There are parents who report that the break-up of the marriage, for all its attendant emotional, financial, and practical implications, actually made their task easier. The person who tries to satisfy the demands of a needy child *and* a needy spouse undertakes a spectacular (and sometimes impossible) juggling act. When the needy spouse leaves, at least it's possible to concentrate on the child.

That is not to say, of course, that single parenting is ever easy. Single parents of mentally retarded children recognize that it's a rough job that someone's got to do and can feel real pride in the knowledge that they're the ones that didn't quit. But self-congratulation only helps up to a point. Nearly all single parents who have a mentally impaired child acknowledge the need for a support system that would, ideally, be centered in a successful marriage. Single parents need a lot of support, and single parents of retarded children especially so. Carol, the mother of Katherine, says:

> I was a single parent for a little over three years. That doesn't sound long, but when I look back it seems like eternity. I found it very difficult. At first there were neighbors and friends willing to help out and watch Katherine for me, and I always insisted on paying them, which I think helped matters. But after a year or so they all said, in one way or another, "We can't handle this any more." They had their own children to take care of. After that I hired a lady to help for a while. When she went, there was no one left.

As Katherine approached adolescence I stopped being able to find baby-sitters or child care workers. I'd had a wonderful older woman, but one day she said to me, "You know, Carol, I couldn't sleep last night. It dawned on me that Katherine's going to start menstruating soon." That was the last time she sat for her. She couldn't face that reality. The cute little handicapped child is one thing, but the handicapped adult is not cute. The handicapped adult is unpleasant and offensive to most people.

I was living in a suburb where there were no community services, and I was working full time as a draftsman. I didn't have a private office, and I wasn't supposed to get personal phone calls. I punched a time clock. It was very demanding work, but I liked it, even though it was very high pressure and very hard on the eyes. I liked working, but having Katherine made it very difficult. She was at school during the day, but after school she was on her own for over an hour until Christopher got home from school at five. And it was awful.

While I was at the office I didn't think about it, or I tried not to. Although Katherine could use the telephone it wouldn't help because nobody could understand her. I wasn't supposed to make personal calls, but I did call her, and my employers looked the other way for me a lot of the time. They were fairly supportive. They didn't have to, but they even paid me for some of the time I spent on visits to the doctor and on other errands that I had to run for Katherine. I tried not to push it too hard. It would certainly have helped a lot if I'd had my own office and my own phone and a job where I didn't have to punch a time clock, where I could have made my own hours as long as I got my work done and they got their money's worth out of me. But I didn't have that kind of employment.

I'd get crisis phone calls, and every day I'd go home to a crisis. One day I walked in and there was blood on the walls and in the bathroom and I thought, "Oh, my God, she's cut her arm off." Actually, she'd been fiddling in the kitchen and had cut her finger slightly. But between the kitchen and the bathroom there was enough blood to make you think there'd been a major accident. Twice I came home and the house was filled with smoke: she had tried to cook dinner.

Another of Katherine's favorite things to do—and she'll still do it though she's better about it now—is to mess up the linen closet. She did it at least once a week. Every sheet and towel that I'd washed, folded, and put in the linen closet would be out on the floor, unfolded, walked on, in a pile. I've never been able to figure out why she did that; maybe she was mad at me because I wasn't there. Even now, I'm always punished for going out. She'll have gotten into something of mine. Now that she's older, it's usually my makeup or clothes.

It wasn't easy to have a job with all that going on. I blocked out a lot, but there were days when I didn't do my job very well. Chris called one day and said, "Mom, my bike has been stolen, what shall I do?" He was in tears and I couldn't even go home. I worked about a twenty-minute drive from my home—not bad, but a little farther than I was comfortable with. But by changing jobs I had raised my salary by a third, and money is money. You've got to eat, and I had two young mouths to feed. It was hard.

Lynne's marriage to Laura's father did not end in divorce. Her husband committed suicide when Laura, their only child, was ten. Whatever the circumstances that leave a parent to go it alone, however, the repercussions seem to be the same. Lynne says:

Being a single parent was awful. I did it for eight years, from the time Laura was ten to the time she was eighteen. During those years, fortunately, I happened to be getting a lot of support from the school. I know I couldn't have done it without them.

The hardest part was dealing with the behavioral problems day in and day out. There is hyperactivity involved in Laura's handicap, and she couldn't concentrate for long periods. I think I kept my weight down because I was always running after her. That in itself was hard because I had nobody to share it with. I felt that I had no freedom, that I couldn't even take a walk. I also felt extremely poor all the time I was alone. This was not realistic, and when I look back I realize that although I didn't have a lot of money, I had enough; I could have afforded to get away for a weekend, but I didn't allow myself that. Many of the tensions I was feeling were of my own making because I didn't give my head or body any relief.

When I began to show the strain I ran to therapy. I never stopped to think that I needed time off. I immediately became judgmental and told myself, "I am unable to handle all this because there is some deficiency in me: I'd better go to a therapist." That is a pattern I repeat because I have such high standards of performance for myself. I've got to be Superwoman, so the minute I run into a snag or feel pain because I'm not coping I don't say to myself, "Maybe you need time off or some fun in your life. You've been on the treadmill too long." Some other parents in that situation get away and forget for a bit. But if you're a parent like me your sense of responsibility is heightened to such a degree that you're on twenty-four hour duty. You don't even sleep well; you always have one ear open.

I'm convinced that it would have been absolutely different if Laura had not been handicapped. You become very protective because you know that with retarded children there's always a deficit; judgment is lacking, they're immature, they can't make their own decisions. Some of these feelings were unrealistic regarding Laura. She could have made some decisions. You don't have to coddle a retarded child as much as I have coddled Laura, but I don't think I even knew I was doing it. The mothering instinct is so strong that when you couple it with the fact that the child's handicapped you're like a mother bird with a nestling that can't fly very well. You hang on to that little creature. You keep it in the nest and don't let it fly because it's going to fall on its face, which God forbid.

When I remarried I tried very hard to integrate the two families, but I became very attuned to who was taking advantage of whom, and I tried to protect my daughter's rights. The other kids would go into her room, 'take her cigarettes, borrow her records, and I objected. My husband told me, "They're like that with everyone." Recently he said, "You're going to have to let her experience hurts now, while they may still be small; every hurt is a learning experience and you have to prepare her to get really hurt."

When I was a single parent I think what kept me from going completely to pieces (and Laura too) was that I had to work. The priorities were a roof over our heads and food on the table. I wasn't working to get out of the house because housework bored me. I had to work. I worked as a secretary in a large office and I found a surrogate family in the people there. Every time a crisis developed, I knew I could call up either the school principal or someone from work. I could never depend on my family. I never felt strong support or backing and never believed that my family would help me. That may have been wrong or right, but it was the way I felt, and so I always had to have a surrogate family, and it usually consisted of co-workers or neighbors.

One good friend of mine was a sort of Dutch uncle to Laura, and a few of my friends were fatherly towards her, which was good. These were all co-workers. The whole texture of my relationship with my co-workers changed when I remarried: I ceased to look on them as an emotional crutch. When I remarried I directed those feelings to my husband, and rightly so.

During the years I was single I was not actually lonely, but I was deprived of the caring companionship of a man. I had dear friends and I had acquaintances, but not what a woman in that situation needs—a very special, caring relationship. I never sought it, and it was a fluke that I remarried because I never went out of my way to look for the sort of relationship that might lead to it; in fact I shied away from it.

Caring companionship was not something I really had with my first husband. He was a very troubled individual who de-

pended on me for his emotional support. He died of his emotional illness. He committed suicide. Because of that experience I was not eager to be involved with a man, especially if I saw that he had any tics. I used to tell myself, I am taking care of myself one day at a time, and I don't need any problems. I've had enough problems. The remarkable thing is that I never really lost my feeling for men. I just didn't want a burden. I had carried, for thirteen years, the burden of a very immature man, not selfish, but involved only in himself, and he couldn't be any other way. I don't think I ever felt I wasn't loved, because the way he behaved was the only way he knew how to behave. He was good and kind, but he was self-destructive.

Glenn, the man I married, is the opposite of my first husband. He is very strong. I went through one year when I said, "Oh, isn't this wonderful. I don't have to make any decisions. I have someone to do it all." I became very passive. It was great. Of course, now I'm back to my old self.

Even so, every so often something comes up that I know I cannot share with my husband, something that I can discuss only with someone who is carrying, if not the burden of a handicapped child, then something else at that level of emotion. I could not share such things with someone who had no cross of their own to carry and would think that I'm strange or weird.

All the same, I'm glad I have sensitive people around as a backup. When you're dealing with an ongoing, unsolvable situation, the more backups you have the better you are able to survive. I think one reason it has been so hard is that I have a neurotic need to feel I can straighten things out. And I happen to have a kid that needs to be straightened out, but in her case it just can't be done.

Like Don, Pamela's father, George is in the relatively unusual position of being the male single parent of a child with a mental handicap. His son Shaun, now sixteen, is mildly retarded. Shaun and his twelve-year-old sister, Sheila, have lived with their father for eight years.* George says:

When we decided to have our first child my wife and I were having some difficulties, and I think we both hoped that having a child would take some of the pressure off the relationship. My wife had an extremely difficult time accepting even the possibility that our son was not normal. She had emotional problems of her own, and I have a fairly severe speech problem. When a child

---

*In this family's story, names have been changed in order to protect the family's privacy.

with a mental handicap came along I think she felt it was too much.

It was first suggested that Shaun was not normal when he was about eighteen months old. He came down with pneumonia and had to be hospitalized, and his pediatrician suggested that while the child was in the hospital he would like to do some neurological tests. Shaun had been slow sitting up and standing; he was crawling before he was two, but I don't think he walked until he was two. His eyes weren't coordinated and he looked a little bit odd.

The doctors ran a whole battery of tests, including bone marrow and chromosome tests, and I was told later that they were trying to determine if a retardation syndrome was present. At the time they wouldn't say yes or no, and that problem lasted for years. Doctors kept telling us, "Wait and see."

After Shaun's birth my wife had severe difficulties. Some was post-partum depression; she was also having real problems in her relationship with me. It was a severe crisis, and I had to decide whether to seek psychiatric treatment for her. I decided against it, and that's what pushed us into a nondenominational church community where we stayed for a number of years. We moved there when Shaun was about six months old. If we hadn't made that move and if my wife hadn't had some of the pressure taken off, she would probably have left a lot sooner.

The kind of communal living arrangement we were in meant that a lot of the responsibility for the children was assumed by the community. I hoped that if my wife had that kind of support we could keep the marriage together. I worked at whatever job I was assigned, and that's where I learned accounting (all my schooling had been in English literature).

In that community we had our second child. At that point I fully expected that we would stay there, that my wife would have the protection of the environment and we would stay together. I was not an only child, so it seemed logical to have at least one more child. It was as simple as that.

The support system that the community offered was helpful to my wife, but the point came when I decided that it was time to put the children first, and that meant leaving even though my wife was opposed to the idea. I did not feel it was a suitable place to raise children, particularly a child with the kind of problems that Shaun now clearly had. He was nearly six years old and on the point of starting school, and there was no question but that we had to leave.

It was obvious that Shaun wasn't ready to start in a regular school, and we were referred to a school for learning disabled children. At that time we ran Shaun through another battery of tests, and the doctors tended to the view that he was mildly retarded. *The school didn't agree and continued to treat him as learning disabled, which led to a lot of problems later.*

After we left the communal environment where we had been living, and my wife had to assume more responsibility, she began to feel the pressure. She left home, but came back after about ten months. She stayed for six months but after that she left for good and eventually we got divorced. There was no question that the children would stay with me. Considering my wife's emotional history I couldn't leave them with her. It wasn't really an issue.

I have been a single parent for eight years, and it has taken its toll. I had to quit my job to go back to school and get my degree in accounting. It had gotten to be more than I could handle to work my job, which carried a lot of responsibility, and take care of the children. Recently I've been working independently, which helps me, except during the tax season, to have some flexibility in my schedule, and in the immediate future I don't see the possibility of going back to a straight nine-to-five job. I was lucky to have the economic resources that allowed me to make that choice.

The first year after my wife left I must have had a sitter: it's hard to remember, and some of it I've blocked out. Then the children spent a summer with my sister, and after that I arranged a work exchange with a university student, and he was here for a couple of years. After that I was never able to locate anyone who would live in. I had the children in before- and after-school programs until Shaun was about twelve and asked if he could stay home in the mornings. I wondered if he could contrive to get himself to school on time, and he was able to do that.

The doctors have finally concluded that Shaun is mildly retarded and has probably been educated beyond his capacity because he spent all those years in a school for learning disabled children—which also included a number of kids who were emotionally disturbed. In that school he fell farther and farther behind, and he had difficulty getting along with the other students. He was aware that he was the slowest one in his class, and the other kids teased him. By the time he was of high school age he had had such a bad year that the school said they would make a place for him only until the district found an alternative. They suggested a school for mentally retarded children, which they weren't sure would take him because he might be too high-functioning. However, the special school did feel that there were programs he could benefit from, and on that basis they accepted him. It has turned out to be one of the best things that ever happened to him. The change in him has been remarkable, a complete turnaround, because now he is happy.

The children see their mother regularly, usually one day a week, and they get along well with her. However, they don't get along well with each other. Some of that may have to do with

182

Shaun's handicap. Sheila may resent the extra attention he gets. They have had fights to the point where the school social worker suggested that we all get together to see if we could talk some things through. I don't think Shaun ever intends to hurt Sheila, and I have stressed that she shouldn't antagonize him because he might hurt her unintentionally. Basically, I think they care for each other. When Sheila went to camp Shaun missed her, and when he's away she misses him, although she won't admit it.

If Sheila ever feels over-responsible it's partly because of her trying to be the lady of the house, and I think that is a difficult situation for her. She has also had to deal with kids telling her that her brother is retarded. I've only heard her say anything about it one time, when they were watching a TV program. There was a commercial that had to do with the retarded and Shaun made some derogatory remark. Sheila said, "Shaun, do you know what retarded is?" I forget what his answer was but she said, "You are." I think Shaun has actually known that himself since he was quite young.

I have sometimes thought about remarrying, but it would take a very integrated person to deal with the situation here. To begin with, it would have to be someone who could deal with Shaun's handicap and my speech problem, and then with Sheila who still has a whole lot to work through with her mother and would probably have a hard time relating to someone else. So remarrying is not among my immediate plans.

how Sandra found a mother

Madelon comes at the single parent issue from a totally different perspective. She chose to be a single parent, and she chose to adopt Sandra, a handicapped child. She wonders if perhaps single parenting may not be easier than trying to raise a handicapped child and give equal time to other family members as well.

Madelon was approaching forty and was giving serious

thought to whether or not she was satisfied with what her life was offering her when she came across a newspaper clipping that suggested a way of changing her life. She says:

I've got a very good job and a good income, and I've never married and probably never will. I was doing things that weren't really meaningful to me in terms of the time and money invested, and I began to think that when you're single and don't have anything outside of yourself you can get very self-centered and self-involved. I could see it happening to other people and I guess I didn't want it to happen to me. I was thirty-nine when I started having these thoughts. Forty was just down the road and I considered what it would be like to be fifty and still in the same role and the prospect wasn't too thrilling. I came across that newspaper story at just the right moment.

It was an article about the difficulty of finding adoptive homes for teenagers and older children. It didn't call them "hard to place" and I don't recall any specific reference to handicapped children, but I decided to check into it. I went through a session with a group of would-be adoptive parents in which we examined our attitudes about ourselves, and the people from the agency talked about what it's like to adopt—the reality of it. There were three or four couples in the group, and three single women. One couple already had children; one couple couldn't have any of their own. One of the single women was a nun who had left the convent and was interested in having a child.

Once that was over I went through all the procedures to become licensed for foster care. You need a license to have a child in your home, because the child is in foster care with you until the adoption becomes final. Once I was licensed, it was a matter of looking for a child. I was given forms to fill out, and I had to state which characteristics I would find acceptable in a child and which I would not.

A lot of the characteristics on the list had to do with problems kids develop because of emotional instability—things like wetting the bed, temper tantrums, lying, stealing, running away, being defiant, being uncommunicative, and so forth. Then there was a section about problems you would be willing to accept, and I don't remember if retardation was even there. It probably was, but I didn't circle it. I said I would accept epilepsy because my father's brother had had it. No one ever talked about it, but he must have been retarded, too. He was always very child-like, and I know that he lived at home although I doubt if he went to school. When my grandfather died he was institutionalized, and I think he died not long after. I thought, why wouldn't I accept something that had existed in my own family? I also said I would consider a child with orthopedic problems, but not a child who was blind or deaf because I thought that would be too much to handle. From my answers, and from interviewing my family and friends, the agency decided that I would be better off with a child who needed to be brought out rather than one who was defiant.

It's very depressing to flip through the state register and look at the children who are up for adoption. There are very severely handicapped children who need homes, but I decided that wasn't for me because I was working. How could I handle a child like that? What could I do if there was a problem? I kept thinking that if I didn't have to work and could do this full time, then I could take care of a child in a wheelchair, or whatever. But I had to be practical.

Also, the age group I put down was six to eight years, which was getting away from what had originally interested me—the older children. I was hearing about teenagers acting out and I thought, all I need is some twelve-year-old that's decided to be promiscuous. I didn't stipulate that I wanted a girl. I said it didn't matter, and right up to the end I felt that I wouldn't care if the child was a boy or a girl. I have a feeling that if it had been a boy I'd probably have made the adjustment, but I'm comfortable that Sandra is a girl.

I kept looking through the registers and there didn't seem to be anything I could handle, but the agency director kept telling me that these things just pop up and you never know from day to day what's going to come across the desk. I waited a year and a half after I was licensed. Periodically they came up with something and I always gave it consideration—twins down in Texas, a girl in Wisconsin—but nothing really fit.

I didn't feel that the agency was doing enough, so I started going down there and looking at the book. I would skip over anything that said cerebral palsy, because in my ignorance I was confusing it with multiple sclerosis and thought it was degenerative. Finally the director of adoptions explained to me that cerebral palsy is damage to the central nervous system; it can occur before birth, at birth, after birth, in an accident or whatever, and whatever damage is done doesn't get any worse.

That changed it in my mind. I went back and looked at the cases where it said "mild cerebral palsy." There were three children with that description, and one of them was Sandra. I think I'd looked at her before but been put off because I'd already decided I couldn't take a blind child and her description also said she was legally blind. I didn't know what "legally blind" meant, and again the director of adoptions had to explain that it doesn't mean total blindness. She said that quite often children who are legally blind don't have any particular problems when they grow up. For example, they may not be able to recognize someone across the street but they can see that someone is there. It's not as if they can't see where they're going.

It said that Sandra was a very loving child, attractive, and improving remarkably. We called down to the city where she was living and talked to her social worker, who sounded very positive, but the director warned me that you have to be careful because sometimes a social worker will be so eager to place a child that she'll distort things. We got more information and I arranged to take Sandra somewhere for the weekend. I travelled down on a Friday and went with the social worker to pick Sandra up from her foster mother, whom Sandra called "Grandma." The social worker was taking Sandra to get glasses. What I remember about Sandra was that she seemed very small, was sweet to her Grandma, and had a nice manner about her. She was interested in things and talkative with the social worker. By the time we got to the optometrist she was talking to me a little bit, and looking at me.

She was very patient in the office, but all the time I felt that the doctor was treating her like an alien. I'm sure he was a decent man, but there wasn't the same feeling that there would have been if she'd been a kid going in there with her mother. He said things like, "Well, you know, with kids like this . . ." and I thought, "She's not a kid 'like this,' she's a little girl." I got very defensive for her. Apparently on public aid you're limited, so she couldn't get sunglasses, which she wanted. The optometrist said, "She can get clip-ons." He picked out a frame for her and it was like saying, "Well, here's a cheapo." The frame he chose didn't look good on her but he was going to make her have it all the same. I protested and said, "Let's see what else you've got." Then we found a pair that looked halfway decent.

The first thing I did when the social worker left and Sandra and I went off on our weekend was to take her to the drugstore and buy her sunglasses.

I think I had already decided I wanted to adopt her by the time we'd gotten out of the eye doctor's office. I didn't try to push it with her, though. I told her that we were going to spend some time together to decide if we wanted to live together. I knew I had to be very careful because she'd been through a difficult time. A year earlier the agency found out that her foster father had cancer. They yanked her out of this foster home where she'd been since she was two and quickly moved her in with a family that had a child and was thinking about adopting another one. But the chemistry wasn't right; she didn't get along with them. I don't know exactly what happened, but they dropped her off back at her foster mother's, bag and baggage. Supposedly it was just for a vacation, but Sandra knew they were getting rid of her. That happened during the summer, and her foster father died in October. Then I appeared, and she came with me the following March, when she was twelve-and-a-half. Her foster mother wanted her to stay another summer. For her it was like losing her own daughter.

The first weekend we spent together we hit it off. I had brought Sandra some presents, and letters from my nieces, and she got a kick out of that. On Sunday the social worker came to pick her up. We had lunch, and then I left, having arranged that the following week I'd fly down and bring her home for the weekend. I made sure she understood that I wasn't leaving for good, but I didn't say that we were going through with the adoption. Later the social worker told me that as soon as they were alone Sandra said, "You know, she didn't tell me she was going to take me." She'd kept track of that.

The second weekend we spent together I explained that we were supposed to be sizing each other up, but that night when she was in the bathroom, getting ready for bed, she said, "Well, if you're gonna be my mother, you gotta come into the bathroom and help me wash my face and comb my hair and get me ready for bed." Then she started calling me "mother." It was that fast.

When I told the director of the agency that we wanted to go ahead with the placement she said, "You're going to have to be careful. Go down and pick up her stuff and bring her right back home, because at this point if you give her any reason to think you're abandoning her she might have a tantrum or get hysterical." So I drove down and picked up her things, then we spent the night at a hotel and in the morning we drove back together.

That's when reality finally set in for Sandra about leaving her foster mother. She started having awful nightmares about her Grandma being killed in an automobile accident or a fire. Then she started dreaming that I was killed. It was a devastating period and went on for months.

As soon as we got home—within a matter of days—we started having awful fights. I can't remember what started it but Sandra was feeling feisty and I said, "Do you want to hit me?" and she really went after me, she wouldn't stop hitting me. It was awful; I didn't know what to do with her. I tried to get hold of the people at the agency but I couldn't reach them. Finally I got hold of the family doctor. I was hysterical. He tried to soothe me and I kept crying into the phone. I said, "I'm exhausted; I don't know what to do with her." He said, "She's having a tantrum, get behind her. This is very important: you have to concentrate very intently on what you're doing. Get behind her and hold her down; do not allow her to hurt you. Tell her you're not going to let her hurt you or herself." Well, I did manage to hold her down. Fortunately, she was a lot weaker than she is now, so I was able to do it.

A day or two later the agency arranged for a fellow from the Cerebral Palsy Foundation to visit us. Sandra was still feisty and I still didn't know what to do about it. I'd had her just a couple of days and I was beaten already. This fellow was very good. He talked to me and then he talked to Sandra, and he was appalled at me. He said, "How did you get into this? You're the parent, she's the child. Get control." He was able to help get things in perspective for me and Sandra.

Later we got into some pretty heavy stuff about her handicaps. I can't remember exactly how the subject came up. I think Sandra said, "I don't even know why I don't see very well." I found out that she'd never had the nerve to broach the subject with anybody. I tried to explain to her what cerebral palsy was. I was the big expert, of course—I'd only just found out about it myself. Instant mother. I tried to explain what I knew, and how it could happen and what it meant. That's been an ongoing thing. She's done a lot of talking about it. She'll say things like, "I know it could be a lot worse, but a little cerebral palsy can sure cause a whole lot of trouble." She's trying to get it into perspective.

Sandra was a victim of child abuse in that when she was born she had medical problems that needed attention, and that attention was not given. After she was born she had seizures and her mother was instructed to give her medication, but for a full eighteen months Sandra wasn't given the medication. They didn't find out until she was back in the hospital.

Sandra's mother finally abandoned her. She left her with a neighbor. Before that there had been reports that Sandra was sleeping in a box, and neighbors said that she had fallen off a porch. After her mother abandoned her, she was put in the hospital, suffering from malnutrition. They said she was severely retarded. She'd had a very bad time. It's almost destructive to dwell on the details.

Another thing Sandra didn't know anything about was her original family. We found out through the state that she had a brother who was a year older. He was taken away from his mother when he was six months old and placed with a family who subsequently adopted him. As far as anybody knows, he has no handicaps. Sandra said she had found out that her foster mother wasn't her real mother by overhearing a telephone conversation, but maybe they had told her when she was younger, and she forgot. Anyway, she says it was a big surprise to her. When she came to live with me, the lady from the agency, who visited us periodically, brought Sandra's original birth certificate and we sat down and told Sandra everything we knew. Sometimes Sandra acts very child-like, and at other times she acts very grown up and she was very grown up about this family stuff. She was all business-like; she had questions. She wanted to know her mother's name, how old she was, where she was born, who her father was and what he looked like. She wanted to know if her father and mother were still married and if they had any other children. She had a fantasy that her father and mother were still together, but it didn't seem likely because the records show that at a certain point her mother was with someone else.

Adopting a child was very different from what I had anticipated. Friends told me that I was going to have a drastic change in life-style, and I said, "Like what?" I did not perceive what it was really going to be like. First of all, it began to be a big hassle to get to work on time. Sandra can pretty much get herself dressed, but she does need help with combing her hair. She'll throw her clothes over her head, and if you comb her hair before she gets her clothes on it gets all messed up, and I like her to get out of the house looking decent. And then her hair has to be washed every night because it's oily, so while she's getting her hair washed she might as well get in the tub, and then when she's in the tub she wants to listen to music. She has no conception of time, so she's in there half an hour and yells because she doesn't have enough time to play. I used to spend three hours a day with the physical things of dressing her, and getting her hair washed and set, and craziness like that.

Then there was all the trauma with sleeping, and that took a long time to straighten out. I couldn't just plunk her in bed at night and be on my own. The television had to be off. Finally I decided that it was easier for me to go to bed at the same time as she did so that she could go to sleep.

For a long time I wasn't working at my normal level of efficiency because I was totally immersed in caring for her. She was a needy child in many ways and work was just not a priority item. Luckily, someone was able to take my job when I went off for the month that Sandra first came to live with me and wasn't in school yet.

I had been under the impression that she could go into school right away, but it was bad timing because spring vacation came along. I'd been told that when she moved in I should let the school people know and give them her papers. But the papers didn't come and they wouldn't even look at her until they got all the records. They wouldn't do any testing to see where she should go to school. Eventually I camped on the doorstep of the director of special education and said, "Look, this child is having six-hour nightmares. She has nothing to occupy herself with, and I want her in school." Everyone told me it's not that simple, but finally they tested her and the psychologist said he felt a special school would be the place for her. The alternative would be junior high school, but he felt that the junior high was too large. He said, "Her balance isn't good, and she doesn't see very well, and if she were my child I would not like the idea of a couple hundred kids running down the stairs at the same time and knocking her over."

We visited the special school and Sandra spent some time in class and loved it. Then we went to look at the junior high, but Sandra wanted to stay at the special school so we went back there for a conference. I hadn't faced up to the fact of her retardation; in fact I probably still haven't faced it because I still don't really understand what her functioning level is—it's all over the map. I know there's a problem, but it's hard to pin down what it is or how serious it is.

I'm happy with the school placement. The other day I asked, "How would you like to be in a regular high school?" and Sandra said, "I'm learning just fine where I am," as if to say, "Don't you do that to me." I think the school she's in is the best one for her.

It took my breath away when we had the original conference and the psychologist who had tested Sandra said that she was "borderline trainable mentally handicapped." I couldn't rationalize that with her verbal skills. Since that time I've come to understand better her vision problem and the impact that has on her. Quite often children with vision problems were thought to be retarded when they weren't. I know that she loses a lot because she doesn't have good vision, but that doesn't explain everything by any means. I can see that she is sometimes confused about things. Math is supposedly her strong suit, but she gets confused if you go too fast. Occasionally when I tried to teach her at home she would say, "There's no sense in such a thing," when it was something she couldn't comprehend. Or she'd say, "My teacher hasn't taught me that yet, you're not supposed to do it. Let the teacher do it, she teaches better." So I just backed off.

How do you make up for the damage done to a child who was, to all intents and purposes, left in a box? How do you distinguish the results of that from retardation? Maybe now she's doing some catching up. In addition to the harm from that early period, she has the trauma of knowing that she doesn't really have a family. Sandra's also told me some very painful things about her earlier experiences in mainstream schools. She remembers going up to children in the playground and saying, "Do you want to be my *friend?" and having them laugh at her and run away. Sometimes they'd beat up on her. And she's a fighter, so she used to have fist fights. In her mind, the teacher would always punish her even when the fight was started by someone else. I take that with a grain of salt, but I do know it was difficult for her. How much can you learn in a classroom, knowing that when the bell rings and you go out to recess you're going to have a fight with all those kids? And yet, for all I know, she was working very hard in school and those teachers were very good and she's come as far as she has because of that.*

In any case, now when she's at school, unless she's having a bad day because of worries about one thing or another, she's working hard. For a while we went to a psychologist to help her with her emotional problems, and they seem to be straightening out very well, which should improve her concentration in school. She's also busy with outside activities that stretch her in different ways.

Sandra would love me to get married. She dreams about my having a boyfriend (although now she's getting to be more interested in her own boyfriends) and she sometimes pushes the idea. It seems that she would love a father, and I can't imagine that Sandra at this stage would be difficult for anyone to take on—everybody loves her. Realistically, I doubt that I'll ever marry. It's not uppermost in my mind. It would be nice to have some help, but that's not a very good reason to get married. Anyway, I'm not sure if husbands are a help or just more work. It would be nice to believe that if I were married I'd be able to come home and have someone say, "You're tired, sit down and rest and I'll take care of things." But that's not what happens in most marriages, and I've got no reason to believe that it would happen in mine.

When your child is having a six-hour screaming nightmare, how do you juggle that with a husband, or another child? A handicapped child's needs are so overwhelming initially that I can't imagine trying to keep everybody's needs met at the same time. I imagine that you would run into conflicts about how much should be done. My personality is such that although I'm not a loner, I've always been able to handle things pretty much on my own. The psychologist said that I'm the type that will see it through no matter how difficult it gets. But he was also telling me that I don't have to do everything. A child like Sandra has so many needs that you can immerse yourself in them twenty-four hours a day, and you have to watch out for that.

One of my goals is to give Sandra certain social skills. She's interested in sports and music, and it has been important to me that she should learn to do something well. I have pushed her to get some confidence in those things that she's apparently able to do well, like swimming. She loves to run and to skate. I've urged her into the choir at church, so that she is a little bit main-streamed and she's getting some music, and she loves that. She's also learned a little about singing, and a little bit of piano and guitar. I remember my aunt telling me that children like to be with other children, but because of Sandra's vision problems she can't easily run out and find friends, so I have had to do it by finding the special recreational programs where she can be with her friends.

I don't feel overwhelmed. None of her problems is that over-whelming if you take each one of them individually, but you do need to take the difficulties one at a time. Sandra is now seven-teen, and I can see the fruits of all this work both at school and socially. She's just been elected president of the student council at school. She's at the point where she has almost caught up to where she should be. She's really able to use her energy constructively, instead of just trying to deal with her emotional problems. I feel that all this is a great accomplishment, on her part and on mine. I can finally sit back and say, "We're doing fine." I can even take some time for myself. For a long time my own activities went by the board, but things are easier now. My concentration has improved. I've joined a health club, and I take an eight- or nine-mile hike on Sunday mornings while Sandra is still in bed. I want to do more, but at least I'm able to do that.

PART THREE

letting go

but when she leaves home, where will she go?

According to psychologists, the three major crises for parents of a mentally retarded child occur at the time of diagnosis, at puberty, and when the child leaves home. In Victoria's case, the onset of the second crisis provoked concern about the third. As adolescence transformed my shy flower into a young hellion, I spent much time wondering how I was going to survive living with Victoria until she was twenty-one, the age at which she would complete her schooling and, presumably, move into some kind of job and some kind of alternative living arrangement.

By the time was was fifteen it was clear the Victoria was not the sort of teenager who relished the restrictions of the parental home. I used to tell myself that things could be worse: if she were not retarded, and therefore subject to far more control than a nonhandicapped girl of her age, she would probably be staying out all night, experimenting with drugs, getting pregnant, and doing a lot of other unacceptable teenage things. As it was, she was just making our lives (and hers) miserable, and I mentally dropped the twenty-one age limit to eighteen. If I could keep her at home until then, I figured, I'd be doing well.

The obvious sequel to this line of thinking was to consider where Victoria would live if she didn't live at home. I began to pay a lot more attention to what are known in the field of mental retardation as residential alternatives. The prospect was not exciting. Paradoxically, one of the reasons that parents of mentally handicapped young people spend a disproportionate amount of time worrying about the future is that the options are so few. Although we are past the days when the only options were the parental home or an institution— and probably the kind of institution that would be an unacceptable alternative for any family whose child could stay home—there is still a serious shortage of places for a retarded person to go upon reaching the age at which a non-handicapped person would begin to live independently.

Between the two extremes of the family home and a large institution are various living arrangements where normal independence, as far as the individual can handle it, is reinforced by appropriate supervision and support services. These arrangements bear names like "supportive living arrangement," "community living facility," or "community-based small group home"—unfamiliar terms that rapidly become part of the vocabulary as your retarded child grows up.

Although there may be living facilities available, they may not be suitable for your child. Some facilities demand a high level of social and self-help skills, putting them out of reach for any except mildly retarded people. Some require that prospective residents be responsible for their own medication, which can be a major drawback for those with epilepsy or other conditions requiring regular medication. Some facilities require a degree of physical mobility that excludes those with severe gross motor impairments. Some places charge a high monthly fee which many families cannot afford. Other living arrangements are fine up to a point but fail to supply what you actually want for your child. The best living facilities have waiting lists that appear to extend from here into the next century. And, of course, there's an added catch: you may locate a facility that's perfect for your child except that your child doesn't want to go, and the facility won't accept the kid unless he or she accepts the placement too.

One reason that there are so few community based living facilities for mentally handicapped people is that many members of the community don't want retarded people as neighbors. Such people are abstractly in favor of deinstitutionalization and of community living arrangements for handicapped people—but not on their block or, sometimes, even in their town. In order to open a small group home, which is the most home-like living arrangement and the one that most parents of children like Victoria, given the choice, would probably opt for, it may be necessary to circumvent zoning regulations that limit the number of unrelated people who can live together in one house. Getting past such regulations can take years. When parents of retarded youngsters who are going to need a place to live hear about a perfectly good, operating group home being forced by community opposition to close its doors, their feelings tend to approach the homicidal.

A few years ago such an instance occurred in a suburb close to where we live. A local association for retarded people acquired a six-bedroom home in a district zoned for single family residences. Two retarded young men and two house parents moved in, and the association wanted to move two more young men into the unoccupied bedrooms. This meant that the "family" would consist of more than four unrelated persons and the association would require a special use permit in order to keep the home in operation. They did not get the permit because a group of local residents successfully blocked the proposal on the grounds that such an arrangement would lower their property values and set a precedent for other institutional facilities on their home turf.

It's hard for parents with retarded children to take seriously the claims that such opposition groups are solely concerned with zoning issues, and that it matters not a jot whether their prospective neighbors are mentally handicapped or not. When you have a retarded child there's no way to avoid the knowledge that many people don't want to get too close to those who are retarded. Translated into subjective terms, there are a whole lot of people who don't want my daughter living next door.

I wrote a newspaper story about this incident, and in the course of my research I called the administrator of a group of town homes for mildly retarded people in our locality. I knew that the opening of those homes had been stalled for years because of opposition from neighbors. Even now that the homes were established and accepted as part of the neighborhood, the administrator didn't want to talk about the issue in a newspaper story. She preferred, she said, that they keep a low profile and not make any noises that might disturb their hard-won peace.

In the newspaper article I pointed out that it sometimes appears to those of us intimately involved in the subject that community attitudes towards mental handicaps have survived whole and entire from the Dark Ages. Tired old misconceptions persist, one of them being a lack of distinction between mental retardation and mental illness. Mentally retarded people, I said, do not usually engage in overtly dangerous, hostile, or anti-social behavior. This got me into trouble with advocates for the mentally ill, who claimed that I was denigrating the population they served. That, of course, was not my intention, but the truth is that community opinion frequently fails to distinguish between the two conditions and to realize that while mental illness can make a person dangerous to himself or to others, this is not usually true of mental retardation—certainly not in the case of retarded people who are potential clients for small group homes.

In fact, young people like Victoria are deliberately trained to a high degree of social competence. They are drilled constantly in socially appropriate behavior. They are, in essence, taught to conform. We know that mentally retarded people have to survive in an ungenerous world and we do everything in our power to help them become acceptable to a society which, unfortunately, often exhibits towards them a marked lack of compassion or imagination.

Those who oppose living facilities that are integrated into the community fail to grasp an essential point: retarded persons *are* part of the community. They have a right to live in homes of their own, near their families, just like anyone else. They may need certain support systems that other people do not, but basically the appropriate place for a home-like living facility is in the neighborhood. Small group homes are, in fact, what residential zoning is all about: the building of families. The whole point is to give people whose options are limited by disability the chance to live as normal a life as possible in a home of their own.

Perhaps the saddest part of the whole business was that the two young men who lived in the group home threatened with closure were long-term residents of the suburb. Everything was fine while they lived with their parents; they weren't lowering anybody's property values then. But when they wanted to make an independent home for themselves their own community said no.

One neighbor opposed to the home was quoted as saying that single-family zoning was one of the features they paid for when they bought their homes. I had the bright idea that I'd go to see her and tell her about Victoria, and she and all her fellow thinkers would immediately have a change of heart. By telephone the woman told me that she didn't have time to see me and that she wished the subject were closed. I could wish the same thing, but from my side of the fence it looked then, as it looks now, as though the subject will be wide open for many years to come.

198

It also occurred to me that I would like to feel that my daughter's neighbors, whoever they might turn out to be, would be generous and open-minded people. There may be those who don't want Victoria living next door to them, but there are also those who don't meet my criteria for whom I want living next door to Victoria.

(Fortunately, this story had a happy ending. That group home did stay open, and several others have opened in the same area since then.)

So as Victoria proceeded at a gallop through her teens, I was forced to look more and more closely into what exactly the outside world had to offer a young person like her, and I discovered that the parents of all her young friends were beginning to develop anxiety symptoms along exactly the same lines.

how Bernie made a home for his boys

Bernie is the father of three sons, the eldest of whom is thirty and all of whom are retarded. As his boys were growing up and it became clear that there was really no place for them to go when they reached the age to leave home, Bernie set about making a place for them to go. He founded a community living facility for mentally handicapped young men and women on the outskirts of a major metropolitan city. His "village" is now home to his own three sons as well as about sixty other retarded people between the ages of eighteen and forty. The facility, of which Bernie was the director for ten years and with which he is still intimately involved, is a pleasant, friendly, comfortable place. Parents from all over the state are hell-bent on getting their youngsters a place there. Bernie says:

When our oldest son, Artie, was born, there was no indication of any retardation. He is the highest functioning of the three, and he is what you would call educable. The pediatrician did not notice anything out of the ordinary; he was just a little slow in walking and talking. With our second son, who is moderately retarded, the doctor noticed slower development than is normal, and he called our attention to it. By this time my wife, Alta, was pregnant with our third. We didn't think our second son's slow development was particularly significant, but we did take him to another doctor who looked at him for about thirty seconds and told us that he was retarded. That hit my wife right between the eyes, and me, too. When you hear that word, especially if you're young, as we were, you get extremely frightened. You don't know what to do.

Fortunately, we had a great pediatrician. He sat down with us, explained the situation, and sent us to a stack of doctors—an audiologist, an ophthalmologist, a neurologist, people like that—so that we could get a better insight into what was happening.

When our third son, Gary, was born, we already knew that Barry was handicapped, and meanwhile Artie had started kindergarten and we found out that he was also having a problem. As soon as the newest youngster came along we had him checked. The doctor said it was too soon to be sure, but he was fearful of the same thing.

In those days, of course, the retarded were still in closets. Eventually, they did come out of the closet, thanks in part to the Kennedy family and presidential mandates and a lot of new laws. People know more about handicapped persons now, and are more accepting—although not as much as we'd like them to be, of course.

As far as we know, the cause of our sons' retardation is genetic; at least, that is what the doctors surmised. It took me quite a few years to accept the fact that I had handicapped sons. When your kids are born you think they're going to grow up to be President of the United States, president of a large corporation, great scholars, great athletes. I was athletic when I was in school. I was very active in school functions, and clubs, and fraternities. What you want for your kids, basically, is that they have a good childhood and a good life. And when you have three, and they're all retarded, that's a considerable thing to face up to. It took me a long time to come to terms with it, and those first years were extremely difficult for me. Then, as they grew older, I accepted it.

With my wife it was different. It was instant love for the kids; they were her whole life. If it hadn't been for her I don't think we'd have done as well as we did. She was the backbone of the family. I was out working, making a living, and when I came home I tried to help her as much as I could, but she had the brunt of it all day. She had to go shopping with them, take them places, as you do with kids. We never kept our kids in, we never closeted or hid them. If we had family functions we took our kids.

It wasn't always easy. My wife's family took to the kids like a duck takes to water, but it was a little more difficult for my folks. They thought it was something that the children would outgrow, like an allergy. I think the word retardation frightened them to the point where they never even wanted to speak about it. I had a hard time with them, because they didn't fully comprehend the situation until the boys got older. Then they could see that they were good, lovable kids. They were just a little slower than everybody else, that's all.

I was in the insurance business as my sons were growing up, and as they got older I realized that I had better get involved in their futures. I had gone through the state institutions that were just about the only options available for mentally handicapped people, and I went home to my wife and I told her our boys were never going to live in a place like that. But there were no alternatives. There were a few custodial places; they provided baby-sitting. I wanted more for my boys. I thought they deserved it, and I decided they were going to get it. That's when I got active in a parent group at the younger boys' school. Once you joined the parent group it was mandatory that you attend the meetings. There were eight-week courses on how to realize and accept that you have handicapped kids, and how to help them and yourself. I think those weeks finally opened my eyes, and I began to understand and believe. After that, the reality just had to sink in a little further.

We had children in diapers for the first eight or nine years that we were married, and it was rather difficult. The oldest boy went into a mainstreamed special education class, and at age three the younger two entered a school for mentally retarded youngsters. We had to pay tuition and transportation, unless we could transport them ourselves. When they reached high school age we only paid half and the high school picked up the other half. Then, in 1968 the mandate came out and there was no more tuition to pay, and finally also no more transportation costs.

Prior to that we fought for classes and recreational facilities at the park district. A group of us went to the park district and said there was nothing for the retarded population, and we set up a summer program and an after-school program once or twice a week, which was very beneficial to the children. Before that there had been absolutely nothing apart from a bowling program once a week. The school used to transport them to a bowling alley owned by the husband of one of the teachers—they got to use it for *nothing. It worked out beautifully, and it brought the children into the community which was very much needed and very rare at that time.*

The school our two younger boys attended was the pioneer in the country, and the curriculum was adopted for most of the schools for the retarded throughout the United States. It started out in 1949 as a little one-room schoolhouse with one boy, and then it grew and grew. The final structure was built by a general contractor who had a retarded son and got all his sub-contractors to work either in the evenings or on weekends. The land was donated. The building went up and the mortgage was paid off in a rather short time because everyone in the village from the mayor on down was willing to pitch in.

All the time the boys were growing up, we tried to live as normal a life as any family. We went places; we went on vacations; we went out to dinner. My kids, God bless them, are very well-mannered; in fact to this day a lot of people can't believe how well-mannered they are. We tried to do things as a family and still do. Although our sons now live in the village, we still get together and still function as a family.

Although it took me a long time to deal with their retardation, I am very proud of my sons. I would never trade them in. My three sons are super people; I love them. They're pleasant to get along with, and they have no prejudices. My eldest son has such a tremendous social facade that you wouldn't think he was retarded. His academic skills are minimal, but he can hold a job because of his social competence. Right now he's doing custodial work in a store. Residents of the village work at the public library, in department stores, in restaurants; they're diversified, they're all over. The fact is that they can handle a job.

My eldest son is the only one who has ever asked questions about his retardation. He doesn't feel that he's retarded because he's comparing himself with his brothers, who are less able than he is. I told him, "You have some of what we call emotional problems, because you're a little different from the guy next door but not a lot different, like your brothers." So he brought up examples. He said, "You mean like driving a car?" And I said, "Yes." "And playing ball?" And I said, "Yes." So he was able to grasp that. Whether he accepted it or not I don't know. I think he had a hard time with it. He's gone through some therapy and I think that was necessary for him. After two years of therapy I think he's got a better handle on it. It's helped him tremendously, and done something I couldn't do for him. My other two sons have never asked and never made any comment about their retardation. Those two young men are both in a workshop. My middle son once ran a dishwasher at the high school, and he did an excellent job, so that's something we're keeping in mind for the future.

I have no regrets for my sons. I'm very happy for them. They are happy. I've seen tremendous progress in all three, and they are growing into fine young men of whom I am very proud.

The village where Bernie's sons—thanks in great part to their father—now live is made up of apartments for the higher functioning residents and more structured living arrangements for those who require more supervision and assistance. Bernie says:

If you go through the village you will see that it is not like an institution. It does not have metal beds and dressers. It has the sort of furnishings that everyone else has. It has colorful things. It's home-like, and that's the way it's going to be as long as I am involved with it. That's what I wanted for my boys, and for everybody else, and now I feel I have all these sons and daughters as well as my own three sons.

What I would like to see, though, is more residences in the community, and I don't mean residences like the village because although it does not look or feel like an institution, if you view it truthfully it is a mini-institution. It's on a street surrounded by commercial and industrial property and it's all by itself. It's not integrated into the community in the way I would like it to be. Admittedly, a lot of the young people who live there work in the community, but I still feel they need an apartment building here, a home there, with their peers. That's where they belong—in the community. They are no different from anybody else, apart from maybe being a bit slower. They have feelings. They have abilities. They can do things other people do, except that they do them more slowly.

Years ago I would have said that taking care of retarded people was the responsibility of the state. Now I'd say that the responsibility belongs to the parents, if they are inclined to undertake it. There are some parents who drop their kid off and never come again unless I call them and say, "You get in here and be part of your kid's life, or you take the kid home. I expect to see you at least once a month, if not more." This is not a drop and leave place. It is not an institution in that sense. I want the kids home for the holidays, where they belong. I want them to know that they still have families of their own.

When parents come in to talk about placing a young person, we ask, "What living skills does your child have?" But we usually discover that the child can do a half or a third of what the parents say. The parents are embarrassed to say their children can't achieve. I say, "It doesn't reflect on you," but they believe it does. They feel they're not whole people because they have a handicapped child. I can't fathom that. The thing I try to get across to parents is, never feel guilty. Feel proud that this is your child, that he's making progress, and that you are helping him to do it.

I expect parents to be cooperative in terms of what is needed when they have a child in a facility. That doesn't mean they have to pull money out of their pockets if they can't afford it, but I want them to help in any way they can—sell tickets to a fund-raiser, get people to come. But primarily I want them to take an interest in their young person, to come around every two weeks, or every ten days, or whatever; to call the youngster and let the youngster call them. If there's a family, I want them to take part. I don't want them to forget.

I had a family come to talk to me about placing their daughter. This young lady is now in her early thirties, and she'd been institutionalized since she was seventeen months old, usually far away. This is the closest she's been to her parents geographically in all those years. Now the parents are getting up in years and they wanted to make her part of their lives again. I couldn't believe what I was hearing. I sat down and closed the door, and I said, "Let me tell you a little philosophy of mine. This is not a place where you drop and leave kids. If your daughter lives here, I'll expect to see you, too. I really feel sorry for you people, because you don't know what you've missed. You don't know the joy you could have had with your daughter, and you've missed thirty years of it." Now those parents visit their daughter.

placement: a time for compromise

It was partly due to the sexual confusion experienced by Jeff, Leslie's brother, that he was eventually placed in the facility where he now lives. Jeff's sexual curiosity, expressed in terms appropriate to his mental age but not to his physical age, transgressed legal boundaries and landed him in court. Leslie says of that experience, "There is nothing in the world more frightening than seeing a mentally retarded person up in front of a judge who has no understanding of mental retardation."

The court case did, however, open the door to finding an appropriate placement for Jeff. The process also taught Leslie a lot about what the future holds for a person with mental retardation, and the differences between the family's expectations and the realities. Leslie says:

Jeff graduated from school when he was twenty-one, and was placed that fall, but the placement didn't work out. There had been a conflict between my parents over where Jeffrey was going to go. My mother didn't feel he should be placed at all. When he left that first placement, he lived with her for almost a year. Then she couldn't care for him any more—she didn't have the money or the resources—so he came back to live with my father and step-mother for a short time and worked in a sheltered workshop. Then he got in trouble with the police. He followed a little girl and lifted her skirt. Then he got on the bus to come home. The police stopped the bus and took him to the police station, and he ended up in court. The court put him into a behavior modification program for six months, and eventually he was placed where he is now.

He had never been on medication. When he was young my parents were very much opposed to medication. Now he takes Thorazine, a heavy-duty tranquilizer. We're still uncomfortable about it. Jeff has a great sense of humor; he's very interested in what's going on in the world and he used to be interesting to talk to. Now that he's on Thorazine he's very dull. He has a speech difficulty, but he has a large vocabulary and he's able to express himself. We've seen a real decrease in that since he's been on the medication, and it disturbs all of us. But the alternative is to have him fighting with people and being disruptive.

I've been noticing lately that the parents of some of my students don't deal with their kids the way my parents dealt with Jeff. All my parents expected and wanted from his school setting was that he should be watched and not get hurt or be allowed to hurt anyone else. Expectations are different these days, and that causes complications. Some parents are realistic but others are deluding themselves. Now parents want not only to keep the child safe, but want him to accomplish something, make a contribution, fit in somewhere, wherever that somewhere is—a community living facility or whatever the parents picture as an acceptable setting. For most parents a community living facility is an acceptable setting, and that's unfortunate because most of the kids won't get into that sort of facility. In fact, few of these retarded young people are going to find living facilities that match what their parents want for them.

There are some wonderful living facilities available, and we all hope there'll be more of them in the future, and that more of them will offer high quality care and opportunities and programming. There are also second-rate and poor facilities, and facilities that don't have caring and competent staff. Some parents are unwilling to accept the possibility that not all the people caring for their child are good people.

At a facility for handicapped children where I worked and which influenced my decision to go into special education, there had been several cases in which parents thought their children were being abused by the staff, particularly by the woman who owned the place. Apparently she had allowed a bunch of kids to bite a child, in retaliation for his having bitten someone else. She set the kids on this child and his parents found out about it. It became a big issue because a former staff member reported it to the newspapers.

This had happened before I got there. I was there for the last six months before the place closed down, when they were desperate for staff and couldn't get anybody to work there any longer. I went in and taught the kids that were left, those whose parents hadn't pulled them out and those who had been placed there by the state. I was not involved in the investigation, but I did learn that there were parents who would not believe that any wrongdoing had taken place. Their children had been there for years, and they were relieved to have this clean, happy place where their kids had ribbons in their hair. They would not face such issues as

*what kinds of playrooms the children were working in, whether
they had any personal freedom, whether they were in fact being
set upon one another, or whether the staff were putting Tabasco
sauce on the tongues of the children with Down syndrome to stop
them from letting their tongues hang out. Parents with children
in a facility sometimes walk a very thin line.*

Victoria at sixteen: crisis time

Victoria spent her sweet sixteenth birthday in the adolescent
unit of a major metropolitan hospital. She partied with a
group of other teenagers all of whom had, by some man-
ifestation of antisocial behavior, driven their parents to throw
in the towel and let the medical profession figure out why
their children were screwed up.

Victoria's misbehavior did not seem very impressive com-
pared to that of some of her companions. She wound up in
the adolescent unit because she wouldn't get out of bed. By
the time Victoria was fifteen-and-a-half, her headlong
plunge into adolescence had pulled us all into the pit after
her. She was alternately hyped up and depressed. When she
was up she was ornery, loud, recalcitrant, and generally impossible to live with. When she was depressed her skin tone
became waxy, her hair limp and dull, and her manner confused.

Getting her to school on time in the morning was the
major achievement of my day—and frequently the only one.
Either she wouldn't get out of bed, or she'd get out of bed
but wouldn't get in the shower. Or she'd get in the shower,
but she wouldn't get out. Or once out of the shower, she
wouldn't get dressed. Or she'd get dressed up to a point.
She'd arrive downstairs for breakfast fully dressed except for
her socks and shoes, and there was no way in the world she

was going to put on her socks and shoes. At this point she was walking to school alone, and clearly she could not walk to school without shoes. People notice that sort of thing. They think it's odd. Anyway, the mornings were getting chilly.

When you've got a five-year-old who won't put on socks and shoes it is still possible to employ brute force. It is possible to sit on the child (literally, if necessary) and get the child shod. This system does not work with a fifteen-year-old, especially one who is taller and stronger than you are. I would make Victoria sit down and I'd put on her socks and shoes. As soon as I had mastered one foot and turned my attention to the other, Victoria removed the first sock or shoe. On good days we settled for keeping the shoes on but leaving the laces undone. Let the school deal with the laces. Brushing teeth or hair became areas of equal conflict, but going to school with messy hair can pass for the latest in teenage self-assertion, and no one notices dirty teeth from a distance.

"Let her come to school looking a mess," her homeroom teacher told me. "We'll handle it here. The other kids will let her know that she looks a real mess and she'd better go smarten up before she gets into class." That worked for a while, but I was not up to letting this unkempt, sullen young creature walk to school by herself, so on bad days I used to drive her.

Even on those days when she managed to be fully dressed and reasonably well groomed, getting her out of the house was a risky business. "I don't want to go to that yuck school!" she'd scream. "I'm not going!" I would sit her on the couch and say, "Okay, Victoria, you may not want to go to that yuck school, but you're going anyway and you know that. Sit here until you are calm, and then you may leave." With luck, the tantrum would abate sufficiently that I could let her out the door. I would watch for a couple of blocks to make sure she was headed in the right direction. Sometimes she'd leave the house yelling and screaming and quiet down outside the door. If she kept it up all the way down the block I'd dive into the car, haul her in, and drive her to school. On the worst mornings, when I obviously couldn't let her leave the house alone, I'd also drive her to school.

By this time Emma was flatly refusing to leave the house at the same time as Victoria because she was understandably embarrassed to have her friends see her teenage sister yelling and crying in the street and generally making an exhibition of herself. After Emma left, I'd wait for her to turn the corner to her school, then I'd let Victoria leave. I was reluctant to stop her walking to school altogether, because doing so represented a major step forward in terms of independence.

As that fall edged into winter, the situation got worse. Victoria's depressions got more frequent and severe. Once, fifteen minutes after going to work, I got a telephone call saying that Victoria was in the office at Emma's school, and asking what they should do with her. That was the first time she'd not gone to school once I'd got her out the door; after that I generally followed her at a distance at least part of the way to school.

The dressing problem worsened, too. The school's advice to let her go looking a mess and smarten up at school wasn't working. Eventually they said, "Bring her in her pajamas, if that's what you have to do, and have her bring her clothes in a paper bag. All the kids will laugh at her, and she'll straighten up when she realizes how foolish that makes her look." That didn't work, either. In fact, I think Victoria got some perverse enjoyment out of the incident. If you want attention, showing up at school in pajamas and bathrobe is a foolproof way of getting it.

Naturally, these morning traumas were not too gratifying for the rest of the family. Don left for work before any of the rest of us got up, so he usually missed the fireworks. Emma learned that the mornings were up for grabs and she pretty much had to fend for herself. I was grateful if I could get to work on time. Victoria was not supposed to arrive at school before eight-thirty in the morning, and the walk took her ten minutes at most. I was supposed to be in my office, ten minutes away by car, also at eight-thirty. There was some very delicate timing involved.

Usually I was relieved to be at work, just so that I could concentrate on something other than my child's difficulties. Sometimes, though, by the time I got to the office I'd be shaking or in tears. Sometimes I sat staring at my coffee cup for thirty minutes before I could begin my work. I was deeply grateful that, thanks in part to the pioneer work done by Jeff's stepmother and father, once Victoria was actually in school she was going to be there until three o'clock. I did not have to fear, as Jeff's stepmother did, that the phone would ring and someone from the school would say, "Come get Victoria; she's acting out again." I did, however, get to the point where I was convinced I would knife the next person who told me, "She's a teenager, what do you expect?"

Because I did not want Emma to feel responsible for a potentially explosive older sister during the after-school hours before I got home from work, I arranged for Victoria to attend programs at a recreational center for handicapped youngsters most days after school. She went to skating and sports classes and a variety of other activities. It meant a lot of car-pooling, but that was a small price to pay for having my troubled and troublesome kid well occupied and her sister freed from inappropriate care-taking responsibilities.

The tantrums, the noncompliance, the screaming and yelling—all that I might have been able to handle. What I couldn't handle was that Victoria was clearly unhappy much of the time, and that she looked like a sick child. She was screaming and yelling all right, but she was screaming and yelling for help, and I didn't know how to help her. For years we'd been trying to pin down some medical reason for her mood swings and the physical changes that seemed to accompany them. The doctor who diagnosed her retardation, and whom she has continued to see regularly ever since, identified mineral deficiencies, so we gave her mineral supplements. He identified an enzyme problem, so we gave her enzymes. Still, there was something that we couldn't put our finger on. When Victoria reached puberty we tried to tie the mood swings to her menstrual cycle, but there didn't seem to be a connection.

"You know," said the doctor, "there's a great deal we don't know about biochemistry. I see children who are seriously affected by changes in the weather. I see children who go off the wall when the moon is full. It sounds crazy, but it's true. I see children whose medication has to be adjusted to the full moon."

He also gave me comfort by accepting my exasperation with people who saw all Victoria's problems as natural outcomes of adolescence. "Some of them are," he said, "but what nobody seems to realize is that some kids go through adolescence with no trouble at all. I actually know adolescents who are perfectly ordinary, nice people."

"That's good to know," I said. "Please God, Emma will be one of them, because I don't think I could go through this again with any child, retarded or otherwise."

So by the time Victoria was fifteen-and-a-half it was clear that someone had to take some action here or everybody in the family would be crazy. I was still so sure that there must be some physical component involved in her emotional condition that I decided to have her checked out from A to Z. I was told that the best place to have such testing done was a hospital with a special adolescent program. I located such a hospital and checked her in.

That was probably one of the smartest things I ever did because I finally heard someone in authority say what I'd been suspecting for months: "For her sake and for everybody else's, this child should not be living at home. It's time to consider placement." Unfortunately, none of the other teenagers in the program was retarded, and that gave rise to all sorts of complications, including my first head-on clash with the social worker syndrome.

We checked Victoria into the adolescent unit in mid-January—two months before her sixteenth birthday. The doctors promised to run every test known to man and to observe her closely. All that they did, but it took a long time and cost an amount of money I'm still scared to contemplate. Victoria settled in very comfortably. She had a good time. She got just what she needed: a highly-structured environment and a great deal of one-on-one attention. For the first few weeks we were not allowed to see her—when you're a medical professional put in charge of a screwed up kid the first thing you do, apparently, is separate the kid from the parent who is probably the reason the child is screwed up. That was fine with me and Victoria's stepfather. We'd seen enough of Victoria, and in such heavy doses, that we could live without her quite comfortably for a while. Emma was not averse to some peace and quiet, either.

Don and I, however, were expected to attend parent groups, and they were eye-openers. Don, to his great credit, accompanied me to every meeting (although now I wish I hadn't put him through that), and we found out in a hurry that we were not the only ones with problems. The other parents were there because their children were potential suicides, or stole their money, or ran away from home, or got into trouble with the police. The simplest issues seemed to be over- or under-achievement. We learned a very great deal about what parents of other children go through. We also learned that what the other parents were going through had very little to do with our situation. So on the intellectual level the meetings were fascinating, but on the emotional level they were not much help.

Despite the disparity in the issues we were examining, however, our relationship with the other parents was considerably more satisfying than our relationship with the professionals. The two people most closely involved with Victoria, apart from the various specialists who tested her, were a social worker, a sophisticated woman in her mid-forties, and a rather young psychiatrist. Initially, I saw more of the social worker, but it was a clear case of incompatibility. We did not get along. The fact that none of the children in the program had mental retardation led to a number of run-ins between us; I felt that whatever her other skills and abilities, this social worker knew less about mental retardation than I did.

Both the social worker and the psychiatrist were, along with the rest of the staff, genuinely concerned with the welfare of the youngsters in their charge. As far as Victoria's immediate physical and emotional care was concerned, I had no argument with either of them. On a personal level, it was a very different matter. For one thing, I perceived them both as guilt mongers. They managed to make me feel inadequate in a way I had not felt in years. I had worked through a lot of my guilt feelings and was most distressed about having them churned up all over again. I also felt that I'd tried to deal honestly with my feelings about having Victoria live at home—my feelings involved a lot of hostility—and that my honesty had been misinterpreted. I was being unfairly labeled as an uncaring mother who was trying to dump her child. When I expressed concern about the cost of the treatment and the type of follow-up program they were recommending, the social worker told me, "You do not care about this child. You do not care what is right or wrong for her. All you're concerned with is that you don't have to spend money on her."

For all practical purposes, the chances of that social worker and myself ever developing a good working relationship died with those words. Fortunately, I'd been around compassionate and reinforcing professionals long enough in my travels with Victoria to realize, even as my heart turned to ice, that I did not have to assume that she was right and that I was, indeed, a mean and mercenary mommy.

Professionals who use guilt to manipulate parents cause a great deal of pain. They also waste a lot of their own time. Parents of children who have problems almost invariably feel guilty already, at one level or another. They don't need anyone to pile it on with a shovel. What they usually need is someone to help them dig out from under.

Although the social worker and I could not get along, it was necessary that we continue to communicate. The hospital staff were doing exactly what Victoria was there to have them do—they were putting her through a very complete battery of tests. The fact that Victoria was retarded and the other kids weren't, however, led to several more confrontations with the social worker.

For instance, she was delighted at how well Victoria responded to "modeling" from the other teenage girls on the unit, and indeed Victoria learned to do things she had never done before. She learned to cut up her own food because it never occurred to anyone to do it for her. She got along fine with some of the other girls, and the social worker began to talk about mainstreaming and what a shame it was that Victoria was in a special school and not among normal kids.

She was right, but only up to a point. Victoria did learn from the other girls, and I did think later on about the possibility of mainstreaming her more. But in that program Victoria was not actually being mainstreamed with normal kids, and I tried to explain this to the social worker.

"There's something in what you say," I agreed, "but you have to remember that she's not among 'normal' kids here. These kids have real, important problems. *They're* not among normal kids. They're here because they couldn't deal with normal life any more than Victoria can. These girls can make a pet of Victoria now, while they're all in the same situation and in a protected environment, but put them back among their peers and see how much time they have for Victoria then."

One of the effects of the modeling Victoria received in the program was that her vocabulary increased and she began to use some age-appropriate language. Once we got past the early "no contact with the parents" stage, I was allowed to call her, and Victoria would speak to me on the phone (this was progress because Victoria despises the telephone).

"Hi sweetheart," I would greet her, "How are you?"

And Victoria would go off into a fit of giggles; "Fuck you, mother!" she would tell me cheerfully, and hang up.

So back I went to the social worker, who was getting very tired of me. I said, "Look, I'm sorry to sound negative, and I know that's the way teenagers talk, but it's doing Victoria a disservice to let her use that kind of language. Her school has spent years teaching this child socially acceptable behavior, and telling people 'fuck you' does not constitute socially acceptable behavior. When she goes back to school, that sort of language is going to get her in big trouble. What's more, I'm investigating a placement in a living facility run by nuns and, if she gets in, that sort of language will surely get her thrown out. Will you please get her to clean up her act." They got her to clean up her act.

By the time it had been officially decided that it was in nobody's best interest—especially not Victoria's—for her to continue to live at home, insurance coverage for her stay was running out. Both the social worker and the psychiatrist disagreed with me about where Victoria should live if she didn't live at home. They wanted her sent to a prohibitively expensive living facility that was not only out of state but halfway across the country, and I said no. It may indeed have been a terrific place for kids with problems, but the expense involved made it an unacceptable proposition, and I was not going to be brow-beaten by the intimation that good parents sacrifice for their children and that lots of parents who couldn't afford it managed to send their kids to this particular facility. There's a difference between sacrificing for your child and taking reckless financial risks—especially when there's another child in the family. Further, I had no intention of sending Victoria halfway across the United States, where I couldn't see her more than twice a year and would have no way of keeping adequately in touch with her programming or her progress. Because Victoria is not very good on the telephone, I would have only the haziest notion of what her life was like; if she were miserable, she would not be able to let me know. Nobody was going to talk me into putting my daughter in that position.

Moreover, I already knew what I wanted for Victoria. I had done my homework and had visited a living facility which was considered not only one of the best available but was located, providentially, a ten-minute drive from my home. The principal of Victoria's school, whom I have known for years and for whom I have a great deal of respect, had told me that if he had a mentally retarded child, that was the facility he would choose. Other people whose opinion and knowledge of the field I valued had said the same. I had talked to parents of children who lived there, and almost everything they had to say was positive.

When I visited the facility I saw the unit where a child at Victoria's functioning level would probably live. I met the children and the staff, and I liked what I saw. I also knew that the facility planned to open group homes, each housing eight children and three full-time care-givers, and that it might be possible to arrange a placement for Victoria in one of those. I had discussed the placement with my former husband, who assured me that he trusted my judgment and that if a facility was all right with me, it was also all right with him.

Unfortunately, it was not all right with the social worker or the psychiatrist. They intimated that I would be condemning my child to a snake pit. I insisted that they visit the facility and see for themselves; eventually they did so, and still they held out. They were insistent that we rethink our position on sending Victoria out of state. We were still stalemated when the insurance money ran out and we had to bring Victoria home. Although I had foreseen this and asked the staff to prepare her for the transition, there had been no preparation. She quit cold turkey. She had to make the transition from the protected environment of the hospital to regular, disorganized home life with no cushioning at all. To our relief, she took it well.

She seemed healthy and a lot better adjusted than when she had entered the hospital. She was fairly calm and cooperative. They had done well by her. We now knew, officially, that we had a mentally retarded child with no identifiable physical ailments who was subject to mood swings and depression and was having trouble dealing with the relatively unstructured environment provided by a normal, two-breadwinner family. We also had an official statement that Victoria needed to live away from home (although the hospital had failed to provide any alternative other than their out-of-state placement and never came up with an alternative). All we needed, in order to pursue the paperwork required to get her a placement in the facility I had chosen, and a state grant to help fund that placement, was the same information on paper. That proved to be our next stumbling block.

The reports and test results did not arrive. I made repeated calls to the hospital administrative department, only to be told that some of the test results weren't through, or that so-and-so hadn't finished his report, and that it wouldn't be long. I began to get paranoid. Bureaucratic wheels turn slowly, but surely not this slowly? Could it be that, because the people I'd been dealing with disagreed with my choice of a placement for Victoria, they were delaying the information in order to try to block the placement? What were they going to say in their reports? Would they say that I had a mentally ill child in need of psychiatric care? Such a statement would not only be inaccurate but would effectively block Victoria's chances of being accepted at the facility I'd chosen. And what would they say about me? I knew what the social worker thought of me, and I didn't much want her view, which I considered to be biased, perpetuated in print.

Eventually, I called Victoria's father and said, "All right, now that you're a hot-shot executive, will you please call the hospital and tell them that I want those reports and test results, and I want them fast, and I want them to reflect an accurate view of Victoria's condition—that she's a mentally retarded adolescent who needs to be in a different environment because she cannot cope emotionally without more structure than we can give her at home."

"No problem," he said. "Leave it to me."

Half an hour later he called back. "Don't worry about it," he told me. "You'll get those reports and they will say exactly what you want them to say."

"Terrific," I said. "How did you do it?"

"It was easy," he replied. "I told them that they were dealing with our kid, and our insurance money, and we were legally entitled to those reports and test results. I also told them that whatever differences you and I may have had in the past, I consider you to be a first-rate mother and I have absolute confidence in your ability to make decisions that are in the best interests of the children."

"Thanks," I said admiringly.

"Think nothing of it," he said.

But I did think of it. On the personal level, I was glad that even though we were no longer married, Victoria's father and I could still work together for her. I also thought about what might have happened if I had not been sufficiently experienced, and sufficiently bloody-minded, to resist the pressure put on me to make a decision that I believed to be wrong for my child.

John was right. I got the reports, and I duly sent them to the state department of mental health along with an application for an individual care grant. I told them that the facility would accept Victoria if she got the grant. Then I discovered that I was not through with red tape. On the basis of the hospital reports, the department of mental health decided that Victoria might be more suitably placed in a foster home than in a living facility. Their reason was that someone without a full-time job outside the home, and with experience of caring for handicapped children, might be able to provide the high level of structure that Victoria needed.

Once I had processed the information that a foster home for my child did not mean that I was a worthless mother, I agreed to consider it if a suitable family could be found. One of our regular sitters came from a family that had two children of their own (including the sitter) and regularly took in foster children for varying lengths of time. Such a family, I thought, might well be able to provide a home where Victoria could be happy. But no such home could be found which met my stipulation that Victoria continue to attend her regular school, which she could do if she entered the larger facility.

We needed to find a foster family that lived within the school district, and there simply wasn't one. An alternative was offered: Victoria could go live with a foster mother who was already taking care of a little girl with spina bifida who was confined to a wheelchair. This woman lived in a third floor apartment in an urban district where she was afraid to leave her home at night. Not only was the home out of our school district, but Victoria's life would be severely restricted. How could a woman who lived alone, except for a child in a wheelchair, and who was afraid to go out after dark, ferry Victoria to and from all the social activities we had set up for her? I might be a burned-out parent with a full-time job, but I could still offer her a great deal more than that. I had a pleasant suburban home with a garden, and I had car-pooled so much for so long that providing special classes and social activities was simply programmed into my routine. I told the state that it was nice of them to offer, but we had to do better than that. The facility that was willing to accept her, I pointed out, could offer a whole lot more than that.

Everyone at the department of mental health, including the caseworker assigned to Victoria, was wonderfully cooperative and kind. They wanted what was best for her, but I still figured I knew what was best, and they still disagreed. Eventually I called up Victoria's caseworker and said, "Look, you haven't met this kid. You haven't seen her on her own turf. I'd like to invite you to come to our home and meet Victoria so that she's a real person to you and not just a name on a file. I think if you meet her you'll get a more accurate picture of how she functions, because it seems to me you're assuming that she has a lot more social and emotional competence than she really does have."

So the caseworker came to visit us and Victoria gave him a tour of the house, introduced him to her dolls, and showed him her record player, the simple puzzles she liked to do, and the toys she played with.

"Now what do you think of a group home placement?" I asked at the end of the visit.

"I think it would probably be fine," he said. Then he went back and told the same thing to the other people involved in the case and Victoria got her grant.

Victoria moved into the group home eight months after I had checked her into the hospital for testing. They were probably the most grueling months of my life and I feel I'll never fully recover from them. I lost a lot of illusions. But I gained what I believe is the best living arrangement I could have found for her in the state in which we live. The fact that she's living only ten minutes away from home is icing on the cake, and it's my opinion that it's icing I deserve.

"I don't think it's right to take a free ride"

Kathy and her husband, Jim, considered their pleasant, secure, suburban life and wondered why they felt that it was
incomplete. They had a solid, happy marriage; they had two
healthy small sons; they felt that they had been given a
generous share of life's kindnesses. They decided that the
sense of incompleteness was coming from a conviction that if
life has given you a lot of good things, it's only fair to give
something back. They wanted to make a contribution. Accordingly, they applied for a position as house parents in a
group home for mentally retarded children. They and their
two children would live with up to eight retarded girls, most
of them teenagers. Jim would continue his regular job as an
architectural draftsman. Kathy would be surrogate mother to
the girls, responsible for running the household and caring
for the children. Thus she became mother to ten children
instead of two—among them, for six hectic months, my
daughter.

Along the way Kathy discovered that not everyone viewed
with approval her method of giving back to others some of
the good things she and her family had received. Her
mother thought she was crazy. She almost lost her best
friend. Other friends told her they couldn't believe she could
do such a thing to her own children. Some refused to visit
her in her new home. For a while Kathy herself thought she
was crazy. She lost her privacy. She lost her sleep. She barely
got to say hello to her husband now and then. At times she
didn't believe she could make it through the unofficial two-
year commitment. Eighteen months into it, however, she and
Jim are considering extending it to three years. Kathy says:

*I have a big family and we've had our share of tribulations, but
we've had a lot of good times. My family is really close and we've
had a good life. I'm not religious, but I believe that God has been*

*good to us, and when we've had hard times there's always been a
lot of love to carry us through, and a lot of family support. We've
always been able to see that there would be sunshine at the end of
the tunnel.*

*I don't think it's right to take a free ride. When I was younger
I was a real hippie. We all talked about changing the world.
Then the chance came for us to practice what we had believed in
and marched for. Instead of settling in the suburbs we had an
opportunity to do something. Jim is my best friend and we have a
great marriage, and we've always believed we were here for a
reason. This is just one of the things we can do together, and I
believe that there will be other things. Many people are very
involved in material things, but I know that life means more
than living comfortably and joining the PTA. There are other
things to do in the world, and it doesn't necessarily mean that you
have to go off to Africa or somewhere exotic to do it. In a way,
though, it seems we might as well have gone to Africa. We really
have very little time for our personal family and we don't see
much of our friends. We don't see people as often as we would
otherwise, but I think it's worth it. I can't stay here forever, but
for now it's okay.*

*Not everyone thought it was such a great idea for us to come
here. Amazingly enough it was my mother who was most against
it, mainly, I think, because of her memories of what she had been
through with my brother, who was severely retarded from birth.
She knew it had tied her down and sapped her being. We didn't
tell her until we were really involved and sure that this was what
we were going to do, and I was surprised by her reaction. She
couldn't see why, if God didn't put us in this position, we'd put
ourselves in it.*

*I am the second oldest of seven children, and Mark, my
brother, was the third oldest. He never functioned beyond the
level of a six-month-old baby. My parents had a good pediatrician, but that was about it. They could never go on vacation.
There was no respite care. They couldn't even get a baby-sitter.
Baby-sitters were afraid to go into his room because he had
convulsions and was on medication.*

*My mother kept thinking that there was something that could
be done, and my father didn't have the heart to tell her there was
nothing they could do. My mother had a friend with a handicapped child; she had a little box with holes in it for the child's
arms and legs, and she'd put him in it several times a day to try to
get him to walk. His room had a ceiling with stars that lit up at
night because they hoped that would stimulate him. My mom was
that way; she kept searching. Finally a doctor told her, "Take this
child home and love him; he's never going to get better." He was*

already seven and that was the first time anyone had said it to her plainly. Everyone else had realized it, though. It was obvious. He was like an infant: he couldn't speak, he wore diapers, he couldn't even turn over. He needed constant nursing care. Nobody except our pediatrician would treat him. Some of his teeth were bad and my mother took them out herself because she couldn't find a dentist who would do it. It was bad for her. The doctors said originally that he wouldn't live beyond three or four, so it was amazing that he lived as long as he did.

There was another issue that made it difficult for my mother to deal with our coming here. When my brother was alive, a time came when she was advised to put him somewhere because he was so sick and so physically disabled that it was getting very difficult to care for him at home. This facility took children only up to age seven, and Mark was already nine. The alternative was the state institution. The day my parents went to visit that institution was the first time I had seen my dad cry. A month later my brother died, so the problem was solved. But my mother remembered the last place she had looked at, and when I told her we were coming here she immediately thought in terms of a snake pit. She visited us very gingerly at first, but now she's accepted it. This is our home, and these are the people that live with us, and it's fine.

My mother was not the only person who had difficulties with our decision. For a while I lost my best friend. She was frustrated because we never had time to sit down and talk. It pulled me away from her, and that lasted a couple of months. Now she's come back. She says that if this is my life, these are the terms and we can be friends. I am glad it turned out the way it did, because that would have been a great loss to me.

There were people who felt that our children should not be exposed to this sort of situation, and people who felt that they themselves should not be exposed to it. I have friends who still won't come here, and I have friends who will only come on home-visit weekends when the girls aren't here. They are just not comfortable around handicapped people.

The most bluntly put statement came from a friend of ours who said, "I think you guys are great; it's a great thing you are doing and somebody's got to do it, but I have to tell you that I can't come to see you. I've been around handicapped people. They work where I work. But being here is just too uncomfortable." He's uncomfortable because he hasn't been around handicapped people enough. He thinks they're different, and they're not. They may not speak clearly, or you may have to look deeply at what they're doing to figure out their motivation, but they're not different. This friend did ask me to get him tickets for our last big fund-raiser, but he's still not comfortable with us and the girls in our home.

It seems to me that a lot of the discomfort comes from seeing handicapped people who are not cared for properly and who are not socially acceptable. Almost every day I drive past a nursing home whose residents include a lot of mentally retarded people who are not well cared for and probably should not be walking around without supervision. Their behavior is not socially appropriate. They're shabby and dirty, and I can see why people pull back from them. They don't know what to expect. They're afraid these strange, unkempt people are going to come up to them and embarrass them. I've felt that way myself. It's not only because the person's handicapped; it's because you don't know what kind of a situation that person is going to put you in. It's a fear of the unknown.

I joke about how all the girls who live with me look like little preppies when they go to school, and I make sure that they're all well-behaved and well-groomed. But these kids are the lucky ones because they've got parents who care about where they live, how they conduct themselves, how they look, and the impression they make on other people—and they've got us to follow through. A lot of handicapped people don't get that kind of care and support, and they're the ones who tend to be out on the streets where people get embarrassed by them and want to keep out of their way.

It's hard to overcome feelings like that. Some people have to be around our girls for a long time before they're comfortable enough to realize that they're just ordinary kids. But I don't let that stop me from taking the kids with me when I go out. If I'm going to a friend's house I take some of the girls, unless I know it's somebody that can't handle it. On the other hand, I know people who have been changed by learning to be around the children who live here.

I think my own children are going to benefit from our experience. The people who told me that it wasn't fair to the boys to come here said that we wouldn't be able to give them as much of our time, and that is true. But there are things that balance it out. I always wanted a big family, and I don't like labor and delivery, so this is how I got it. The boys benefit from the give and take of a big family, and they'll benefit from not being spoiled. I don't see that they feel uncared for. I think at some point in their lives they'll say that what their mother and father did was a good thing.

When I came here I did not recognize the risks I was taking. I did not know what I was taking on. When we first started getting involved with this facility as volunteers, we saw a depth to people who had a handicapped person in the family that we didn't see in *other people—an extra dimension. That is what made it impor-tant to us. We wanted to be more involved with the children, and we started to talk about applying to become house parents in one of the new group homes. It was a big procedure. There was a lot of psychological testing—they look at every aspect of your person-ality.*

The orientation included lots of meetings with the people involved in setting up the group homes, and they told us all they knew of what might be involved. But nobody knew exactly what we were in for. Even the people in charge of the orientation admitted they didn't know. We covered as much as we could about living in a little community, relationships with other people in the community, the social side of it—living in this little compound you're very close to people. We worked with the kids. We talked about the philosophy behind the group homes. Some retarded people can go beyond the structured life of the main facility, and the idea behind the homes is to help people who have that potential to learn to live as independently as possible. And it works. It does help them develop independent living skills. We talked about it as much as we could, but a lot was speculation, and things have come up that we weren't prepared for. We've had a couple of kids for whom this was not the right living arrangement, and that was incredibly hard for me. At first we wanted to open our hearts to everyone, and it was hard to admit that however much we tried, this was not the right setting for some people.

In the beginning, I was packing every day. I said, I cannot live with this; I cannot live like this; it's not natural. There's a staff person on from midnight to eight in the morning; it's not natural to have somebody in your kitchen or vacuuming your living room at three in the morning. But you live with it. That's a big benefit—you become flexible. I thought I was flexible before I came, but now I'm double-jointed.

I knew that some people wouldn't be over as frequently as we'd like, but I didn't know it would cut down my contact with the outside world as much as it did at first. That has eased up as we go on. Now there's a volunteer who comes in one night a week. Even so, we're only alone here once a month, on home-visit weekends. When the kids are here, to have a day off and really be alone you have to physically leave the house—it's not like having a natural quiet time at home. A relief homemaker comes in periodically, but if I'm actually in the house everybody knows it. I can stay in my bedroom, but there's always some kind of emer-gency that I have to take care of. When all the kids are in school, from about nine-thirty to two-thirty, there are quiet hours. But usually I have paper work, or calls to make, or someone has the day off from school. It's very seldom that I have a week with five days when nothing is going on.

What keeps me going is the growth I've seen in the girls. Also, when things are at their lowest, one of them will say something that cracks you up. A sense of humor is important here.

We've looked carefully at what effect this has had on our marriage, because we have so little time together. When we go away from here or on vacations, we almost always take the boys, so there's been very little time for just the two of us. If we hadn't been married for ten years before we came here it would have been very difficult. To live here as a couple you need a solid background. A lot of times I've snapped at Jim, but I wouldn't have if we'd had time to talk it out like we used to. So there is an effect on our marriage. But we also see each other in a different light. I see new things in Jim that make me admire him much more. Still, we couldn't do it forever. In some ways it really is an unnatural life.

The facility asks for a two-year commitment, but there's nothing in writing. We've been here eighteen months and we don't see ourselves leaving at the end of two years. Three years would probably be good. Beyond that, I don't know. There's a nice rhythm to things now. I've worked out all the kinks. But sometimes when I'm away from here I really understand how different it is.

I went away for two weeks in the summer and took the boys with me. I couldn't stand it: there were no emergencies, nobody needing me. It was too quiet. I called my sister and my brother and talked them into joining us. And I went to see a friend who's the administrator of a facility like this one. Busman's holiday. After the second week I started to relax, and then it was time to come back.

This experience has changed us and made us aware of so many things that we can't go back to being Mr. and Mrs. Suburbia. There'll always be something else. Just as I didn't know what it would be before, but it showed up, I think it will show up again.

It must be very difficult for parents to entrust their child to someone they don't know. There are also parents who must think, "How can you do this when I can't? How can you live with my child when I can't live with her?" A newspaper interviewer asked me about that, and I said, "When I go to bed at night I do not have to lie awake worrying about what is going to happen to my retarded child when I am seventy or eighty years old. I love these kids, and I care for them, but when I leave here my commitment is over. I will always be concerned about them, but I will not have *the day-to-day worry about what is going to happen to them. I won't be making the decisions."*

I've never before been involved with anything like this— making decisions for other people's children. I have a good relationship with the parents of my girls, but as with any other relationship, we've had to work at it and build it. I'm very much aware of the fact that I'm not dealing with the same issues as the parents.

I really believe that parents need to understand that some handicapped children become more handicapped by being the center of their family's attention. They're not allowed to grow as they should. Parents feel guilty when they place a child, but if they could see the growth that occurs here it would ease their guilt. The child has taken up so much of their lives, and now they can do what they want. They can nurture their other children, give them their fair share. But their guilt is compounded because they feel good about placing the child, and they don't think they should feel good about it. They have to work that through, I guess, but I think it would help if they could see the way their children grow when they're on their own.

A lot of parents seem to want a quiet sanctuary away from the world where the child can just be safe. At a meeting with parents from the group homes, we talked about things like taking the bus and going out to the store. Some of the parents were terrified, especially the parents of some of the young adults who are really getting into mobility training. We said, "There are amazing things about your child that because of your particular relationship you've never seen. Don't you want to take the chance to let your child grow as much as possible?"

We don't take foolish risks, and don't let the children take them, but there's always going to be some risk. My own children live here, and every time they go outside someone might grab them, or they might get hit by a truck. There's always a risk. Some of the children here are really capable. They can be mobility trained, and they can go out. It's very scary for parents, and you know at some point, with so many people coming through the system, that something, some day, might happen. A tree branch can drop on their head when they're out for a Sunday walk. You can't protect people, handicapped or nonhandicapped, from everything.

Two of the girls in my house take the bus to school; they have to transfer twice. Every morning when they leave I think, "God, what if. . . ?" And I know that if something happened, I would have to live with that forever. Nobody could take the guilt away. It wouldn't be deserved or necessary guilt, but it would still be there. And I imagine that what I feel is only a tiny piece of what parents are afraid of. I trust the kids. I just don't trust the rest of the world.

I don't expend energy involving myself in why parents have placed a child here—I can't, because I need that energy for the children. I don't think it's fair for the children to have to cope with all the emotions of the parents. Retarded people may be handicapped in some ways, but in others they're very perceptive. They know if they're not accepted.

Even so, it's hard for the parents. As a parent myself, though not of a handicapped child, I can see how a mother could be jealous of me. Sometimes a mother picks up a child for a home visit and doesn't like the way she is dressed. She may say (or think), "As soon as we get home we'll dress you in something that looks nicer." That's her way of trying to retain some control.

It's hard for me, too. For example, when parents come to collect a child for a home visit I don't know whether or not I should go upstairs and help pack. It might be intruding on the relationship between the parent and the child. It's also difficult to be with the children when the parents are there. Perhaps someone is being really rude at the table, and the parents are letting it slide. I wouldn't let it slide, but when the parents are there it's not my place to correct the child. I never forget that I am not the child's mother. I do not pretend to be. I have a relationship with the child, and the parents have a different relationship, and the two should not be confused.

Sometimes I wonder how I would cope if I had a retarded child myself. Right now I feel I'm doing well and I'd like to have another child, although I don't know when I would find the time. Then I wonder—what if there's a card up somebody's sleeve? I think, "Well, Kathy, you're a big shot now, but could you do it if it were your own child?" I think that's in everybody's mind as long as there's a chance that they'll have more kids—what would they do? What would I do? Until it happens, I can't say. No one can say. There are probably people who believed they could never deal with it in a million years, but then it happened and they dealt with it.

leaving home: major crisis number three

Do not be too quick to believe anyone who tells you that having a handicapped child leave home for some kind of living facility is no different from having a nonhandicapped child go away to college. The analogy doesn't hold up, and the first rock it stumbles on is a large and knobby one. The child leaving for college is taking her life—however ineptly and against your better judgment—into her own hands. The child who is mentally retarded and is leaving home to move into a residential facility is usually just exchanging one parent figure for another, or a number of others. You are not relinquishing your responsibilities to the child herself, but to someone who is to a significant degree about to take your place in your child's life. This person, or persons, will be doing the job you've done all these years. And no matter how estimable that person may be, to some extent your child is no longer your child.

You find yourself astride a fence of your own brick-by-brick building, and totally at a loss to know which way to jump. All these years you have held the reins, but now your hands are empty. Your young filly, or colt, is off the leading rein and where does that leave you? It leaves you bewildered and befuddled by a whole slew of unanswered questions. Who's in charge now? Who's calling the shots? What is your role in this new arrangement? Do you, in fact, have a role at all? You're in the middle of a genuine identity crisis, and it is very discomforting to be so situated.

When Victoria moved into Kathy's house I was ecstatic. I was positive that this was absolutely the best placement I could have found for her, and I was dizzy with pride that I achieved it for her. Those months of battle had left me bruised and scarred, but I had won. The house parents were everything I could hope for—caring, responsible, and just plain nice. The house was beautiful; I would never live in such elegance. Several of Victoria's schoolmates were already in residence, so she had instant friends. She would continue to attend the same school, so there would be no traumatic change there; in fact the familiarity of the school routine would ease the transition from one living arrangement to another. And the facility was a mere ten minutes away from home.

It was a miracle; yea, verily. And, of course, relieved of the day-to-day care of a demanding, mentally retarded, emotionally volatile teenager I would immediately become a pillar of the community, a credit to my friends, a joy to my family.

The honeymoon lasted ten days during which I did not, as it happens, become any better a person, and then Victoria went off the wall. "There's bound to be a period of adjustment," I had said, "and she can be pretty obnoxious." But it was generally acknowledged that a child leaving home was entitled to her day in the limelight and that Victoria would not be normal in any sense of the word if she didn't react in some way to this radical change.

But we had all—especially me, despite my extensive and painful experience—underestimated the degree of obnoxiousness to which Victoria could aspire. Within the space of one short month (less, if you discount the ten-day honeymoon) she had the whole place terrorized. Some of her behavior was attributable to confusion, like getting up and getting dressed several times in the middle of the night. Some was attributable to the teenager syndrome, like screaming her head off when requested to follow a simple instruction. She also produced some less obtrusive but more destructive tricks, like hitting the other children and picking on Kathy's eighteen-month-old son. Here was Victoria, who adores small children and has always been gentle and motherly to them, slyly waiting until everyone's back was turned and then pinching this little kid until he cried. She also developed some brand new and bizarre behaviors concerning food, like stuffing a whole slice of bread into her mouth, or wolfing a chunk of watermelon, rind and all.

My young filly, to pursue the analogy, had got the bit between her teeth and was off and running. I was appalled. I became not just a parent with an identity crisis but a guilt-ridden parent with an identity crisis. I was the one who had told the administrators of the facility, and Victoria's house parents, "You'll love this kid. She's just right for you. She's charming, she loves small children, she loves to be helpful, she's cute and pretty, she's a nice person. Of course, she can be difficult, but what kid can't?"

A month later, as the professionals to whose care I had assigned my child gathered to debate whether or not they could stand to live with her, I learned which side of the fence I was really on: the other side. Everyone at the facility, including Victoria, was on one side, and I was on the other. The house parents, the administrators, the psychologist, the teachers from the school were all huddled together trying to find a way to get Victoria down off the wall, and they didn't need me. If they did, they'd let me know. Meanwhile, I'd better not see or talk to Victoria, so that she could have a chance to figure out who was in control (or who was supposed to be in control because a lot of the time it seemed that she was). The one person no longer even in the running for control was me, and that was becoming painfully clear.

How did I feel? I could analyze it exactly. I felt incompetent, inferior, excluded. That's on the one hand. On the other hand, I felt considerably relieved, like a child who has been told to go away and let the grown-ups make the decisions. Of course, these was a strong possibility these grown-ups might decide that Victoria should live somewhere else (in a padlocked cage, perhaps?), but there was nothing I could do about it.

Victoria, however, was in a position to do plenty about it if she so chose. An ironical role reversal had occurred. While I sat at home, virtually helpless, my poor retarded and defenseless daughter had come into her own. This time she did, in fact, have the opportunity to take some responsibility for her own life. Victoria had the opportunity to behave herself and stay in her new setting, and if she had been happy no doubt that is what she would have done. She also had the opportunity to continue misbehaving and get herself removed, which is what she did. Victoria had made a decision about the way she wanted to live, and since she couldn't talk about it, she acted it out until someone finally got the message.

Victoria stayed in Kathy's house for six months while everyone involved (including, from a distance and to a very limited extent, me) tried to figure out what her problem was. In the meantime, my illusions about myself went down the drain. When Victoria moved into the group home my soul was bathed in altruism. This was my chance, as I saw it, to be an angel of mercy, a giver of gifts, the sort of helpful and involved mommy that any facility would be happy to have on the rolls. It did not work out that way. I was doing everyone a favor by not being involved. I could write to Victoria, but I was asked not to telephone her or see her between the monthly home-visit weekends. I kept telling myself that if I had any sense I would enjoy the respite, but I was experiencing a feeling of powerlessness that was impossible to ignore. And, of course, I was grieving over the loss of my child. I knew that it was unlikely, whatever the outcome of her sojourn with Kathy, that Victoria would ever live at home again for an extended period, nor did I much relish such a prospect. But that was not the point. My fledgling had left the nest. In the manner of other teenagers, Victoria had left home.

When you are raising a retarded child you know what's going on every minute of the day, because to a large extent you are responsible for what's going on, for planning where the child goes and what she or he does. When you've been doing that for sixteen years, not knowing is not easy. As I went about my daily routines at work and at home, I'd wonder what Victoria was doing. Was she, at that very moment, screaming the house down because she didn't want to do her laundry? Was she pinching the baby? Or was she, God willing, playing a board game or quietly watching TV with the other girls? What sort of day had she had at school? Better than yesterday, or worse? Was she happy, or was she miserable and lonely and afraid? Did she miss me? Did she think that she no longer lived at home because I didn't want her, or didn't love her?

I could, of course, call her housemother every day for a report. It had been made clear to me that I could call at any time. But if I did, surely I'd be a nuisance. If I didn't, though, would they think I didn't care? Were they justified, anyway, in having me keep out of my daughter's way until she got her new routine figured out and her new surrogate parent identified? Could my absence be making things worse because Victoria construed it as abandonment? Should I send her a pretty card or a little present and risk having it arrive when she'd been particularly difficult and shouldn't be getting rewards? Why didn't someone tell me what to do?

While all this was going on I distracted myself (in both senses of the word) by imagining what it will be like when I do have a daughter, Emma, going off to college. I won't know what's going on then, either. I won't know, at eleven or twelve at night, if she's huddled over her books or snuggled up with some unsuitable male student in some unsuitable location; I won't know if she's off at some party drinking or smoking dope—or worse. I don't expect Emma, in college, to be doing anything particularly awful, but I won't know. I won't be able to call because that will make me an overanxious mother. But if I don't call, will she think I don't care? Admittedly, when Emma is in college she'll be old enough to make her own decisions whether I like them or not. Legally, she'll be a free agent. That will never be the case with Victoria. Emotionally, though, how different is it going to be?

I reached the point where I was willing to admit that people who make the college analogy may not be quite as off base as I had thought. I didn't, and still don't, believe that it holds up altogether, but I decided I was willing to discuss the finer details.

Meanwhile, Victoria was having some good days and some bad days. I kept track of her progress, or lack of it, in a general sort of way through phone calls to Kathy, who told me about the techniques they were using to try to help my difficult daughter. One time I learned that Victoria's punishment for misbehavior was "time out," which meant that she sat on a chair on the landing for a length of time measured by a clock-timer. "But now," Kathy told me, "she waits until I'm out of sight and then slips down and changes the timer." My reaction to this was a seemingly inappropriate delight: I hadn't known that Victoria was bright enough to do that, and frankly I was impressed. So was Kathy, though naturally her pleasure was somewhat tempered by frustration. Later, I passed on the news of Victoria's sleight-of-hand to her stepfather. "Well," he said, "I'm really quite proud of her."

Having a retarded child is a bit like living with Alice in Wonderland: things are never quite what they seem.

Kathy, Jim, their co-workers, and the administrators of the

group home struggled with Victoria's recalcitrance for six months which was, in retrospect, above and beyond the call of duty. Kathy badly wanted it to work, and so did I. I wanted it so much that I blocked the evidence that it wasn't going to work to the point where I was genuinely shocked when the administrators called to say that Victoria was clearly not appropriately placed in the group home and we were going to meet to talk about alternative placements.

The timing of the call was unfortunate, to say the least. Depleted almost to breaking point by the expenditure of energy that Victoria had cost us over the preceding fourteen months, Don and I had taken ourselves off for an expensive "let's get away from it all and rediscover who we are and why we got married" weekend. It was glorious. We came home on Sunday night feeling wonderful. The call came Monday morning.

Telling yourself you should have known is every bit as easy and unproductive as telling somebody else "I told you so." I had chosen not to know. The group home situation that I had perceived as ideal for Victoria is ideal for lots of children whose intellectual functioning level is similar to Victoria's but whose emotional functioning level is more stable. All the time that I'd been longing for someone to tell me what to do, so had Victoria. She had been offered a level of independence that was more than she could handle. That was what she had been trying to tell us. I had wanted that group home setting for her so badly that I had convinced myself that she wanted it, too, but Victoria was not going to settle for something that did not suit her just because it suited me.

I'm sure she never thought it through on that level, but that's what it amounted to. Just as Victoria had, essentially, made the decision that my home was no longer where she wanted to live, so she had made the decision that Kathy's house was not where she wanted to live, either. Victoria, of course, did not have to decide where to go from there. Nor, as it happens, did I. And it's just as well that I did not have to make the decision, because I had no idea of where to go from there. For a while, all I could think of was that I had found my daughter this wonderful home and she had thrown it back in my face. She had rejected my gift. I had given her a coat made of silk and rainbows and she had said, "Thanks, it's very pretty, but it doesn't fit."

The facility of which the group homes are a part also comprises a number of other units for children with varying types and degrees of disability. It was decided that Victoria should move to "the big house" and into a unit of about a dozen other girls, some of whom, like herself, had the functional skills to live in a group home but not the emotional stability. The big house offered a lot more structure. It also looked a lot more like a traditional "institution." In fact, it used to be an orphanage. Victoria moved in on a six-week trial basis. Both Kathy and I were present at the meeting at which the decision to move her was made, and we were both in tears. We both felt we had failed Victoria and, in some way, each other. It was a highly charged situation, but through the obscuring mists of emotion I understood how much everyone there cared about what happened to my daughter. I was told that if the unit to which Victoria was assigned proved unsuitable for her, there was no other place for her in that facility but that I'd be given as much help as possible in finding an alternative placement.

During the next six weeks I existed in a state of constant anxiety. I kept in touch, once more, by phone calls, which I made as seldom as my anxiety would allow. During that time, however, I established friendly relations with the psychologist who was seeing Victoria. Once, when my latest call to the big house had given me the information that Victoria was doing okay, a teacher phoned to say that at school Victoria was not okay—in fact, she was off the wall. I put my head down on my office desk and cried, and when I got tired of crying I called the psychologist.

"I don't know what's going on," I told him. "One person tells me one thing, and then another person tells me something else. How am I supposed to make sense of all this? Here I am with my kid in limbo; I don't know whether they're going to keep her or throw her out, and if they throw her out I don't know what I'm going to do. I'm miserable and scared and confused, and what are you going to do about it?"

We decided that I was suffering from information overload and would be a lot better off knowing less, not more. We agreed that since he saw Victoria on Wednesday afternoons and at that time pulled together information on her progress from the various people concerned with her care, I should call him on Thursday mornings for an update. Apart from that, I should keep my head down and simply wait out the six-week trial period.

The six weeks, which turned into eight or nine, crawled past and joined the period between Victoria's admission to the hospital for tests and her admission to Kathy's house as one of the worst times of my life. When they were over, however, the facility decided to keep my daughter. She was still having problems, but they seemed manageable. Victoria appeared content. She was firm friends with some of the staff—often she seemed to consider herself to *be* one of the staff. She helped with the less able children; she fetched and carried; she got to stay up later than the younger children. She stopped hitting people. Her appetite stabilized. Apparently Victoria had decided to stay.

care-givers and parents: a delicate balance

When Victoria decided, at considerable emotional cost to herself and everyone around her, that Kathy's house was not the right place for her, she moved in with Linda—or, rather, in Linda's charge. Linda is coordinator of the unit in which Victoria lives and of another unit for younger and less able children, twenty-four girls in all. Linda began working with retarded children as a volunteer while she was still in high school, took a part-time job while she was in college at the facility where she still works, and decided to stay after discovering that her chosen profession, law, was not for her after all. At twenty-six, she has been working with handicapped children for eight years. Linda says:

I was going to be a lawyer, but I got sidetracked. In college I took political science, with French as my minor, and because I wanted a part-time job I started working at the facility where I now work full-time. By the time I finished my second year of college I had been working here for eighteen months and I was becoming more and more drawn to it. I had gotten very involved with a few of the children. I wasn't sure that working with retarded children was what I wanted to do with my life, but I had found out that I didn't want to be a lawyer. So when I was offered a full-time job as a prevocational trainer here I accepted it. I worked with fairly high-functioning children and I taught them self-help skills— how to take the bus, go shopping, cook, do laundry.

I now have a supervisory position, and if I hadn't gotten it I probably could not have stayed. Before that I was doing child care. It was rewarding, but I had been doing it for five years and it doesn't pay enough—so if I had not gotten a raise and been made to feel that I was going somewhere I would have left. Right now, though, I don't know where I'm going. After this level comes administration, and I don't know if that's what I want to get into.

Caring for mentally handicapped children is not easy. There's a high burnout rate, and a high turnover rate. I don't know that all the staff here stay long enough to become burned out, but on the other hand some people have stayed for years. My mother is a child care worker and has been here nearly as long as I have. My best friend, also a child care worker, has been here for six years.

I have visited other facilities and I think ours compares very favorably. The relationship that some of the staff people build up with the children here is excellent, and I haven't been in any other place where I've seen as much physical affection demonstrated; it is not encouraged in other places.

To do this work you need to be patient. That doesn't mean that you have to be naturally patient; you have to be willing to work at it. It's easy to get impatient and annoyed if you ask a child to do something and she doesn't catch on right away. You have to be able to backtrack and think, "All right, what did I say that she didn't understand?" I've certainly lost my temper on occasion, but I don't usually have to make an effort to be patient.

Also, you have to be tolerant. Some children have behaviors that can be very irritating, like rocking. You have to raise your tolerance level and that doesn't come naturally, either; you have to do it consciously. After eight years there isn't too much that fazes me, yet I don't believe I was either tolerant or patient as a child or teenager, and I'm still impatient with normal children. When I have a child of my own, and naturally I hope and pray that the child will be normal, I'm going to have to remind myself to push harder than I do with the children here, because a normal child can achieve so much more.

When we go out on field trips I see a lot of normal children who are ill-behaved, and I'm sure that the fault is with their parents. It seems to me that our children are much nicer to be around. When you ask them to do something, they may not get up and fly to it, but at least they'll say "okay."

I remember an occasion about two years after I became a child care worker, when I had taken the children to a park just across the road. One of the little girls was playing in the sandbox and a couple of normal kids, about nine or ten years old, started teasing her and calling her names like "cootie girl." She understood that they were making fun of her, but she didn't understand why and she stood in the sandbox and cried. I flew off the handle at those kids. I screamed at them, "Who do you think you are? Where are your parents? If you don't leave this park right now I'm going to call the police on you." Of course, the little girl got more upset because I was upset, and it took me a few minutes to calm down and try to comfort her.

After the incident I thought, "That's it, we're never going back to that park. Those little rattails will never get another opportunity to do that to a child." Then, of course, I realized that I'd be depriving our children of playtime in the park. I still don't know if I was trying to protect myself or the child, which is obvious from how I still feel about it six years later. I could not bear to hear a child that I cared for called names by a normal child.

I am very attached to all of the kids, and I still take it personally if anyone affronts them. I also take it personally if they don't look good, if they're not clean and well-dressed. I don't yell at the kids about it any more, but I do yell at the staff, and that has given me something of a reputation with them—that if the children don't look good, if their hair isn't brushed or there's a run in their pantyhose, you'd better watch out because you'll have to answer to Linda. I really care about how they look, and maybe it stems from that incident in the park. I want other people to see them in the best possible light.

On occasions like the Special Olympics, where you see groups of children and adults from a lot of different facilities, there's no denying that I feel great pride in our group. Some of our children have weight problems, but nothing like what I see in children from other places. I see children weighing two hundred pounds, with greasy hair, and it breaks my heart because that lack of care means they're being denied their dignity as people. In a lot of ways I have the same feelings that a parent would have. It's hard not to: I am given a parental role to play, and I think it's understandable that I feel the way I do.

I get very involved with the children, and that can create difficulties. It used to be harder than it is now. I am still very *much involved with one of the girls who has now moved into one of the group homes. Then there's one little boy who comes to us for Christmas—although he's more my mother's than mine. I'm also very fond of a little girl who's a ward of the state, and with that little girl I haven't ever been able to distance myself. I never want to distance myself from the children, but I have to keep things in perspective.*

I was deeply involved with the little girl who is now in the group home, and she is very attached to me. I used to take her on outings, to the zoo and so on, and it became a problem because when the child went home for a visit she talked a lot about me and that made her mother uncomfortable. I would hope that parents would be pleased that a child talks affectionately about the people here and that they could accept a staff member as just somebody else whom the child loves, but I see that it is also threatening.

This child had never lived at home, and she certainly never called me mom, or mommy, or anything like that, but there was a real feeling on the mother's part that I had taken her place in her child's life. So I purposely tried to put some distance between that child and myself. We're still very close, but I don't take her out any more.

I met this child when she was four years old, so it's probably fair to say that I had a pretty big impact on her life. It was very hard to me to let her go, even as far as the group home, although I wanted her to go because her ability to handle that much independence proved how much progress she had made. When I first met her she could say about three words and still wasn't toilet trained. She has come a very long way, and I played a part in that. I was also instrumental in getting her to the point where she could go out to school, instead of attending the school we have here at the facility. The first time she was tested the scores were too low for her to go out to school, and so I concentrated even more on that child and, sure enough, next time she was tested her IQ had gone up eighteen points, and now she's going out to school.

The children in the unit where Victoria lives have to be functioning at a certain level of independence. They can all dress themselves although some need help with such details as fastening bras or tying shoelaces. Victoria is unofficial shoelace supervisor for the kids who have difficulty tying their own. All the girls work on self-help skills like making beds—two, or sometimes three, girls share each bedroom— and doing laundry. The youngest child is twelve. The unit where Linda's other charges live has a dormitory rather than smaller bedrooms. There are similar living arrangements for the boys, and girls and boys socialize together. Of the distinction between the units Linda says:

> *In the dorm we have mostly younger children. There are a couple of teenagers who could be on the other unit, but have behaviors or other problems that prevent it. And there are children on the unit who, like Victoria, theoretically function well enough to be in a group home but have behavior problems that require them to be in this more structured setting. One of our girls can do anything in the area of self-help—she sets the table and does laundry, she showers independently, shampoos her own hair, the whole bit, everything—but she cannot be trusted, for instance, not to put something in her ear. That kind of situation breaks my heart.*
>
> *I think all our children are happy. Some of them go through moods, but so do normal children, especially teenagers. I think most of our kids feel very good about themselves, which is actually unusual for teenage girls. They are told all the time that they are pretty, that they look nice, that they're doing good work, and most normal kids don't get that sort of reinforcement. No matter what level the children are functioning at, they're not going to go anywhere as adults unless they've got self-confidence. I've always believed that very strongly, and I try to pass it along to the staff by being very encouraging to the girls in front of them. Of course, some of the staff don't need any modeling from me. It just comes naturally to them to give the children a great deal of reinforcement and encouragement.*

Linda has come to understand some of the ambivalence parents feel about having their child in a facility, and she's learned to maintain the delicate balance between the parents and herself and her colleagues that is necessary to keep the relationship working smoothly. She says:

> *I've learned to understand some of the anxiety that parents must go through in placing a child, but there are also things that parents need to understand. They have to realize that the child is going to be living with a lot more people than she or he was before, and that this sort of communal living gives rise to certain differences—for instance, personal possessions don't always stay exactly where they should be. The unit where Victoria lives, with the girls two or occasionally three to a room, is very home-like. That's probably easier for parents to accept than the dorm might be. Our dorms are small, with only ten beds, but when your child has had her own room, or has shared a room with just one other person, and you first come here and look at the dorm, what you*

see is those ten beds, and that must constitute a sort of culture shock for parents. They think, "But she won't have any privacy," or, "Where's she going to put her teddy bear?"

Sometimes the parents are more involved with the teddy bear than the child is, and what they need to remember is that here their child will be among friends, whereas at home she might have been very lonely. Here the child will have a peer group, and the sort of programs and opportunities that the parent can't provide at home. That's what is going. to be important for the child, even if her teddy bear does end up on someone else's bed once in a while.

When they place a child, parents have to deal with grief, and loss, and guilt. They'd have an easier time if they could focus on the positive aspects of the child's life here instead of on what they see to be the negative issues.

It's hard for a parent to relinquish control of a child, especially if they've cared for the child at home for years, and their feelings come out in different ways. At a meeting recently one of my new parents complained because her daughter's clothes were getting lost or spoiled. She said she took great pride in her daughter's appearance, and it bothered her that the clothes weren't being taken care of. In fact, we do try hard to take care of everyone's clothes, but it's like with a big family—sometimes things get mixed up. We tried to explain that when you've twenty-four kids' knee socks to deal with, you're going to be left with a lot of odd socks. Basically, I don't think that mother's main concern was with her daughter's clothes. Complaining about the clothes was a way of expressing how she felt about losing her daughter.

I talked to her later, and she was carrying around a lot of guilt about placing the child, especially because this little girl seemed particularly helpless. But she was honest enough to admit that it made her uncomfortable to hear her daughter talking about us nonstop during home visit, and asking about coming back. She had a conflict: as a mother she was happy because her daughter was letting her know that placement was the right choice; but she also needed to hear that the little girl was missing her constantly.

This little girl really is happy with us, and she has made great progress right from the beginning. The family decided to place her because she had become the focus of their lives. She was dragging everybody under because she needed constant supervision and care. They have other children whose needs have to be considered too. It wasn't fair to have one child constantly at the center of attention. The child is doing well here, and the mother will discover that she made the right decision.

I have to keep reminding myself that there's no way of understanding everything that parents feel, just as they have no way of knowing the frustrations that we experience here. Of course, the comparison is faulty; after an eight-hour day, even if it turns into a ten-hour day, we can go home. We can always go home eventually. Parents carry this around with them always, and that is true even when the child is living here instead of at home.

Even after all this time I can't always read a parent's feelings accurately. I realize I can't anticipate everything. For example, one of the parents offered to pay for all the children to go out for pizza on her daughter's birthday, which was wonderful. She asked which pizza restaurant we were going to, and I asked, "Would you like to meet us there?" She said, "No, I don't think so, because my daughter will think I'm going to take her home afterwards."

I felt very foolish and awkward. It was the girl's sixteenth birthday, and of course her mother would want to be at her own daughter's sixteenth birthday party. But she was willing to miss that rather than disappoint the child by not taking her home after the party. In fact, this family is very involved with the child. The child goes home every other weekend. Her mother certainly has nothing to feel guilty about, but I felt bad because I had reminded her that she could not be at her own daughter's party. It's a shame when that happens to someone you think does a really good job as a parent.

It's difficult not to make judgments about parents. We're all human, and it's easy to fall into the trap of judging who is a really fine parent, or who is not so good, or of wondering how parents can treat their child this way. With twenty-four girls in my charge, there's no way of knowing all the parents and what their situations are. Even if I think I know, or I think they've told me, I've probably only gotten half the story. There are always secrets in the heart that cannot be shared.

The mother of the little girl that I got so involved with had always been very courteous to me and even sent me Christmas cards and gifts. I would never have known, without being told, that at the same time she was feeling real resentment towards me as a rival for her daughter's affection.

Some parents are very comfortable with the facility; they see it as the child's home away from home. In some cases that is literally true because their children have been here all their lives. But in many cases—more, as we open more units—we're dealing with parents whose children have lived at home for many years, and they have different issues to deal with.

I am not usually the one to initiate a contact with a parent unless there is something specific that a parent needs to know or something that the child needs. We feel that it is the place of the parent to contact us. Also, parents are involved with their children to different degrees. Some are highly involved. Some take the child home once a month and that's the extent of their involvement. Others are not involved at all. It's mandatory that a child go home on home-visit weekends, so long as there's a place for the child to go, but sometimes a child can't go home. The mother of one of my girls has cancer, which presents a particular problem. Some parents can't cope emotionally with the child.

Also, some parents have a very difficult time putting any restraints on their child at home. They don't expect any positive behavior. We have one little girl who bangs her head, and although we keep her helmet off most of the time here, her parents are too fearful to allow that at home. She has caused physical harm to herself, and they're afraid to take that risk. They are too fearful even to let her sit at the dining table for meals at home, although she always sits at the dining table here. The mother is honest with me and tells me what they do at home, so I know that for a few days after a home visit this little girl is going to be very resistant to doing anything for herself.

Some children are very happy to be back after a home visit, because they are familiar and comfortable with the routine here and they're attached to staff persons. Some are unhappy the day they get back, but after a couple of days they're just fine. Some are very equable about the whole thing; they're happy to go home, and they're happy to come back.

Some parents take advantage of us and of the facility, but no one wants to take it out on the child. If a child is appropriately placed here but the parents aren't cooperative, what can you do? It may be that the parents were very much involved at first but have gradually fallen off. This happens in cases where the child has been here for years. But what are you going to do if the parents stay away? Push the child out the door?

It's a tricky situation. Sometimes the staff will resent parents who aren't involved, or who say negative things about their child or the care the child is getting. Even if nothing is said, the staff members sense negative feelings on the part of the parent and resent them, and I may not be able to tell them anything useful to help them overcome their resentment. I may know something about a parent's situation that I'm not at liberty to tell the staff. Without giving a reason, it's hard to say to a staff member, "Well, you have to try to understand what that parent is going through." The resentful feelings are there, but you hope that they don't ever show. Nobody's immune to personal feelings. Mainly, you hope that the staff you get are professional enough and compassionate enough not to let such feelings affect their attitude towards the child.

It's good when parents are honest enough to tell us about a

family situation that may be affecting a child. Some people feel that it's a matter of pride to keep their troubles to themselves, but that can be misplaced pride. It helps us to know. It's not necessary to go into explicit detail. It's enough to say, "There was a family problem. . . ." Many times when a child comes back from a home visit, there's a reaction that we can't account for, or a behavior that's been eliminated will suddenly reappear and we're at a loss to know why. If the parent knows what's upsetting the child, that's knowledge we'd like to share.

People sometimes take the attitude that because children are retarded, they won't notice or won't understand. That's not true. The emotions of retarded people are often at an even higher pitch than those of normal people. Retarded people may not sort out their ideas so much, but it's all there on the emotional level.

I hope to marry and have children, and I hope that will make me more sensitive to how parents feel. It's a real effort for me now—I'm always having to think about it and hope my perceptions are accurate. I know I cannot understand in the way a parent does the fear of not knowing what to do with your child. But knowing what limited good facilities are available, I think about it all the time. I have a heavy responsibility. Right now there's one girl in my unit that I don't know if we can keep. It may be that this is not the right setting for her. During Victoria's trial period here, too, I could not say with any assurance that she would adjust. But there were a lot of other girls in the unit that we had to think about as well as Victoria. You always have to consider the child in relation to the other children. At the same time, you become personally attached to the children and you hate to see them go.

It's been the same with the children that have gone over to the group homes. The day I got their moving date, I went down into the stairwell and sat there crying because I couldn't bear the thought of giving up my kids. It was extremely hard for me, even though I was proud of them and wanted them to have that opportunity and knew I could still see them every day if I wanted to.

The rewards I get from this work are certainly not monetary and never will be. I have pride in what I do. I believe that it's important work and that this is the best thing I could be doing with my life and with whatever skills I have, and I feel lucky that I found out so early that this is what I wanted to do. I am proud when I see a child develop something that I started. It certainly feeds some need in me, to see that I am making some kind of impact on a child's life.

Also, there is a great need for the work I do, and for places like this facility. I think about how many handicapped adults are still living with their parents and how circumscribed their lives have become—both the child's and the parents' lives. Maybe the big excitement of their week is bingo, but they could have much more. Our children do have much more. There are far more options now for mentally retarded people and their families, and I want to be involved in that.

I don't want a handicapped child of my own—no one wants one, and I pray I never have one. Perhaps I'm paying my dues now, because I am certainly putting off having children. I could get married in the next year or so, but I don't think I would want to have children for another four or five years. I have some fear because I have three retarded cousins. They have a syndrome that involves extra digits, impaired vision, and mild retardation. With that in the family I would certainly consider genetic counseling before I had children.

Basically, I feel more pride in my work than in anything else I have ever done. Not even going to school gave me more satisfaction than what I'm doing now. I enjoyed it from the time I was a volunteer while I was still in high school. I enjoy being with normal kids, but I do love being with handicapped people. There's a certain emotional quality that they have, a certain honesty and openness, that you don't find very often, and it's a quality that I've always enjoyed being around. Many people never experience it; they close themselves off from it. I get sad and disheartened when I see parents closing themselves off from their children because the children are retarded. I used to feel angry about it and wonder, "How can you close yourself off from this perfectly adorable child? How can you not accept this child?" But I don't know what's going on in those parents' hearts, or what has gone on in their lives and may still be going on. Who's to say what stage of grieving a parent is at? Some never get past the grief, and maybe turning away is their only method of dealing with it. In that case the best thing they ever did for their child was to put the child in a loving environment like this. But if we give the children love, we certainly get it back. Speaking for myself, that's the one thing I seek from the children—that special quality of openness and warmth.

the loneliness of the long-distance parent

Emma and I are taking Victoria back after a home-visit weekend. Victoria is fairly cheerful, and we deliver her without incident into the hands of Amy, a leggy, long-haired blonde who is one of Victoria's favorite people, and one of the people who help parents recognize that it's okay to have a child in an "institution." One of Amy's colleagues is Roni, a child care worker disguised as a punk rocker. The first time I set eyes on Roni she was wearing a black mini-dress, earrings down to her shoulders, and one of those haircuts that stick up one inch on top of the head and go every which way everywhere else. As soon as I realized that she worked there and wasn't somebody's sister, I said to myself, "This is probably our kind of place."

Roni is not on duty this time, and since Victoria is in an amiable mood, Amy agrees to her request to see Emma and me to the elevator, provided she comes right back.

At the elevator, we exchange hugs and kisses, and Victoria heads off down the corridor to Amy. We watch as her progress slows.

"Victoria," I call, "Amy's waiting for you."

Victoria turns around and comes racing back to where we're standing. "I want to give you another kiss," she says, and does so. Then, "I'll push the button for you," she offers.

"Fine," I tell her, "but then you've got to go see Amy. I guess she needs you to help her with the other kids."

"Okay," Victoria agrees pleasantly.

She presses the "down" button, the elevator arrives, and quick as a cat Victoria is in the elevator. "I'm coming with you," she announces.

"Boy," says Emma admiringly, "that was smart."

I grab at the "door open" button and the three of us get out of the elevator and head off once more down the corridor towards Amy. Victoria, outsmarted intellectually, is now on the verge of verbal rebellion so I start up a patter about all the things Amy needs her to help with.

Again we deliver Victoria into Amy's custody, exchange more hugs and kisses, extract an unconvincing promise to "be good" from Victoria, and start back towards the elevator. All is quiet. Evidently Victoria has decided against throwing a tantrum this time. Inevitably, however, I am in tears within the first few yards.

Emma, still pondering her retarded sibling's sleight of foot, glances sideways and observes my condition. "Oh *God,* mother," she exclaims, exasperated. "You're not going to cry again."

Automatically I respond, "Emma, don't say 'oh, God.' Say something else. Say 'oh, shit,' if you want to, but don't say 'oh, God.' Kids who go to Catholic schools aren't supposed to say 'oh, God'."

By the time we are out in the grounds and walking towards the car I have, thanks to the intervention of my younger daughter, stopped crying. Emma's mind is still on Victoria's trick with the elevator.

"That was very clever of Victoria," she says again.

"Yes," I agree. "It was also very manipulative."

On the way home we discuss, for the umpteenth time, what a very basic error it is to assume that because people are retarded they are also stupid. By the time we get home we have both recovered from my attack of separation anxiety. We know that Victoria, very likely, is now happily bossing the other kids or helping them get into their pajamas and conduct their pre-bedtime routines.

In the course of Emma's own pre-bedtime routine she remembers to ask for a definition of manipulative, which I try to supply. I tell her that one of the things manipulative people do is to lay guilt trips on other people. Victoria had very successfully manipulated me into feeling guilty about leaving her. She needn't have made the effort: I felt guilty, anyway. To some extent I still do. Every time.

Emma is well acquainted with guilt. It's almost the first word a parent learns in the language of retardation (frequently before the word retardation itself enters the parent's vocabulary), and siblings catch on fast. Probably the first thing you tell the child who has a retarded brother or sister is, "It's not your fault. There's nothing that you have to feel guilty about." And you repeat it, time and again, down the years. So Victoria's sister knows about guilt and she recognizes a guilt trip when she sees one. Manipulative, however, is a new word in her vocabulary.

"Am I manipulative?" she wants to know.

"No," I assure her truthfully, and hope that it will continue to be true.

And that is the end, for this evening, of pre-psychology 101.

Home visits take place one weekend a month. Families are asked to pick up their children on Friday evening before six and return them Sunday evening after six. What goes on during home visits can be positive, negative or, as usually happens, a mixture of the two. However successful or unsuccessful a home visit may be, it requires a major readjustment on everyone's part. Victoria, accustomed to the highly structured routine of the facility, requires that I maintain that structure for her while she's at home. No longer in the habit of structuring Victoria's life on an hour-to-hour basis, I have trouble disciplining myself to provide the direction she needs. If we get back on each other's wavelengths, things go smoothly. If we don't, they don't. Whichever way the visit goes, taking her back is an emotionally charged experience, although less so now that we've all had some experience of it.

When Victoria first left home I cried routinely every time I took her back after a home visit. When she lived in Kathy's house it was easier, but when she moved into the big house I had to deal with corridors that told me clearly that this was an institution where my child now lived most of her life. There's something about those corridors. They can make you feel very lonely.

After Don—exhausted by the strain of trying to keep up with Victoria's needs and still have some time and space, and some of me, for himself—moved out, those corridors took on a whole new aspect for me.

After the Fall break, when Emma was staying with her father and Victoria and I had been alone together for most of the weekend, I took her back by myself. She'd been a real sweetheart all weekend. She kept telling me, "You're my mother," and I'd agree, "Yes, I am. I'm your mother." Then she'd say, "I'm the only daughter you've got." And I'd correct her, "No, I have two daughters; I have you, and I have Emma. What you mean is that I'm the only mother *you've* got."

So Victoria would think about that for a while and say, "You're a mother." Again I'd confirm, "Sure, I'm your mother."

"You're a beautiful mother," she said—words I'd have killed for a couple of years earlier when she was in her "I hate you" phase. "And you're a beautiful daughter," I told her, "and I'm proud of you."

"You're proud of me? Will you tell Emma and Don I've been a good girl?"

"Of course I'll tell them, and it will make them very happy."

This weekend, when we went back, the building had been reorganized so that the reception area was considerably farther away than before from Victoria's living quarters. Victoria and I walked the length of the corridor with her suitcase, her new sneakers (bought on sale that afternoon and still in their box), and a large chrysanthemum plant we'd bought as a "welcome back" gift for the kids and staff. We unpacked, and Victoria settled in to tell Roni about her foot—she had a blister on her toe. I started off back down the corridor, and that corridor stretched ahead of me as though it would take the rest of my life to reach the end of it. My clogs rang on the newly shined floor. I gritted my teeth and promised myself that if I could make it to the car without crying I would go home and indulge in a real, sopping wet fit of weeping.

I didn't make it.

visiting Victoria: a close-up view of reality

Visiting Victoria is much like walking into a college dorm. There are two- or three-person bedrooms with adjoining bathrooms, a laundry room, a kitchen with a refrigerator full of snacks, and a living room with a couch and easy chairs and books, toys, and records. There's a television set, a record player, and a VCR. Any time you visit you're likely to hear either the television going or music from the record player. Kids are sitting around, playing with toys or games, listening to the music, getting ready for their next program.

As often as not someone has just had her hair washed and Roni or Amy or someone else on the staff is curling the kid's hair, making her look pretty, telling her how nice she looks. If it's Saturday, when the children go to Mass, there's a big hustle of hunting for pantyhose, belts, hair barrettes, dress-up shoes. There's always a beauty shop routine going on. Everybody gets dressed up for Mass on Saturdays. Usually the Mass is held in the chapel within the facility, but sometimes the girls go to the adjoining big church. On occasion a group of them will go to other churches in the neighborhood, where one or two of them will read the lessons—thus the children do their own public relations for the facility.

The first time I visited the facility was on a Saturday afternoon. It was harried, disorganized, kids milling around and making demands and getting in each other's way. It was just like a big family. It felt so ordinary, so much like any family trying to get the hell out of there and get some place on time, that I was totally reassured. This may be an institution, I told myself, but this is okay. My daughter could live here, and I could live with that.

There are times, though, when I am acutely conscious of how different my perception of where Victoria lives is from the perceptions, or expectations, of other people. The other day I brought her some pairs of jeans from the thrift shop. Because Victoria usually despises shopping for clothes almost as much as she despises the telephone, I didn't take her to try them on. I have her body measurements, in relation to mine, down pretty pat: if something fits me around the waist it will probably fit her, and if it's four inches too long on me it will probably look just fine on Victoria. So, off I go to the facility with my armful of thrift shop jeans to try them on Victoria, and it happens that I arrive in the middle of a party. Some kids from another unit are visiting and there are children running all over the place.

Many of them I know. Some of them greet me as Mrs. Mantle, some greet me with "Hi, Victoria's mommy," some say, "Hi," and some just come up and touch my arm. One little girl whom I don't know comes up and puts her arms around me, so I hug her back and ask her how she's doing. Then she puts her hands around my throat and presses her fingers down on my windpipe. This is a little disconcerting and I am wondering how to keep breathing without appearing to reject this small person's overtures, which do not appear to be hostile, when one of the child care workers comes up and tells me, "She can't hear, so she likes to feel the vibrations when you talk."

The child and I make a friendly, though speechless, goodbye, and I step over various bodies on my way to the door. It's like a slumber party with Emma's friends. Victoria comes with me and tells me the names of some of the visitors, and we head towards her room to try on the jeans. In the corridor is a very small child in a walker, and I'm surprised to see a baby in this party of obviously older children. "How old is that little girl?" I ask, and someone tells me, "She's nine, but she's very little."

Victoria and I try on the jeans and hang up those that don't need alterations. Then we say our goodbyes and Victoria goes back to the party while I head off down that corridor and go home to Emma, who is doing pre-algebra homework.

A few weeks later I am once again in the unit, delivering Victoria after a home visit, and this time I am in a mean mood and as I pace that long corridor I list to myself the people I know who have no conception of what it's like to have a child in an "institution," and how, in my present mood of uncharity and self pity I'd like to give them a close-up view.

I think of the people who pay lip service to my retarded daughter, who tell me how beautiful she is and how brave I am and how they couldn't possibly cope with what I have to deal with, and I think to myself, "This is a heap of shit." And I number on my fingers, as I walk down that long corridor, all the people I'd like to haul in there. It does not matter, in the context of my present emotional state, that the institution is a happy, friendly, loving place where a handicapped child has friends to come home to and a whole army of people whose goal is to make that child's life as complete and satisfying as possible. What is going on has to do not with Victoria, but with me.

There are people who have shilly-shallied on the fringes of my life and pretended to be my friends while clearly avoiding the acknowledgement of my daughter's retardation and its implications for her, for me, for my family, and—if you really think about it—for them. When I allow myself that dangerous luxury of feeling anger toward those people I wonder whether it would make me feel better if I could confront them with the reality of Victoria's handicap.

I wonder how they would react to the sight of a room full of impaired, imperfect, mentally disabled children; or to feeling around their throats the fingers of a child who is not only retarded but can comprehend the concept of speech only by feeling the vibrations of a speaking person's windpipe. I wonder if, by walking that endless corridor away from Victoria's unit after a home visit, they would comprehend how I feel sometimes when I walk away and leave her there. And I want to tell them, "This is my child; these children, all of them, are in some way my children. This is a part of my life, and this is how it's always going to be. You do not have to share it, and I may not even choose to invite you to share it. But if you don't acknowledge it, then we might as well part company right now, and you will be the loser."

fund raising: an exercise
    in (among other things) humility

Some three hundred mentally retarded children, teenagers, and—since fairly recently—adults occupy the facility where Victoria lives. The facility is a not-for-profit organization that relies heavily on charitable contributions and that makes considerable demands in terms of personal commitment on the parents of the retarded people who live there. Before a resident is accepted it is made very clear that the family is expected to help support the facility. This support can take a number of forms: direct financial contributions; solicitation of financial contributions from others; participation on various boards and committees and in fund-raising activities; and volunteer work at the facility itself. Most facilities that are not state-funded (and, for all I know, those that are) require similar involvement. In some cases there's the unspoken threat that parents who refuse to cooperate run the risk of losing their child's placement, although it seems reasonable to hope that no facility would so burden a handicapped child with the sins of the parents. Some facilities do not, or are not legally entitled to, demand specific financial contributions from parents. Some do demand direct financial contributions in the form of monthly payments, which can be quite high.

Six forty-five on a cool, grey October morning at the subway station. It's an interesting time and place to watch the early morning world go by. Workers stream off the buses and head towards the trains, or vice versa. Some are bright and shiny and alert. Many are still half asleep, some still grey with fatigue. A few are locked into a private world, isolated by the headphones clamped over their ears. They are a varied lot. To me, however, they fall into only two categories: those who will put a quarter, or a few pennies, or a dollar bill, into the canister I thrust in front of them, and those who won't.

Over my jeans and raincoat I wear the familiar yellow plastic tunic of the Knights of Columbus, a Catholic organization that raises money to support various charitable agencies. The two front pockets of my tunic are stuffed with Tootsie Rolls. I bulge, pregnant with candy. As the buses disgorge their passengers I advance. "Please help the retarded children, buy a Tootsie Roll!" I'm only a few minutes into this litany when I realize that the words are coming out without any punctuation and sound really strange. I'm asking all these people to help retarded children buy a Tootsie Roll. I can't imagine that anyone else is concerned with grammatical niceties at that hour, but once a writer, always a writer. I rephrase my appeal: "Please buy a Tootsie Roll to help retarded children!"

Before long I am having a hard time remembering to say "please": it takes up too much time. I am, however, getting in a lot of "thank yous." People are actually stuffing money into my canister. They even seem pleased to get a Tootsie Roll in return. They say "thank you" to me, as though I'm doing them a favor instead of the other way around. Some people are fumbling in purses or pockets before they can even hear my voice. They recognize the yellow tunic. Kind people. Giving people. If I think they haven't heard my appeal, I clarify it: "Thank you—you're helping retarded children." If there's time, or the face is particularly friendly, I'll add that one of those children is mine.

What I'm doing, I observe in a lull between buses, is begging in the streets for my child. The money that goes into my canister, or some of it, will go to the facility where Victoria lives. The people who drop their quarters and loose change in my box are doing something real for real kids. I hope they know that. I want to tell them that Victoria, my daughter, thanks them. I'd really like them to know that their nickels and dimes and dollar bills add up to good homes and trips to the movies and music classes for youngsters with mental retardation. But that's not all. They're also giving witness that there are people who care enough to dig into their purses or pockets on an unpromising fall morning when all they're really intent on is getting to work on time and paying their own bills and taking care of their own kids.

When you have a child with special needs, you get exercised in humility. When you have a child in a living facility you learn to do a lot of things you'd really rather not do—like fund-raising, which is a polite name for asking total strangers for money. My daughter's facility is commonly recognized as an excellent one. It costs money to keep it that way. It costs standing outside the subway station in a yellow tunic with your pockets stuffed with candy.

A woman from the facility called me up and said, "How would you like to do the subway station at six o'clock on Friday morning?" And I said, "I would not like that at all. I work. I've got another kid to get off to school."

She said, "But we're having a hard time getting people to do it. There's only one other person. We need you."

"Keep talking," I told her, "until I feel guilty enough to say 'yes.'" So she did. And I did.

Fund-raising can get to be a dirty word when you've got a child whose quality of life is directly and significantly dependent on the amount of money available to provide services for her. My daughter gets a state grant and Supplemental Security Income. She goes to a wonderful public school. I know exactly where my tax dollars go, and I don't grudge a penny. But it's not enough. Parents of kids like mine, whose immediately recognizable contribution to the community is limited by disability, support those children in other ways. We do volunteer work. We sell raffle tickets. We peddle candy at subway stations.

And people, to their enormous credit, respond. It's fascinating to observe who hears your call for help. The most unlikely people give. People I didn't even approach—because they looked as though they had enough problems keeping themselves afloat—came up and dropped cash into my canister. Many sleek, expensive types averted their eyes. Once I realized, to my total dismay, that I had invited a bag lady to help support my retarded kid. A cab driver waved aside my canister and candy bar and said, "Waddya wanna do—kill me with candy?" I thought, but did not say, "No, you airhead—although I can't say you'd be a major loss to society—I just want you to drop one little quarter into this slot." Another time a woman I've known for ten years came by and asked, "What are you doing here?" When I told her, she said she already gave enough to charity. I said, "Wait a minute. This is for retarded kids, like Victoria—remember?" Reluctantly she made a contribution and accepted a Tootsie Roll. Another woman claimed she had to get change, and she did—she went into the subway station and came all the way back to me. You certainly meet some interesting people when you get into fund-raising.

A little while after I'd learned not to compete with the rumbling of the trains and the eloquent flight of pigeons every time a bus rolled in, a young man showed up beside me with a fistful of flyers urging support for a candidate in an upcoming local election. At once we were comrades. He gave me a lapel button. I gave him a Tootsie Roll. He said, "If you believe in something, you have to stand up and be counted." I told him about a song the children sing, "Stand together for what you believe; work for what must be done." We talked about Emma, who was going on a peace walk with her school that morning and was horribly embarrassed about taking part in such a public happening. "You get over the embarrassment," said the young political activist. Indeed you do. Embarrassment does not get you supporters. Or contributions. We congratulated each other on being there on that October morning, standing together for what we believed and working for what needed to be done. We decided that "work" was the operative word. And although we were never likely to see each other again, we parted as friends.

As the rush hour passed and business slowed, I turned in the rest of my Tootsie Rolls along with my canister, which was gratifyingly full, and headed off for work myself. I felt a lot of affection for those people who had not turned their eyes away or deliberately skirted the crowd to avoid my outstretched hand. I hoped they were proud of themselves, because they deserved to be.

Many parents of children who are mentally impaired agree that the fund-raising they have to do is one of the least attractive elements of their situation. But there are enough generous, giving people out there to make you feel that working for what needs to be done is not such a dumb thing to do after all. It's amazing what you can learn at the subway station, early in the morning on a cool October day.

Admittedly, when I first learned what sort of fund-raising I'd have to do on behalf of my daughter's facility, I was appalled. It seemed that I was supposed to go to my nearest and dearest and ask them for money. In fact, I was supposed to go to anyone I could think of. This was totally against my English upbringing, which stipulated that you don't ask people for money; you manage with what you've got and it's a matter of pride to do so.

I was profoundly distressed at the thought of approaching people I knew and asking them to contribute to the financial welfare of my retarded child. Even worse was the prospect of going into a store and asking for a gift of merchandise that could be used as a raffle prize at a fund-raiser. Actually, I needn't have gone to the store: I could have sent a form letter. As a reporter, however, I'd always figured that you get a better story if you get it in person, so I began to trudge around to the local stores. Once I took Victoria with me. We went to a small store where I frequently buy gifts and my younger daughter expends her baby-sitting money on desirable trifles, and where I am on friendly terms with the manager. Unfortunately, while the manager was writing out a check, Victoria, whose spatial awareness is unreliable, reached out to examine some pretty trinket and floored a tray of expensive, imported porcelain refrigerator magnets. The manager gave me a check for twenty-five dollars towards my fund-raising total. I gave her one for fifteen dollars towards the breakages. After that, I wrote letters.

Another form of fund-raising in which I got involved was "doing the churches." On Sunday mornings a group of volunteers, wearing aprons emblazoned with the name of the facility, stand outside churches after the services and solicit contributions from the churchgoers. It's similar to Tootsie Rolling: some give, some don't, and frequently the ones who give are just those you wouldn't have expected to give, and vice versa.

After a year or so of fund-raising, I found that my personal attitude towards other fund-raisers had changed. Previously, I had made up my mind about which charities I would contribute to and resolutely avoided the others. I'm a bit more flexible now. When it comes to writing a check, I still set limits according to my financial resources, but I've developed a kinship with the people who stand outside supermarkets and subway stations with canisters. Unless the name of the organization they're collecting for is one I have a reason for not supporting, or bears a name that sounds phony or suspect, I give. Only a quarter, maybe, but I know now that even a quarter makes a difference—not just to the infinitely slow filling of the money box but also to the way the volunteer feels about what he or she is doing.

I've learned to be more receptive to appeals from others because I've been holding the canister myself. There's a limit, however, to anyone's altruism. One evening the phone rang and a pushy woman began talking to me about the Special Olympics, in which Victoria has participated with much enjoyment on a number of occasions. The caller was eager to convince me of the value of the Special Olympics program and the great opportunities it provided for handicapped children. After a while she slowed down long enough to ask if I were familiar with the program.

"Indeed I am," I replied. "I have a mentally retarded daughter."

"Oh, my," she crowed, "That's wonderful!"

Which is all she had time to say, because I snapped back, "No, actually, it's not wonderful. Where I'm coming from it's not wonderful at all, and the one thing you do not say to the parent of a retarded child is, 'that's wonderful.'" And I hung up the phone.

All the unlucky caller had meant, of course, was that she was pleased to have encountered someone who knew what she was talking about and might, therefore, be a soft touch. But she certainly blew it that time. And so, in terms of courtesy and tolerance, did I.

some just clap their hands

When John, the children's father, and I divorced, I was hesitant to break the news to my godmother, whom I loved dearly. She was an English maiden lady of the old school and I respected her deeply. I thought she would be disappointed in me both because my marriage had failed and because I was getting a divorce—an escape route not condoned by the Catholic church to which she was committed and to which I was, at that time, hanging on by my fingertips.

I underestimated my godmother's wisdom. She wrote to me, in effect, that it was indeed sad the marriage had failed, but that clearly it had been important for us to marry because Victoria and Emma needed to be born. In a couple of brief sentences in her characteristically neat, tiny script, she had come closer than anyone before her to answering the inevitable "why?" questions that plague any parent who has a mentally handicapped child. She wasn't offering an easy or complete answer, and she wasn't attempting an explanation, but what she said was enough. Victoria is a necessary person. She has, to quote the "Desiderata"—a poem attributed to religious writer Max Ehrmann—"A right to be here."

It was not until years later—in fact until I reached this point in Victoria's story—that I realized that perhaps my godmother had also answered the "why me?" part of the question: perhaps Victoria needed to be born because she had a story to tell, and perhaps that's why she happened to be born my daughter instead of someone else's. She had a story to tell, and I could write it down for her. I am my daughter's ghost writer.

When we learned that Victoria was mentally retarded, John and I, both journalists, talked about how if we could write about our loss and pain perhaps it would help to heal the wounds. I don't think it occurred to either of us that it could also help to heal the wounds of others. When I finally began to write this book, on Victoria's fourteenth birthday, I hoped that my experiences might help other parents feel less alone and more able to express some of their own feelings—especially some of the negative feelings that society considers it unacceptable to express. I hoped, too, that because this was a family story it might reach others who had no experience of living with retarded people and give them a clearer perception of retardation and its implications.

There's no satisfactory way to close the issues of "why?" and "why me?" and "why my child?" You get into very hot water with ideas like, "children are born retarded so that they can bring out the best in other people." Kathy, with whom Victoria lived for six months, says, "I have seen an extra dimension in people who have a retarded person in their family," and immediately adds, "Of course, this is hardly a justification from the child's point of view."

When you start examining the whys, all sorts of apparent

contradictions surface. Suddenly someone who has insisted, "I absolutely cannot buy the line about a retarded child being a gift from God," is saying, "I believe I am a better person because I have had to come to terms with my child's retardation." It seems that along the road to acceptance most people have found a way to deal with the whys, and some have strong views about how the mentally retarded person will someday, somehow, be compensated for what appears to be a present misfortune. Most people approach these difficult philosphical issues with extreme caution, and many tend to precede any discussion of such feelings with a disclaimer, such as, "I'm not a religious person, but. . . ."

I'm not a religious person, but I believe in life after death and I owe this belief to my mother, whose dead body is the only one I have ever seen. She died when I was in Buenos Aires, and I flew back for the funeral. I visited my mother's body in the funeral home, and when I touched her cold cheek I knew beyond doubt that although the shell of my mother lay there, she wasn't there at all. She had not ceased to exist; she had simply escaped from that body into some other kind of life. There couldn't be any other explanation, because all that energy that had been my mother could not possibly have simply ceased to be. That brief moment (for I did not stay long beside the empty shell of my mother) convinced me, as a long and arduous religious upbringing had never quite succeeded in doing, that death ends only this life and that after death another life begins.

There was a song that I wanted (but was then too conventional) to ask for at my mother's funeral. Part of it goes: "When I die, when I'm dead and gone, there'll be one child born in this world to carry on." Emma was born about a year after my mother died. I'd like someone to play that song at my funeral. Later I heard another song that stayed in my mind because it said something to me about Victoria. The refrain goes:

All God's critters got a place in the choir,
Some sing low, some sing higher,
Some sing out loud on the telephone wires,
And some just clap their hands. . . .

It is abundantly clear to me that Victoria has a place in the choir, and since it seems that here she is not being given a chance to do much more than just clap her hands, her chance to sing out loud must be still to come.

In the Roman Catholic Creed, or profession of faith, Catholics affirm their confidence in "the resurrection of the body, and life everlasting." By this accounting, Victoria will get her chance to sing out loud in a heaven where she will be freed from the limitations imposed on her in this life and where she will be whole and perfect. By the same accounting, because we believe that in the afterlife we will be reunited with those we have loved on earth, I will be able to hear her sing. That is a comforting thought, but whether or not I ever get to hear her sing is not important. What's important is that she get to do it, and I believe that she will.

a light at the end of the tunnel?

Kathy believes that being Victoria's surrogate mother for six months taught her things she didn't know before about handling children. Techniques she learned to use with Victoria she now uses with her own children. She believes that this was a gift that Victoria gave her. Kathy says:

The only book I ever read by parents of a handicapped child was Angel Unaware, *by Dale Evans and Roy Rogers. I read it when I was a little kid and it touched me. By writing about their child they reached other people. This facility came about because of a woman who was touched by a retarded child. The woman who founded the facility had a retarded nephew, and when she saw that there was no place like this, she made one. She, and a lot of other people with her, built up this facility. That was the gift her nephew and the children here have given to her: the inspiration to make a place like this happen.*

I'm not a mystic, and I don't know why children are born retarded, or why something happens to make them retarded. I can't offer a rationale for that. I take the girls in my house to a clinic where I see other handicapped children who don't have what we can give the kids here and whose parents are not much higher functioning than they are. Such sights are difficult to reconcile with your sense of justice. But somebody, somewhere, is going to be touched by it.

It sounds sappy when you talk about it, and I would rather live it than talk about it. I don't even like to talk to my friends about the philosophy behind it, but I feel deeply that I am blessed by being here. I came into it because I felt I had been given a lot of good things, and now I have been given more.

I know from personal experience that my brother had a reason to be here. We were a close family and we were lucky, because it has blown a lot of families apart. Maybe when that happens to you it's not possible to see any reason for your handicapped child's existence. But I'd like to say to the parents, "Even if you can't see any reason for your handicapped child's existence, you don't know how many other people have been touched by it, or how many lives have been changed because they were touched by your child." I'm not really a religious person, but I think there's a deeper side to people that is reached by being with people who are handicapped.

I can see the reason for my brother's existence and what he has done for my soul, and I can also see how that might never touch some people—it might just be a living hell forever. But I guarantee that some people are a little bit deeper because of what they see here and the people they meet. It's corny, and it doesn't ease anybody's trouble, but it's something I'd like to convey—to tell people, "There's a beautiful spot in me because I have known your child."

Joan, who bargained with God for the safe return of her husband from Vietnam and believes that she sacrificed Annie's normality as part of that bargain, says:

Knowing Annie's personality right now, dealing with her as I can at the times when I thoroughly enjoy her, I love that child too much to wish that she were dead. But I wish I had never gotten to know her. If she had just passed away in the incubator it would have been a tragedy. I would have given up the child, just as I had promised, and maybe Alan would have had to go back to Vietnam and maybe he wouldn't. But I would never have had the kind of loss that you go through when you grow up with the child and then the child dies.

I believe in a life after death. I don't think I'm going to have to worry about Annie after death; I think she's going to be taken care of. There's a place up there for her and when she gets there she will be normal. Sometimes I'm afraid that I'll meet her after death, and she will turn on me and accuse me of not doing well by her in this life. But that's when my fears take hold of me. Mostly I just feel that I'll see Annie again after death and she will not be handicapped. That does not mean that I want her to die before me, so that she can be normal. I don't want the grief of losing her. Since we don't really know what the afterlife is, I couldn't handle the loss of her. I would miss her too much. Even if I thought she was normal and happy, it wouldn't be enough: I'd have to know.

Leslie is much more confident about her belief in a possible future for Jeff in which he will no longer be handicapped. In fact, she wonders if then their roles won't be reversed. Leslie says:

I think I was always looking for something, some kind of guidance and some kind of emotional and spiritual support. I was a very devout Catholic when I was in college, looking for a spiritual affiliation, a family, a system of values that I didn't really feel was intact in my own circumstances. I never found it, and it finally got to the point where I was dealing with life pretty well even though there was something missing. Then the year I got out of college I found out about the Baha'i faith, and it filled in all the cracks.

The Baha'i friends I made were the first people that I really trusted with Jeff. It was the first time I felt that here were people who would help me with the responsibility of Jeff just because they were good, helping people. I could take him anywhere with me. We used to go listen to a Baha'i group that played bluegrass music, and they would give Jeff their cowboy hats to wear. I didn't have to worry about their making judgments. We all had the same values and the same way of looking at things.

I don't understand how people can keep going without seeing life in some kind of religious context. To me, it isn't an anchor or a prop, an artificial thing that you create so that you can deal with reality: it is the reality.

We believe in the Baha'i faith that life is a series of tests and difficulties, and that how you deal with them determines whether or not you're going to have to redo the test in the next life. If you deal with it and come to terms with it, if you learn from it and grow through it, you won't have to go through it again.

I think also that on the next plane of existence, the priorities may be different. On this plane, intellect is highly prized; intellect is what makes it or breaks it and that is why it is so hard for mentally retarded people to be valued. But perhaps they are in touch with something that we are not in touch with. Maybe on the next plane of existence intellect isn't going to be so important; maybe heart is going to be important. There we'll be with our huge intellects, but our not very well-developed hearts, and they'll be leading us by the hand. Maybe on the next plane of existence it will be Jeff leading me. So if I do my work for him now and take responsibility for him now, although I have no way of knowing, perhaps next time we meet it will be Jeff leading me through it all.

Millie, John's mother, also believes as a Buddhist that her son's handicap is a temporary condition. She says:

In the Eastern philosophies it is believed that each person is responsible for his own karma. That means that where you are now is the result of a cause that you, not somebody else, put forth, so you can never blame anybody else for what happens to you. I like that a lot. I can't say, "I sure must have had lousy parents to have all these problems now." And I don't have to feel guilty about my children, that I or something I did caused John's condition.

When I first started practicing Buddhism there was no way you could make me believe in past lives or reincarnation. But the more I go on the more sense it seems to make. If we believe in previous existences, it means that each moment we're putting forth the best cause we can, so that the causes we're putting forth now will bring good effects in the future. By that argument I suppose I can say that John is retarded now because of something he did previously. I'm not sure, and I don't have to accept that; it's just a possibility sitting out there.

We lose my husband at this point; past lives lose him altogether. I'll admit that it doesn't give me a reason why children die of leukemia, as our first child did. That's a real tough one. I've thought about the idea that sometimes a person will be born and will complete in a few years whatever the purpose of that life was, and then it's time to go. If Billy's purpose as far as we were concerned was to make us more humane, more appreciative of what we had, certainly that was accomplished in the four years of his life. Perhaps John's purpose is the same, to help us have more empathy and be able to understand people better. And to enjoy him as he is.

People talk about the death experience, the guides who are there when you reach the end of the tunnel, or the light— everyone has read the stories. Then there's a dormancy or learn-

ing period before you choose, or are urged, or whatever, to try it again. And you can even choose the family you're going to come to. By that token, John chose to come back and he chose our family to come back to. It's an interesting thought.

We have had a lot of people die lately, and John understands about death. He was asking questions and I was trying to tell him that we are all going to die, but that we do live on, and that when he dies he will get a new body and he will be able to speak normally.

Donna, who watched her normal baby daughter become gradually and irreversibly brain-damaged because of a mis-diagnosed thyroid condition, says:

Emily is a human life that was wasted, and she was mine, and I'll never be able to stop feeling bad about that. There is still a part of me that says maybe it wouldn't have happened if I'd been stronger, if I'd been tougher, if I'd screamed and yelled at that pediatrician and said, "something's wrong with this baby." I think I will always feel that I could have saved her, because I know that she was intended from the moment she was born to be perfectly normal and that an outside force entered into this.

And yet none of us knows whether it was fate or chance. That cosmic moment, before she was even born, when I chose that particular pediatrician—was that the moment when I slotted us down that chute with no return? I don't know.

I've had many complex thoughts since she was born. I have never believed that God picked me out or said, "You need an impaired child because it will help you," or "because you'll set a good example." I don't believe that. The only thing that has given me any comfort about Emily is something that I read about reincarnation and the death of the body not necessarily being the end of everything.

I know that at that second, at that fraction of a second, when Emily was conceived she was intact, and when she entered this world she was still intact, and this process that destroyed her is strictly happening to her in this life. And when she dies—I don't want to put a religious connotation on it so I don't like to use the word "soul"—whatever that piece of us is that I believe probably goes on for all of us into infinity, that piece of Emily is going to be intact again. I believe Emily is going to get a second shot at it, and that gives me a lot of comfort. I wish it could be in my lifetime, but it can't and I have to accept that. I don't know if it will be in this world, and it doesn't matter. What matters is that I can look in her eyes and know that there's a spark in there that some day is going to get out.